A Guide to
Crisis Intervention

A GUIDE TO CRISIS
INTERVENTION

THIRD EDITION

KRISTI KANEL

California State University Fullerton

BROOKS/COLE
CENGAGE Learning™

Australia • Brazil • Japan • Korea • Mexico • Singapore • Spain • United Kingdom • United States

BROOKS/COLE
CENGAGE Learning™

A Guide to Crisis Intervention, Third Edition
Kristi Kanel

Senior Acquisitions Editor: Marquita Flemming

Assistant Editor: Jennifer Walsh

Editorial Assistant: Samantha Shook

Technology Project Manager: Inna Fedoseyeva

Marketing Manager: Caroline Concilla

Marketing Assistant: Rebecca Weisman

Marketing Communications Manager: Tami Strang

Project Manager, Editorial Production: Rita Jaramillo

Creative Director: Rob Hugel

Art Director: Vernon Boes

Print Buyer: Rebecca Cross

Permissions Editor: Roberta Broyer

Production Service: Sara Dovre Wudali, Buuji, Inc./ICC Macmillan Inc.

Copy Editor: Marjorie Toensing, Buuji, Inc.

Cover Designer: Paula Goldstein

Compositor: ICC Macmillan Inc.

For product information and technology assistance, contact us at **Cengage Learning Customer & Sales Support, 1-800-354-9706**

For permission to use material from this text or product, submit all requests online at **www.cengage.com/permissions** Further permissions questions can be emailed to **permissionrequest@cengage.com**

Library of Congress Control Number: 2005935900

ISBN-13: 978-0-495-00776-0
ISBN-10: 0-495-00776-5

Brooks/Cole
10 Davis Drive
Belmont, CA 94002-3098
USA

Cengage Learning is a leading provider of customized learning solutions with office locations around the globe, including Singapore, the United Kingdom, Australia, Mexico, Brazil, and Japan. Locate your local office at: **international.cengage.com/region**

Cengage Learning products are represented in Canada by Nelson Education, Ltd.

For your course and learning solutions, visit **academic.cengage.com**

Purchase any of our products at your local college store or at our preferred online store **www.ichapters.com**

Printed in the United States of America
5 6 7 11 10 09 08

This book is dedicated to the many human service students that have given me their feedback over the years and to all the brave individuals who have survived and grown through their crises.

BRIEF CONTENTS

CONTENTS

PREFACE

This book was designed to capture the information that I enjoy sharing with graduate and paraprofessional counseling students as well as my colleagues in the counseling profession. In each chapter, I have compiled information about crisis intervention skills and strategies that I have found useful in my work as a psychotherapist in a variety of mental health settings. I have used these concepts and skills in all the agencies in which I have been a practicing counselor. The particular crisis topics were chosen because of the frequency with which they are encountered at typical counseling agencies. The ABC model offered in this book is useful in dealing with almost any crisis, so the student should be able to generalize its techniques to any problem presented by a typical client.

Although the book is written for beginning paraprofessional counselors, the material included is applicable for counselors at all levels. It can be used as a training manual for counselors working at agencies or for students taking a college course.

At the end of each chapter is a list of terms from the chapter, called Key Terms for Study. The reader is encouraged to review these terms after reading the chapter.

I would like to thank the following reviewers for their helpful comments and suggestions for this third edition: Paul Ancona, Edmonds Community College; Steve Atchley, Delaware Technical & Community College; Freida Brown, Gardner-Webb University; Magdalena Linhaardt, University of Maine at Augusta; Deana Morrow, The University of North Carolina at Charlotte; Bernie Newman, Temple

University; Ray Taylor, Pitt Community College; Jod Taywaditep, University of Illinois at Chicago. These reviewers have given me excellent feedback. I believe this edition will be a major improvement over the last edition.

I would also like to acknowledge Dr. Mary Moline, who originally created the crisis intervention course and invited me to be involved in this innovative class at its inception.

Kristi Kanel

ABOUT THE AUTHOR

Dr. Kristi Kanel has been a teacher, practitioner, and scholar of human services for over 25 years. She has been a college professor for the past 22 years. She helped create the first crisis intervention course at California State University, Fullerton, in 1986 and has been teaching the course since then. She also teaches several courses in counseling theory and client populations.

Throughout her career as a human services practitioner, Dr. Kanel has volunteered at a Free Clinic as a counselor, interned with the Orange County Board of Supervisors as an executive assistant, worked as a Mental Health Worker and Specialist for the County Mental Health agency, worked as a clinical supervisor at a Battered Woman's Shelter, and provided psychotherapy for individuals, families, and groups in private practice and at a large Health Maintenance Organization. She has worked extensively with victims of child abuse, partner violence, and sexual assault. Additionally, she has worked with Spanish-speaking Latinos and has conducted research related to the needs of this population. She specializes in crisis intervention and has conducted research on the most effective approach to working with people in crisis.

Dr. Kanel earned her Ph.D. in Counseling Psychology from the University of Southern California, her Master of Counseling degree from California State University, Fullerton, and her Bachelor of Science degree in Human Services from California Sate University, Fullerton.

She enjoys the outdoors, hiking, biking, running, and beaching.

WHAT IS A CRISIS?

CHAPTER I

CRISIS DEFINED

The term **crisis** has been defined in many ways. The definition reflecting the three essential parts of a crisis is the **trilogy definition** and is referred to throughout this book. The three parts of a crisis are these: (1) a precipitating event; (2) a perception of the event that causes subjective distress; and (3) the failure of a person's usual coping methods, which causes a person experiencing the precipitating event to function at a lower level than before the event.

Other authors agree with this general definition. An example is Gilliland and James, who define crisis as "a perception of an event or situation as an intolerable difficulty that exceeds the resources and coping mechanisms of the person" (Gilliland & James, 1988, p. 3). Gerald Caplan, often referred to as the father of modern crisis intervention, describes a crisis as "an obstacle that is, for a time, insurmountable by the use of customary methods of problem solving. A period of disorganization ensues, a period of upset, during which many abortive attempts at a solution are made" (1961, p. 18). In its simplest form, according to Caplan, "it is an upset in the steady state of the individual" (1961, p. 18).

Janosik (1986, p. 4) sees the scope of crisis work as including "precipitating events, behavioral response, failed efforts to cope, and disrupted equilibrium." She has found the following to occur in a crisis: "A precipitator in the form of a hazardous event intrudes on the life of an individual or group, causing a state of tension that is subjectively uncomfortable and the person experiencing the hazardous event resorts to customary coping behaviors" (p. 7). If these behaviors fail to relieve tension, a crisis occurs.

These three components of a crisis must be recognized and understood because they are the elements the crisis counselor will be identifying and helping the client to overcome. The perception of the event is by far the most crucial part to identify, for it is the part that can be most easily and quickly altered by the counselor. It is the focus in this trilogy definition, and the point that differentiates crisis intervention from most other forms of counseling.

By keeping the trilogy definition in mind, the crisis worker can perform the necessary services in a brief time. Whereas other forms of counseling may focus on building self-esteem, personality modification, or even extinguishing maladaptive behaviors, in crisis intervention the focus is on increasing the client's functioning. This is addressed in detail in Chapters 2 and 5; for now, look at two useful formulas for the crisis interventionist that use the trilogy definition.

Formula for Understanding the Process of Crisis Formation

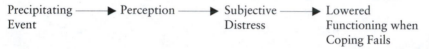

Precipitating ——▶ Perception ——▶ Subjective ——▶ Lowered
Event   Distress   Functioning when
                                                                Coping Fails

If the goal of crisis work is to increase functioning, the following formula aids the crisis worker in understanding the process for leading a client out of a crisis.

Formula for Increasing Functioning

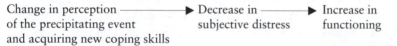

Change in perception ——————▶ Decrease in ———▶ Increase in
of the precipitating event   subjective distress   functioning
and acquiring new coping skills

Again notice that the method involves changing the perception of the precipitating event. Obviously, it is not possible to change the precipitating event. The best one can do is work at changing or altering the client's cognitions and perceptions of the event, offer referrals to supportive agencies, and suggest other coping strategies. These ideas are explored further in subsequent chapters.

One additional thought about crises in general: Often the word crisis conjures up images of panic, emergency, and feeling out of control. This is not necessarily the case. Crises are a part of life and should not be considered abnormal. Crises occur in the lives of normal, average individuals who are just having difficulty coping with stress; therefore, they represent a state to which most of us can relate.

Because of the universal nature of crises, helpers developed a specific approach for intervening in these situations, relying on their own experience. They discovered that the more traditional, long-term counseling approaches were not appropriate for dealing with crises and found that short-term crisis intervention was much more effective. Short-term and brief therapy models are discussed in Chapter 2.

CRISIS AS BOTH DANGER AND OPPORTUNITY

Crisis states are seen by many as somewhat normal developments that occur episodically during "the normal life span of individuals" (Janosik, 1986, p. 3). Whether the individual comes out of the crisis state productively or unproductively depends on how he or she deals with it. In Chinese, crisis means both danger and opportunity (see Figure 1.1). This dichotomous meaning highlights the potentially beneficial as well as the potentially hazardous aspects of a crisis state. A person might face the challenge of the precipitating event adaptively, or he or she might respond with a neurotic disturbance, psychotic illness, or even death.

According to Caplan (1961, p. 19), growth is preceded by a state of imbalance or crisis that serves as the basis for future development. Without crisis, development is not possible. As a person strives to achieve stability during a crisis, the coping process itself can help him or her reach a qualitatively different level of stability. This state may be either a higher or lower functioning level than the person had before the crisis occurred (see Figure 1.2).

Crisis as Opportunity

Even if a person receives no outside intervention or help, the crisis state will eventually cease, usually within 4 to 6 weeks. A crisis is by nature a time-limited event because a person cannot tolerate extreme tension and psychological disequilibrium for more than a few weeks (Caplan, 1964; Janosik, 1986, p. 9;

FIGURE 1.1 | DANGER OR OPPORTUNITY

FIGURE 1.2 │ CRISIS AS BOTH OPPORTUNITY AND DANGER

OPPORTUNITY

Help ⟶ Higher level of functioning

↓

Growth, insight, coping skills

Normal functioning interrupted by
1. Precipitating event
   (event perceived as threatening)
2. Subjective distress
3. Failure in coping

↓

Drop in level of functioning   **DANGER**

↓

Greater vulnerability,   **1. No help** ⟶ Lower level of functioning
disequilibrium   or
                                    2. No help ⟶ Nonfunctioning level

↓

Suicide, homicide, psychosis

Roberts, 1990; Slaikeu, 1990, p. 21). Although a person's character influences how a person emerges from a crisis, that is, either stronger or weaker, seeking and receiving focused help during the crisis state has a much bigger impact on the person. In the midst of a crisis, a person is more receptive to suggestions and help than he or she is in a steady state. A crisis worker can gain significant leverage at this time because of greater client vulnerability. Instead of stabilizing at a lowered level of functioning, an individual who receives help is likely to stabilize at a higher, more adaptive level of functioning. Erratic behaviors and emotions are relieved.

> **Example:** After having been raped, a woman might not seek help or even tell anyone about the trauma. About a month after the violation, she may slip into a state of denial, with reduced contact with the world, lowered trust levels, increased substance abuse, poor interpersonal relations, and a state of dissociation. However, she may continue to be able to work, go to school, put on a front with family and friends, and appear to function normally. In reality, however, she is functioning at a lower level than she did before the rape and will be somewhat impaired until she gets intervention. The longer she waits to get help, the more resistant she will be to it because of the amount of energy she will have invested in the denial process.

This scenario is especially common in cases of incest. It seems fairly obvious that a 3-year-old girl brought in for counseling after being molested one time will respond better than a 30-year-old woman who was molested at age 3 and has repressed acknowledgment of the molestation for 27 years.

An important aspect of client vulnerability during crises is the ethics and integrity of the crisis worker. It would be easy for an unscrupulous worker to take advantage of a client in crisis. Chapter 3 is devoted to ethical issues.

Once the client has returned to a previous, or higher, level of functioning, he or she may opt to continue with therapy. Brief therapy is a reasonably cost-effective approach for dealing with aspects of life that have plagued a person regularly but have not necessarily caused a crisis state. A counselor may work with an individual for 6 to 20 sessions and obtain excellent results in behavioral and emotional changes. Once people have benefited from crisis intervention, they are often more open to continuing work on additional in-depth personal issues because of increased trust in the therapeutic process and the therapist. The choice to continue in postcrisis counseling will of course depend on financial resources and time availability.

Crisis as Danger: Becoming a Crisis-Prone Person

Not everyone who experiences a stressor in life will succumb to a crisis state. No one is certain why some people cope with stress easily whereas others deteriorate into disequilibrium. Several explanations seem plausible. Figure 1.3 extends Figure 1.2 to include the crisis-prone person. If a person does not receive adequate crisis intervention during a crisis state but instead comes out of the crisis by using ego defense mechanisms such as repression, denial, or dissociation, the person is likely to function at a lower level than he or she did before the stressing event. The ego, which has been hypothesized to be the part of the mind that masters reality in order to function, must then use its strength to maintain the denial of the anxiety or pain associated with the precipitating event. Such effort takes away the individual's strength to deal with future stressors, so that another crisis state may develop the next time a stressor hits. This next crisis state may be resolved by more ego defense mechanisms after several weeks, leading to an even lower level of functioning if the person does not receive adequate crisis intervention.

This pattern may go on for many years until the person's ego is completely drained of its capacity to deal with reality. Such people often commit suicide, harm others, or have psychotic breakdowns. These individuals are often viewed as having personality disorders. People with personality disorders are usually seen as suffering from emotional instability, an inability to master reality, poor interpersonal and occupational functioning, and chronic depression. Defense mechanisms and substance abuse are common behaviors people use to overcome crisis states instead of seeking professional help. People who receive help before resorting to defense mechanisms may avoid developing a personality disorder.

Traditional psychotherapy has usually been the course of counseling implemented with people suffering from personality disorders. In today's economy and with health maintenance organizations (HMOs) dictating mental health treatment, clinicians often cannot take the traditional road with crisis-prone people. Because short-term treatment is required in most settings, it is essential to begin working with people as soon as possible after the crisis state sets in to prevent a chronic cycle from developing.

FIGURE 1.3 | CRISIS AS DANGER: THE DEVELOPMENT
OF THE CRISIS-PRONE PERSON

Higher functioning level:
growth, coping skills learned for use with future stressors

↑

Receives help

State of disequilibrium

Receives no help

↓

Lower functioning:
defense mechanisms

New stressor hits; lack of ego strength
to cope with it leads to new crisis state

↓

NO HELP
Lower functioning than before, fewer coping
skills for future stressors

New stressor hits

↓

Another state of disequilibrium

↓

Lower level of functioning, death or psychosis,
severe personality disorder

Other Factors Determining Danger or Possibility

Other factors may also determine whether a crisis presents a danger or an opportunity. These factors are generally found in the client's own environment. In addition to receiving outside help, having access to (1) material resources, (2) personal resources, and (3) social resources seems to determine the level an individual reaches after a crisis.

Material Resources   Material resources are money, shelter, food, transportation, and clothing. Money may not buy love, but it does make life easier during a crisis. For example, a battered woman with minimal material resources (money, food, housing, and transportation) may suffer more in a crisis than a woman with her own income and transportation. A woman with material resources has the choice of staying at a hotel or moving into her own apartment.

She can drive to work, to counseling sessions, and to court. The woman with no material resources will struggle to travel to sessions and will have to be dependent on others. Her freedom to choose wherever and whenever she goes will be largely decided by those on whom she depends. According to Maslow's (1970) hierarchy of needs, material needs must be met before the other needs of personal integration and social contact can receive attention. Not until she is housed, fed, and safe can the battered woman begin to resolve the psychological aspect of the crisis.

It is important to remember that despite financial and other material resources, battered women and other people struggling through a crisis will inevitably suffer. People with material resources sometimes suffer more than those with fewer resources because of psychological and social factors or the duration and severity of the victimization or other precipitating event.

Personal Resources　After her material needs are met, the woman can begin to work through the crisis. Her personal resources, such as ego strength, previous history of coping with stressful situations, absence of personality problems, and physical well-being will help determine how well she copes on her own and how well she accepts and implements intervention.

Ego strength is the ability to understand the world realistically and act on that understanding to get one's needs and wishes met. Many times a crisis worker will be called on to be the client's ego strength temporarily (as when a person is psychotic or severely depressed) until the client can take over for himself or herself. These clients can neither see reality clearly nor put into action realistic coping behaviors. They need someone to structure their behavior until the crisis is managed successfully, often with medication, family intervention, and individual counseling. When someone has coped successfully in the past with various stressors, then usually his or her ego strength is high. However, when someone does not cope successfully with stressors, the person's ego strength is lowered (see Figure 1.3). A crisis worker must "tune into" a client's level of mastering reality in order to set up realistic goals and problem-solving strategies.

Certain **personality traits** may interfere with coping and also with accepting intervention. Some people have problems accepting help or being strong. Others are paranoid or avoid conflict. These people present challenges to counselors, in contrast to clients who are open and trusting.

Clients' **physical well-being** also affects how well they deal with crises. Healthy people have more energy and greater ability to use personal and social resources. The ability to move about and exercise is essential in coping with stress. Disabled and sick clients must constantly cope with these conditions, and so when stress occurs, they simply do not have as much psychological energy to deal with it as physically healthy individuals.

A person's level of **intelligence and education** also affects the outcome of a crisis state. Well-educated people are better able to use cognitive reframes and logical arguments to help them integrate traumas psychologically. People with lower IQs have more difficulty understanding events and their reactions to events, and they tend to be less flexible when solving problems.

Social Resources   A person's social resources also affect the outcome of a crisis. A person with strong support from family, friends, church, work, and school has natural help available, providing these support systems are healthy. A lone individual struggles more during a crisis and tends to depend on outside support systems such as professional counselors, hot lines, emergency rooms, and physicians. Part of the crisis worker's responsibility is to link clients with their natural support systems so their dependency on mental health workers is reduced. Knowledge of support groups such as 12-step self-help groups is vital to a counselor's effective intervention. Clients without much natural support can participate in these groups indefinitely, and the 12-step group may become a natural support resource.

PRECIPITATING EVENTS

Personal crises have identifiable beginnings or precipitating events. These can be new adjustments in the family, loss of a loved one, loss of one's health, contradictions and stresses involved in acculturation, normal psychosocial stages of development, or unexpected situational stressors. Perhaps the most important aspect of any crisis is how the person perceives the situation. The meaning given to the event or adjustment determines whether the person can cope with the added stress. This meaning has been termed the **cognitive key** (Slaikeu, 1990, p. 18). It is the key with which the counselor unlocks the door to understanding the nature of the client's crisis. Once the helper identifies the cognitive meanings the client ascribes to the precipitating events, the helper can work actively to reframe these cognitions. This new way of perceiving the event aids the client in reducing subjective distress and increasing coping abilities.

The way the precipitating event interacts with the person's life view is what makes a situation critical. If people cannot cope with new situations by using their usual mechanisms, a state of disequilibrium will occur. However, if their cognitive perspective of a potential hazard or precipitating event allows people to relieve the stress effectively and resolve the problem, the crisis will not occur in the first place.

Stress is different from crisis, though the two terms are often confused. If people cope with precipitating events without suffering subjective distress, they will likely experience stress but not a crisis. Stress is part of modern life; in fact, it is part of daily life. This does not mean that crises are part of daily life, however, because people typically cope with stress without falling apart emotionally. Even if people undergoing stress experience some subjective distress, if they have the coping skills to master the stress, their functioning level will not be impaired, and hence a crisis state will not ensue.

DEVELOPMENTAL CRISES

For conceptual purposes, we can identify two types of crises: developmental and situational crises. **Developmental crises** are normal, transitional phases that are expected as people move from one stage of life to another. They take years to develop and require adjustments from the family as members take on new roles. Two types of developmental crises will be explored in Chapter 7. Clients often seek counseling because of their inability to cope with the evolving needs of one or more family members. Crisis workers must be sensitive to the special issues surrounding this type of precipitating event.

SITUATIONAL CRISES

Situational crises emerge when uncommon and extraordinary events occur that an individual has no way of forecasting or controlling (Gilliland & James, 1988, p. 15). Some examples of situational crises are crime, rape, death, divorce, illness, and community disaster. The chief characteristics that differentiate these from developmental crises are their (1) sudden onset, (2) unexpectedness, (3) emergency quality, and (4) potential impact on the community (Slaikeu, 1990, pp. 64–65). Situational crises are discussed in detail in the second half of this book.

SUBJECTIVE DISTRESS

A rise in **anxiety** is a typical reaction to the initial impact of a hazardous event. A person may experience shock, disbelief, distress, and panic (e.g., stage 1 of rape trauma syndrome). If this initial anxiety is not resolved, the person may experience a period of disorganization (e.g., stage II of rape trauma syndrome). During this phase, the person often experiences feelings of guilt, anger, helplessness, hopelessness, dissociation, confusion, and fatigue, leaving her in a vulnerable state. She is unable to function at her previous level at work, school, or home. Ironically, in certain circumstances anxiety has the power to generate energy and increase coping abilities, as when a child is in danger and a parent has a surge of adrenaline that helps him rescue the child, or when a natural disaster hits and people have the increased physical strength and endurance to carry bodies and sandbags.

Anxiety, however, seems to fit the curvilinear model (see Figure 1.4) in that too much or too little leaves a person in a state of inertia or with undirected and disintegrative energy (Janosik, 1986, p. 30).

When the anxiety level is moderate and manageable, the crisis worker can use it to help motivate the client to make changes. In sum, anxiety is not always

---

FIGURE 1.4 | CURVILINEAR MODEL OF ANXIETY AS MOTIVATOR FOR CHANGE

Moderate anxiety
(optimal motivation)

Very little anxiety   **High anxiety**
(inertia/low motivation)   (overwhelmed/paralysis)

a bad thing; it is considered necessary, at moderate levels, to spur people to make changes in their lives.

Anxiety is an internal experience; therefore, interventions might first be aimed at alleviating the internal component of stress. This action makes sense because the external component of a crisis often cannot be undone. The only remedy for distress is to change the internal experience.

Changing the internal experience as a remedy for distress can be done in several ways. One would be to medicate the person (e.g., give an injection of a tranquilizer) to relieve the anxiety or grief. The benefit of this intervention is immediate reduction in subjective distress. Sometimes clients cannot benefit from cognitive crisis intervention because their anxiety or grief is too great; in these cases, medication can provide temporary relief until their cognitions can be altered. Crisis workers need to learn to work jointly with psychiatrists when medication is necessary. The crisis worker might call a psychiatrist or physician that he or she has worked with in the past and create a bridge for the client with the psychiatrist. At other times, the crisis worker might consult over the phone with a physician and set up a relationship in which the psychiatrist and crisis worker feel comfortable having ongoing communication while both are working with the client. Some agencies employ both counselors and psychiatrists. In these cases, it is rather simple for the crisis worker to work jointly with the psychiatrist because both workers generally get together during regularly scheduled staff meetings. It is not uncommon for colleagues at agencies to "pop" into each others' offices from time to time to engage in "informal" communication about the progress of mutual clients. No matter which way crisis workers choose to engage with a psychiatrist or a client's primary care physician, it is wise to be knowledgeable about the medications being prescribed and to let the physician take the lead in medication management.

Unfortunately, most of the medications given for distress do not take effect for 10 days to 3 weeks. Expecting a "magical" cure from medication must be discouraged, although if clients believe medication will eventually help, they may have increased hope, which in itself may lower the emotional distress.

The crisis worker, however, would not want to rid clients of all subjective distress too soon without helping them change their perception of the precipitating event or without encouraging coping behaviors. Without discomfort, clients are not as motivated to change. The crisis counselor depends on clients to be in a state of disequilibrium and vulnerability if cognitive change and behavioral change are to occur. Clients with good ego strength and no history of mental illness can often work through a crisis without any medication. Some people, though, absolutely need medication, and the crisis worker must be skilled at knowing when the situation calls for more than just talk therapy.

Medication should be used with discrimination for crisis states. The decision is up to a psychiatrist or other physician. The crisis worker should discuss his or her treatment plan with the psychiatrist and how medication fits into it. Often, the psychiatrist will have suggestions for the counselor and can be a valuable resource for clients. Keeping an open mind about medication can benefit your clients.

For clients who do not seem to need medication to relieve subjective distress, the internal experience is best changed through cognitive restructuring, discussed in subsequent chapters. Some clients may also be able to implement recommended behavioral changes, which can be done in a number of ways.

The essential idea to remember is that the crisis interventionist should not focus on changing precipitating events but rather the way in which clients experience them. Changing perceptions will lower clients' subjective distress and increase their functioning levels. Offering coping strategies also aids in lowering subjective distress and increases functioning as well.

FAILURE OF COPING METHODS

When people in crisis are experiencing feelings of bewilderment, confusion, and conflict, they are in a vulnerable position. They are lacking skills to improve their situation. According to Caplan (1964, p. 18), there are seven characteristics of effective coping behavior (see Table 1.1). Crisis workers should assess clients' current behaviors and guide them toward the areas not being demonstrated. These characteristics should be remembered as the crisis worker begins to provide services to clients, keeping in mind the strengths and weaknesses of the clients.

When a person is unable to use these coping behaviors and is faced with stress, a crisis state will generally evolve. Often the subjective distress, such as anxiety or grief, overwhelms the individual, and the coping behaviors are not functioning. It is little wonder that the person's functioning level in a variety of areas is affected. When such individuals realize they can no longer function at work, at home, in social situations, or emotionally, they may seek mental health treatment. During treatment they will slowly begin to function again by reducing their subjective distress and increasing their coping behaviors.

Once a client's subjective distress has been lowered to a manageable level, the crisis worker may offer coping strategies. These range from referrals to

TABLE 1.1 | CAPLAN'S SEVEN CHARACTERISTICS OF EFFECTIVE COPING BEHAVIOR

1. Actively exploring reality issues and searching for information

2. Freely expressing both positive and negative feelings and tolerating frustration

3. Actively invoking help from others

4. Breaking problems into manageable bits and working through them one at a time

5. Being aware of fatigue and pacing coping efforts while maintaining control in as many areas of functioning as possible

6. Mastering feelings where possible; being flexible and willing to change

7. Trusting in oneself and others and having a basic optimism about the outcome

Source: Caplan, 1964.

agencies, groups, doctors, and lawyers to reading books, journaling, and exercising. Caplan's seven characteristics of effective coping behavior can guide the counselor in creatively constructing a treatment plan that changes cognitions, lowers subjective distress, and increases functioning.

KEY TERMS FOR STUDY

Caplan's seven characteristics of effective coping behavior: Behaviors proposed by Gerald Caplan (1964) as essential for getting through a crisis state. They can be learned through formal crisis intervention, through experience, or while growing up. In any case, the crisis worker needs to acknowledge these characteristics and to transmit them to clients when possible.

cognitive key: The perception a person has of the precipitating events that led to subjective distress. The crisis worker must identify the perception if he or she is to help the client change it and thereby increase functioning.

coping methods: The behaviors, thinking, and emotional processes that a person uses to handle stress and continue to function.

crisis: A state of disequilibrium that occurs after a stressor (precipitating event). The person then is unable to function in one or more areas of his or her life because customary coping mechanisms have failed.

crisis prone: The condition that persists when people fail to grow from a crisis experience and instead deal with the crisis state by using ego defense mechanisms. They will be crisis prone because their ego strength will be weakened, leaving them unable to cope with future stresses.

curvilinear model of anxiety: Model showing that anxiety has the potential to be either a positive or a negative influence for someone in crisis. Too much anxiety may overwhelm the person and lead to lowered functioning. However, moderate anxiety may offer an opportunity for growth and transition from one stage of life to another or may motivate the person to grow from the experience of trauma. People who have no anxiety tend not to be motivated to make any changes at all.

danger and opportunity: Dichotomy associated with a crisis. A crisis can be an opportunity when the person grows by developing new coping skills and altering perceptions. It can be a danger when the person does not seek help and instead copes with the crisis state by using defense mechanisms, resulting in a lowered functioning level and possibly psychosis or even death.

developmental crises: Normal transitional stages that often trigger crisis states, which all people pass through while growing through the life span.

ego strength: The degree to which people can see reality clearly and meet their needs realistically. People with strong egos usually cope with stress better than people with weaker egos.

father of modern crisis intervention: Title given to Gerald Caplan.

functioning level: The way a person behaves socially, occupationally, academically, and emotionally. The functioning level is impaired when a person is in a crisis. The goal of crisis intervention is to increase functioning to precrisis levels or higher.

material resources: Tangible things such as money, transportation, clothes, and food. They constitute one determinant of how well a person is able to deal with a crisis.

personal resources: Determinants of how well a person will deal with a crisis. They include intelligence, ego strength, and physical health.

precipitating event: An actual event in a person's life that triggers a crisis state that can be either situational or developmental.

situational crises: Unexpected traumas having a sudden onset that impair one's functioning level.

social resources: A person's friends, family, and coworkers. The more resources one has, the better one will weather a crisis.

stress: A natural, though trying, part of life. A reaction to difficult events usually involving feelings of anxiety. Stressful events do not become crises if a person can cope with them and functioning is not impaired.

subjective distress: Painful and uncomfortable feelings experienced by a person in crisis.

trilogy definition: The three-part approach to understanding what a crisis is, including the precipitating event, subjective distress (caused by cognitions), and, usually, failure to cope, which leads to lowered functioning.

2 | CHAPTER

CHAPTER

THE HISTORY OF CRISIS INTERVENTION

Eric Lindemann (1944) introduced the first major community mental health program that focused on crisis intervention. He studied the grief reactions experienced by relatives of victims injured or killed in the **Coconut Grove fire** in Boston on November 28, 1942. On that night, 493 people perished as the Coconut Grove Nightclub burned. It was the single largest building fire in U.S. history. As Lindemann joined others from Massachusetts General Hospital to help survivors who had lost loved ones, he came to believe that clergy and other community caretakers could help people with **grief work.** Before this time, only psychiatrists had provided services for those with anxiety and depression, symptoms that were thought to stem from personality disorders or biochemical illnesses.

After his study, Lindemann worked with **Gerald Caplan** to establish a communitywide mental health program in Cambridge, Massachusetts that became known as the **Wellesley Project.** They worked at first with individuals who had suffered such traumatic events as sudden bereavement or the birth of a premature child. This focus on working with women dealing with the grief of either the death of an infant or the birth of an infant with abnormalities was most likely influenced by the baby boom which began during the late 1940s, after World War II had ended. Millions of women were pregnant and some had complications of pregnancy. Physicians were experimenting with a new drug, thalidomide, that prevented morning sickness. Unfortunately, the drug also led to birth defects and other complications. Women who had taken the drug and whose babies had birth defects needed a way to deal with their trauma.

Caplan's focus on **preventive psychiatry,** in which early intervention was provided to promote positive growth and minimize the chance of psychological impairment, led to an emphasis on mental health consultation (Slaikeu, 1990, p. 7). Much of current-day crisis intervention theory has come from the Wellesley Project.

In the early 1960s, the crisis intervention trend gave rise to the **suicide prevention movement.** This movement grew rapidly, and many community centers offered 24-hour hot lines. These centers developed out of the social activist mentality of the 1960s and Caplan's theory. They relied on nonprofessional volunteers for their telephone counseling programs. Caplan's focus on critical life crises attracted nontraditionalists, who were dissatisfied with medical-model and psychoanalytic treatments. Many nonprofit organizations specializing in the treatment of certain personal crises evolved from such grassroots programs as free clinics for abortion of unwanted pregnancies, battered women's shelters, rape centers, and AIDS centers.

Parallel to the suicide prevention movement was the **community mental health movement** in the United States. In 1957, the **Short-Doyle Act** provided funding for mental health clinics in each county throughout the United States. This act was the impetus for the monumental deinstitutionalization of patients from federally funded state mental hospitals. Patients had often stayed in these hospitals for an indefinite period of time—sometimes to fade away, forgotten. With the introduction and widespread use of psychiatric medications such as thorazine and lithium, chronically ill mental patients could be managed on an outpatient basis. Six years later, Congress established the Joint Commission on Mental Illness and Health and, with the support of the Kennedy administration, passed the **Community Mental Health Centers Act** of 1963.

When mental health service centers were built in the community, they became places of specialty for psychiatry. The Community Mental Health Centers Act was originally intended to serve chronically ill mental patients, but soon mental health workers began seeing healthier, less dysfunctional patients suffering from emotional disorders that had typically been treated in private psychologists' offices. As a result, the chronically mentally ill were receiving less care than intended. The **Lanterman Petris Short Act,** passed in 1968, established more specific requirements for the provision of mental health services in the community. The focus was on short-term crisis intervention for clients who were not chronically mentally ill. The legislation also provided for long-term case management and conservatorship of chronically mentally ill people in order to prevent them from harming the general public or from committing crimes. The Lanterman Petris Short Act also addressed involuntary treatment, including the civil rights of individuals for whom involuntary treatment might mean confinement in psychiatric facilities. The issue of involuntary commitment is still controversial in some states. For example, in California, legislation is currently pending that deals with this issue (AB1800 Thomson and Perata)

Although the assembly has passed the bill, it remains buried in a senate committee from which it has never emerged (http://.www.psychlaws.org/ State_Activity/California/AboutCTAC.htm, 10-27-2005).

Currently pending in Congress are two pieces of legislation (AB 1800 Thomson and Perata and AB 2798 Thomson Source: U.S. Government (2000). Mental Health Issues and Legislation Pending in 2000 [Website USGOVSEARCH]. Found at gov.doc from the California State University, Fullerton Pollack Library.)] If passed, this bill would "lengthen the period of time a person may be committed to a psychiatric hospital, broaden the criteria for involuntary treatment and institute a new involuntary outpatient treatment program" and "establish protocols for involuntarily treating judicially committed forensic patients with antipsychotic medication" (U.S. Government, 2000, p. 1).

A major part of the community effort was 24-hour emergency service, which became known as **Psychiatric Emergency Treatment (PET)** services. Most community mental health services are still based on this act. Procedures for dealing with psychotic, suicidal, and homicidal crises and the ways such crises relate to community mental health are discussed in Chapter 6.

In the late 1960s and early 1970s, journals such as *Crisis Intervention* and *Journal of Life-Threatening Behavior,* which dealt specifically with crisis topics, were published. Crisis intervention became more valued in the 1970s as economic conditions led to greater use of community resources (Slaiku, 1990, p. 8).

During this time, the country also saw an increase in university and college programs in which curricula focused on psychology and counseling. Many paraprofessionals who had previously staffed community mental health centers went to college to become professional therapists. Soon, the profession of licensed therapist was big business. Insurance companies paid for counseling services offered by individuals with masters degrees; this led to a rise in the number of people seeking mental health counseling as well as to complaints by insurance companies about the financial burden. The complaints resulted in managed care by indemnity insurance companies. Insurance companies no longer paid for patients to stay in therapy as long as clinicians felt necessary.

The short-term crisis intervention model is by far the most cost effective and, thus, the approach sought by most **health maintenance organizations (HMOs), preferred provider organizations (PPOs),** and other insurance carriers in today's mental health treatment community. Community mental health and nonprofit organizations also use the **brief therapy model.** Utilization review committees often limit treatment to four to six professional sessions and encourage the completion of therapy in such community resources as twelve-step programs and other support groups. The brief therapy method fits in well with the crisis intervention approach for both professional therapists and paraprofessional counselors working in community agencies. Table 2.1 summarizes important dates in the development of crisis intervention as it exists today.

One controversy in the field of crisis intervention centers on paraprofessionals. Some licensed professionals feel that these workers, who have

TABLE 2.1 | TIME LINE IN THE DEVELOPMENT OF CRISIS INTERVENTION

Time Frame	Development
1942	Coconut Grove Nightclub fire; use of nonprofessionals to provide counseling
1946–1964	Baby boom; increase in stillbirths, birth defects, and miscarriages (thalidomide)
1950s	Psychotropic medications introduced; deinstitutionalization of mentally ill people
1957	Short-Doyle Act
1963	Community Mental Health Centers Act
1960s	Publication of professional journals related to suicide prevention and crisis intervention; increase in professional studies in psychology and counseling
1960s–1970s	Civil rights; grass-roots movements; nonprofit agencies; use of paraprofessionals
1970s–1980s	Increase in college programs; professionalization of mental health; proliferation of licensed counselors; movement away from crisis intervention and toward traditional longer-term mental health counseling
1980s–1990s	Managed care takeover of medical field, including mental health; return to crisis intervention in private industry and in community mental health

traditionally provided crisis intervention, do not have enough training to do intervention. Some professionals have proposed that only those with at least a masters degree should be allowed to provide services to those in crisis. Such a move could have a negative impact on poorer communities that cannot afford the costs of this level of expertise, however. The volunteer worker seems vital, especially during times of economic downturn. Understandably, politics and perhaps professional jealousy and fear play a part in the opposition to paraprofessional counseling. No doubt, many clients in need would go untreated if these workers were prohibited from practicing crisis intervention.

Many professional therapists are not aware of the historical foundations of crisis intervention, which was based on paraprofessional services during the Wellesley Project period. Although crisis intervention is used in most mental health offices, not all mental health workers have received specific training in the field. It is often included in other courses in graduate schools and other counseling preparatory colleges. Hence, students must provide crisis intervention based on their interpretation of how to shorten the traditional therapy process. Because crisis intervention is not often emphasized in traditional counseling and psychology graduate schools, many nonprofit agencies provide specific training in crisis intervention to ensure that nonprofessional volunteers can work effectively with clients.

One cannot say that traditional models have had no influence on crisis work. In fact, each traditional counseling approach has contributed to the field of crisis intervention. This seems reasonable considering that the founders of crisis intervention were trained in these models themselves.

CONTRIBUTIONS FROM OTHER THEORETICAL MODALITIES

No single discipline or school of thought can claim crisis theory as its own, for this theory has been derived from a variety of sources. The result, therefore, is an eclectic mixture drawn from psychoanalytic, existential, humanistic, cognitive-behavioral, and general systems theories.

Psychoanalytic Theory

Psychoanalytic theory has contributed to the treatment of people in crisis. Sigmund Freud postulated an idea that is applicable to crisis intervention and crisis theory in his assumption that psychic energy is finite and that only a limited amount exists for each person. This assumption helps explain the disequilibrium that develops when customary coping skills fail and a person's psychological energy is depleted. It also helps explain why people with personality disorders, neuroses, and psychoses react poorly in a crisis: Much of their psychic energy is being used to maintain their disorder; they do not have the "spare" energy to combat unforeseen emergencies (Brenner, 1974, pp. 31–80).

In crisis theory, probably more than in any other psychological theory, the counselor is advised to assess the client's ego strength and at times take over the function of the ego. The concept of ego strength is directly related to psychic energy. People with personality disorders or psychotic disorders usually cannot cope effectively with precipitating events because their psychic energy is being used to deal with previous stressors, losses, and traumas.

Existential Theory

Existential theory has contributed to crisis treatment. Although true existential psychotherapy is a long-term therapy with the goal of basic revision of life perspective (Bugental, 1978, p. 13), some ideas are also useful in a short-term adjustment model. Certainly, the existential thought that anxiety is a normal part of existence and can help self-development is useful to the crisis worker. This idea coincides with the Chinese idea of danger and opportunity. Without anxieties caused by new life situations, people would never grow. Therefore, anxiety as a motivator for risk taking and growth is a key concept from existential theory that has contributed to crisis theory. The belief that all people will suffer in life at one time or another and that suffering can strengthen people can be used to reframe a crisis for the person experiencing it.

Another useful concept from existential theory relates to the acceptance of personal responsibility and realization that many problems are self-caused. Choice then becomes a major focus for the person in crisis. Empowering clients with choices and encouraging them to accept responsibility are useful strategies in many crisis situations. A person who has recently been confronted about her cocaine abuse can be helped to accept responsibility for her addiction. The worker can offer alternative choices and be supportive while the client struggles with the anxiety of withdrawing from the cocaine habit.

Humanistic Approach

The humanistic approach and person-centered therapies have much to offer crisis intervention. This style of helping stresses the importance of trusting clients to realize their potential in the context of a therapeutic relationship. Optimism and hope that clients will recognize and overcome blocks to growth are the foundations for trying to help someone work through a difficult situation (Bugental, 1978, pp. 35–36). If the crisis interventionist does not truly believe that his clients can work through their problems, why would he waste his efforts on them? True, clients may not resolve their difficulties his way, or at his time exactly, but he needs to respect clients at their level and work from there. As long as they grow and develop, he can feel that he has contributed to the resolution of their crises.

Carl Rogers, the founder of person-centered counseling (considered a humanistic therapy), has contributed to the field of crisis intervention by his focus on reflective and empathetic techniques. These techniques, shown to be effective in treatment outcome, help clients acknowledge and freely express their emotions (Corsisni & Wedding, 1989, pp. 175–179). In addition to these outcomes, humanistic techniques create an environment that is special.

Practitioners of person-centered counseling believe that people can grow in a beneficial direction if they can experience a relationship of true acceptance, genuineness, and empathetic understanding. Crises are seen as blocks to growth and the potential for growth. By their presence, counselors help clients begin to accept themselves, trust in themselves, and make new choices based on this self-acceptance and trust.

Cognitive-Behavioral Theories

Every crisis model is based on the behavioral problem-solving model.

1. Define the problem.
2. Review ways that you have already tried to correct the problem.
3. Decide what you want when the problem is solved.
4. Brainstorm alternatives.
5. Select alternatives and commit to following through with them.
6. Follow up.

The cognitive approaches that blossomed in the 1970s and 1980s are also important in crisis work. As mentioned in Chapter 1, a person's cognitions, meanings, and perspectives about the precipitating event are important in the counselor's determining whether a crisis state exists. Cognitive approaches are largely based on Albert Ellis's rational-emotive therapy (Ellis, A., 1994), Beck's cognitive therapy (Beck, 1976), and Meichenbaum's self-instructional training and stress inoculation (Meichenbaum, 1985). These approaches are concerned with understanding the person's cognitive view of the problem and then restructuring and reframing any maladaptive cognitions (Peake, Borduin, & Archer, 1988, pp. 69–71). Cognitive approaches stress homework assignments and follow-up.

Family Systems Theory

Systems theory is particularly useful in developmental crises and crises related to cultural issues.

General systems theory is based on Newton's law of physics, which states that for every action there is an equal and opposite reaction. Terms like self-regulating mechanism, feedback, counteraction, and calibration can be used to describe an interpersonal system as well as a mechanical system.

The idea is that if a member in a family unit changes her or his behavior in a major way, others in the family will behave in ways to prevent the change from happening. This reaction is most likely due to fear of change at a subconscious level. Change often makes people feel anxious. Counteractive behaviors lessen anxiety. Family members often do not realize what they are doing. Therapists point out these processes and make clients conscious of them. Helpers must be sure that a client's anxiety is contained, that the client is supported, and that the client's perceptions are reframed. Typical counteractive behaviors used by family members include shaming, threatening, excluding, or punishing the target person. The one who is behaving outside the family's calibrated range of behaviors may continue a behavior that is acceptable to the family even if it is pathological, rather than endure counteraction from the family. Family systems theory helps explain why pathologic interactions are so common in families and why change takes a long time to occur. People tend to prefer stability (homeostasis), even if the consequence is retention of painful symptoms.

Runaways   **Runaway** is the term used in the family systems model to describe a true family crisis. This term has a particular meaning in family systems theory. A runaway exists when the counteractive-negative feedback mechanisms fail to bring the situation back into calibration, that is, family members cannot create homeostasis with their normal coping mechanisms. The runaway state often causes a family to seek family counseling.

Family therapy models have usually focused on brief interventions, much in keeping with the crisis model. Reframing and assigning positive connotations are two major intervention strategies in family systems approaches, particularly the strategic models. Both of these techniques aim at changing the internal cognitive experience of family members.

Just as a maintenance worker resets a thermostat if its mechanisms do not maintain temperature stability, a family worker resets the calibration of family rules after a runaway to help the family return to homeostasis, albeit a new stability. Crisis intervention often makes use of systems theory by employing techniques from structural and strategic problem-solving therapies (Peake et al., 1988, pp. 90–95).

Structual Family Therapy   Some families may inadvertently maintain a crisis state in a family member because they resist allowing the person to pass through a critical developmental stage. Structural family therapy attempts to help everyone in the family move through new developmental stages at the same time by learning new, more adaptive roles. The range of allowable behaviors is recalibrated, reducing counteractions (resistance). New boundaries are established that allow for age-appropriate independence and nurturance. Minuchin (1974) points out that these are the two main functions of a family: to provide support and nurturance and to create individuals who can function in society independent of the family of origin. Crisis workers must keep this in mind when assessing the nature of a client's crisis, which could involve problems of closeness and support or distance and independence.

Certain terms may be helpful in identifying healthy versus unhealthy structures in families. They also shed light on why certain problems exist. These words describe boundaries, which may need expansion or restriction. The crisis counselor often tries to create clearer boundaries that allow evolving needs to be met in family members.

Enmeshment: In an enmeshed situation, everyone in the family interferes and is overly involved in everyone else's decisions, feelings, wishes, and behaviors. Children may know too much about their parents, and vice versa. One sees a lack of independence of thought and feeling in family members. These families typically see themselves as very close or too close. A child may grow up feeling no sense of separateness and may have problems making decisions and functioning in other adult situations (Bowen, 1985). Depression and anxiety are common in relationships. A crisis state may occur when someone attempts to break out of the enmeshment. Others may react by subtly punishing the individual, perhaps with the "silent treatment" or exclusion from family affairs. A healthy balance between closeness and separateness is the goal of counseling in these circumstances.

Diffusion: A family is diffuse when members are not clear about who is to do what. Roles are not well defined or are inconsistent. For example, when a 16-year-old girl raises a baby in her parents' home, the baby may be confused about the role of his mother, who is receiving parenting at the same time that she is parenting him.

A pathologic variation of diffusion is **cross-generational coalition,** where one parent and a child team up against the other parent, thereby crossing the parent-child boundary. Incest is one of the most harmful examples of cross-generational coalition. It results in moderate to severe disturbances of the victim throughout his or her life. Clear age-appropriate boundaries are essential for healthy emotional functioning.

Disengagement: In a disengaged family, distance is the pattern. The rule in these families is not to get too close emotionally or socially. The relationship between parents and children and between spouses tends to be more functional than in some other troubled families. Independence is encouraged. However, children may feel unsupported and unloved in families where disengagement is strong. This feeling may lead to gang involvement, substance abuse, or teen pregnancy because children seek love and support outside the family or attempt not to feel anything (substance abuse). Crisis workers can intervene by helping families learn how to show support for one another to increase a sense of belonging.

Rigidity; In families with rigid boundaries, spouses and children are treated only one way. There is no crossing over between generations: Children are to be seen and not heard. Wives clean; husbands work; children obey. Father disciplines; mother takes care of children. These rules are typical and can lead to rigid personality structures in children. Counselors need considerable skill to be able to reframe and educate parents with rigid boundaries. They must carefully respect cultural factors. The following vignette shows a family with a problem. The approach used here combines structural family therapy with the family systems model.

A family seeks help to straighten out the 13-year-old daughter's behavior. She likes to be in her room alone, talks back to her parents, prefers her friends over her family, and is interested in boys. Her parents have been restricting her out-of-house activities, but that hasn't helped. A crisis interventionist might restructure and reframe the whole system. Instead of two adults and a child, the family consists of two adults and a maturing adolescent, who is behaving normally. The rules of behavior need to be changed to accommodate the change in structure, thereby lessening negative feedback. This less restrictive atmosphere encourages the 13-year-old to communicate more with her parents. The parents must be made aware of the family's enmeshment. They must see that their teenager needs a sense of independence to learn to function in the adult world she will soon be entering.

In the strategic family therapy model, the goal is to shift family rules to bring about a new homeostasis that does not include pathologic behaviors. Insight into why the family behaves the way it does is not necessary. Short-term homeostatic systems therapy may require fewer than 10 sessions. It includes the following six stages:

1. Introduction to treatment
2. Definition of the problem
3. Estimation of the behaviors maintaining the problem
4. Setting goals for treatment
5. Selecting and making interventions
6. Termination of treatment

Reframing a developmental crisis as a family or marital problem or a simple matter of adjustment is a common intervention. **Prescribing a symptom** is one technique (albeit a sophisticated one) for alleviating crisis states (Haley, 1976). The counselor suggests that the client or family members engage in the problematic behavior but with a slight modification. For example, clients who are very depressed might be told that they need to let themselves really *feel* the depression. To do this, they should close all the windows and curtains and sit in the dark. They are to focus on their sad feelings and cry for one hour. This episode allows clients to experience their symptoms in a new way. Usually, it results in alleviation of the symptoms. A counselor must take great care with this technique and be well trained or receive expert supervision in using it. It is not recommended for suicidal clients.

Brief Therapy

Brief therapy can be useful with individual clients as well as with families. In this approach, clients explore past patterns of behavior and how the patterns have prevented them from succeeding in life in the way they have wanted to succeed. They may explore interpersonal relationships, self-concept, and family patterns. The focus is on creative change and incorporating new styles of relating to the world. Sometimes the precipitating event is the best thing that could happen to a person because it leads him or her to a counselor's office, where some chronic debilitating patterns can be identified. If past ineffective patterns can be recognized, they can be eliminated; the client can learn more effective behaviors for dealing with current as well as future stressors.

Brief therapy seems to be as effective as long-term therapy. According to Garfield (1980, p. 282), "the evidence to date suggests that time-limited marital family therapy is not inferior to open-ended treatment." The average length reported in his research was seven sessions, a number that certainly fits with crisis intervention philosophy.

Critical Incident Debriefing

Community disasters have been dealt with throughout the nation by a process referred to as **critical incident debriefing.** The Red Cross and state and county departments of mental health usually work in tandem to aid victims of unexpected trauma. Many of the coping strategies involved in this process are similar to the ABC model of crisis intervention. The issues and interventions used in critical incident debriefing are presented in detail in Chapter 11, which deals with posttraumatic stress disorder in victims of natural disasters and other traumatic stressors.

The ABC Model of Crisis Intervention

The **ABC model of crisis intervention** is useful in most nonprofit agencies, county agencies, hospitals, and HMOs and with most insurance plans. It is a convenient crisis interviewing technique that can be used either in person or on the phone. It can be completed in a 10-minute phone conversation, in one session, or over six sessions.

The ABC model, developed by the author, is loosely based on Jones's (1968) A-B-C method of crisis management as well as on lecture notes from, and discussions with, Mary Moline at California State University, Fullerton, in the 1980s. A brief outline of the model is presented here. Chapter 5 explores in detail the different aspects of the model. In general, the crisis intervention model is an action-oriented effort between a helper and a person immobilized by an emergency situation; the purpose is to provide temporary, but immediate, relief. This treatment differs from psychotherapy, which is usually a more intensive, introspective analysis between a professional thera-pist and a client; its goal is to provide self-understanding and reconstruction of long-standing personality traits and behavior (Cormier, Cormier, & Weisser, 1986, p. 19).

The focus of the ABC model is to identify the precipitating event, the client's cognitions about the precipitating event, subjective distress, failed cop-ing mechanisms, and impaired function. Remember that these are the aspects of a crisis. The goal is to help the client integrate the precipitating event into his or her daily functioning and return to precrisis levels of emotional, occu-pational, and interpersonal functioning.

Developing and maintaining contact (A) is the first phase of the crisis intervention interview. Building rapport with basic attending skills is the foun-dation of the therapeutic encounter. Without establishing contact with the counselor, whom the client perceives as empathic, present, nonjudgmental, and genuine, the client will not move into phases B and C of the model. Beginning crisis intervention students are often told that before they give advice, they should make sure clients trust both them and themselves to fol-low through with it.

Identifying the problem and therapeutic interaction (B), the second phase, focuses on delineating the problem. Because crisis intervention is brief and time limited, the interventionist needs to zoom in quickly on why the client is seeking help at this particular time. A sharp focus on the problem will prevent distracting issues from confusing the crisis and depleting the client's needed coping energy. The B phase is most important. Identifying perspective, subjec-tive distress, and current and previous functioning takes up most of the mid-dle part of the model. Using the basic attending skills of phase A, the crisis worker collects the necessary information to understand the nature of the cri-sis and then provide new ways for the client to think about, perceive, and cog-nitively process the situation.

Coping (C) is the last phase of the model. Once the crisis interventionist achieves contact with the client and identifies the crisis, they explore new cop-ing methods together. The worker encourages the client to examine ways of coping and then presents his or her own suggestions. Last, the counselor does a follow-up of some type.

Table 2.2 suggests how traditional counseling models have contributed to the ABC model of crisis intervention.

TABLE 2.2 | CONTRIBUTIONS FROM COUNSELING
MODELS TO THE ABC MODEL OF CRISIS

Intervention

Theoretical Model	Contribution
Psychoanalytic	Finite psychic energy and ego strength
Existential	Responsibility; empowerment; choices; crisis as danger and opportunity for growth; anxiety as motivation
Humanistic	Rapport; safe climate; hope and optimism; basic attending skills
Cognitive-Behavioral	Focus on perceptions; reframing; goal setting; problem solving; follow-up
Family Systems	Runaways in families; developmental crises; counteraction; reframing

KEY TERMS FOR STUDY

ABC model: One way to structure crisis intervention that includes (A) developing and maintaining contact, (B) identifying the problem, and (C) coping.

behavioral problem-solving model: Approach focusing on goal setting, problem solving, and brainstorming alternatives.

brief therapy: May be confused with crisis intervention, but focuses on changing longer-standing behavior patterns rather than on only the current precipitating event.

Coconut Grove fire: Nightclub fire in 1942 in which over 400 people died, leaving many survivors in crisis; considered one of the major events leading to the development of crisis intervention as a form of mental health treatment.

cognitive approaches: Approaches focusing on a person's perceptions and thinking processes and how these lead to crisis states.

Community Mental Health Centers Act of 1963: Legislation enacted during the Kennedy administration directing all states to provide mental health treatment for people in crisis.

critical incident debriefing: A process of helping victims of natural disasters and other unexpected trauma deal with loss and stress reactions.

existential theory: Theory from which crisis intervention took the ideas of choice and anxiety. The crisis worker believes that anxiety can be a motivator for change and encourages the client to master anxiety realistically by making choices and accepting responsibility for the choices.

grass-roots efforts: Upward movement from local groups that led to the creation in the 1960s and 1970s of many agencies to meet the needs of various populations not being helped by traditional governmental agencies.

grief work: Crisis intervention largely based on working with survivors and family members of victims of the Coconut Grove fire. It was with this population that Caplan and Lindemann learned how to conduct short-term interventions.

health maintenance organizations (HMOs): The current trend in health insurance. These organizations focus on maintaining health rather than curing illness. The orientation of mental health care under this style of management is definitely crisis intervention.

humanistic approach: Model using a person-centered approach in developing rapport with clients; counselor uses basic attending skills to focus on the inherent growth potential in the client.

Lindemann, Eric: Worked with Gerald Caplan on the Wellesley Project and helped create crisis intervention as it is known today; recognized for his contributions to grief work.

paraprofessionals: Originally community volunteers. Because of the tremendous number of clients needing help at the same time after the Coconut Grove fire, it was necessary to employ community volunteers who were not professionally trained to conduct crisis intervention sessions. These paraprofessionals became part of many agencies in later decades.

psychoanalytic theory: An approach considered the opposite of crisis intervention but with certain ideas useful for the crisis worker. The notion that we have only a certain amount of psychic energy to deal with life stressors leads us to keep our clients proceeding at a slow pace so they don't deplete this energy. Also, ego strength is a useful concept, as shown in Chapter 1.

strategic family therapy: An approach for treating the entire family when a crisis affects any or all members. It is brief and oriented toward solving problems and reaching goals. It is largely based on systems theory.

structural family therapy: Focuses on the boundaries and roles of family members and the crises that arise when families must adjust to changing roles because of normal evolution.

systems theory: Useful in understanding families in crisis. The idea is that a family is a self-regulating system and that when any member behaves outside the norms, other members cope with counteraction. When counteraction (coping) fails, a runaway develops in the family dynamics. This runaway is a crisis and often requires the intervention of a family counselor.

Wellesley Project: Developed by Caplan and Lindemann, the first organized attempt at introducing crisis intervention into a community.

ETHICAL AND PROFESSIONAL ISSUES

CHAPTER 3

THE NEED FOR ETHICS

Strong ethical practice is especially important in the field of crisis intervention because clients in crisis come to a counselor in a vulnerable state of disequilibrium and instability. To take advantage of someone in such an unsteady state would be easy. At the outset of counseling, clients often feel hopeless and scared. They may view a counselor who reaches out with empathy with seemingly all the answers as a hero or savior of some type. Crisis interventionists must adhere to strong ethical behaviors to help clients see them and their abilities in a realistic light.

USE OF PARAPROFESSIONALS

Some mental health professionals may feel that crisis intervention should be provided only by professionals, counselors with at least a masters degree or a license. However, as discussed in Chapter 2, crisis intervention began with the use of community workers, sometimes referred to as nonprofessionals or paraprofessionals. These workers often functioned in multidisciplinary team settings such as county agencies and grassroots nonprofit organizations. Effective crisis intervention can be conducted by undergraduate student trainees or community volunteers as well as by graduate-level students and professional counselors if their training is appropriate and they are properly supervised.

The use of the paraprofessional crisis worker has continued to be especially important as the world has moved into the 21st century. The economic recession of the early 1990s plus a decided shift in governmental policies during the beginning of the 21st century has led to cutbacks in government spending on human services programs, which has meant less money or no money to pay mental health workers. Under these circumstances, the use of volunteers and paraprofessionals makes excellent economic sense, because most professional therapists will not provide crisis intervention consistently for the lowered fees often paid to many paraprofessionals. Also, many situations—including the AIDS epidemic, terrorism, and family deterioration—ensure that crises will be plentiful and intervention desired. When immediate low-cost help is needed, using paraprofessionals makes the community stronger by ensuring that its population is functioning and coping with stress.

SELF-AWARENESS AND COUNTERTRANSFERENCE

Self-awareness is available to crisis workers if they are willing to bring themselves into the interview therapeutically. **Therapeutic awareness** means being conscious of one's own emotions, values, opinions, and behavior. Understanding one's own psychological processes and dynamics can help one guide others through their processes (Corey, Corey, & Callanan, 1993, pp. 30–32). Students can learn therapeutic awareness in crisis intervention classes; such training can help students take an honest, in-depth look at themselves in relation to the crisis of interest. It can be a valuable learning experience, enhancing the crisis worker's skills in helping clients. If workers learn to deal with all the issues surrounding AIDS, for example, they have a better chance of helping a client deal with them.

Countertransference, an issue that must often be addressed in the helping professions, is defined as an "unconsciously determined attitudinal set held by the therapist which interferes with his work" (Singer, 1970, p. 290). Countertransference can be worked through effectively with personal therapy, lab sessions, and active self-exploration. Beginning crisis intervention students have often experienced one or more of the situational crises practiced in coaching sessions. If students have not worked through the crisis completely, their feelings may interfere with their ability to remain calm, objective, and client focused. However, once students' unresolved issues are discovered and processed, both in their own counseling and in lab group, they often are able to work quite effectively with clients going through that same type of crisis. Countertransference is not restricted to students in training. In actuality, this concept was first developed by Sigmund Freud in his training of psychoanalysts. Even the highly trained professional is liable to experience countertransference from time to time. This is the primary reason that personal analysis has been encouraged for psychoanalysts from the very beginning of the discipline.

DUAL RELATIONSHIPS

Another ethical issue involves a **dual relationship**—that is, a counselor's having more than one kind of relationship with a client. When counselors are providing crisis intervention to a client, they should not be involved with that client on a personal level of any kind. This includes prohibition of any relationship—sexual, social, employment, or financial—that is not directly related to the provision of crisis intervention. Such a separation is necessary because a person in crisis is often in a vulnerable state and could be taken advantage of quite easily by a counselor (who is viewed as an expert). Another reason to avoid a dual relationship is because of the possible emotional damage clients may sustain if they experience the counselor in a different role and then are disillusioned or disappointed. Also, the power differential between counselor and client is enormous. The counselor knows quite a bit about the client, and this knowledge can be a source of awkwardness for the client when he or she is out of the therapeutic situation. The most potent word on the subject is this: *Don't make friends or lovers of your clients. It is unethical and in some cases illegal.*

CONFIDENTIALITY

Confidentiality is one of the hallmarks of any trusting relationship. It is also an important part of the ethical code for mental health providers. A broad concept that refers to safeguarding clients from unauthorized disclosures of information made in the therapeutic relationship, confidentiality is an explicit promise by the counselor to reveal nothing unless the client has agreed to it. **Privileged communication**, which is sometimes confused with confidentiality, is the statutory right that protects clients from having their confidences revealed publicly (Corey, Corey, & Callanan, 1993, pp. 102–103).

As they relate to crisis intervention, however, some exceptions to privilege and confidentiality do exist. Privilege is waived if the client signs a document giving the helper permission to disclose the communications between the client and the counselor. Clients may be asked to waive privilege to ensure continuity of care among mental health professionals, to provide for appropriate supervision, when access to records is needed for court testimony, and when information is needed for submitting health insurance claims. Confidentiality must be broken in cases of child abuse or elder abuse, when the client is a danger to self or others, and may be broken when a client is gravely disabled. Sometimes, a client's mental condition will be the focus of a lawsuit, and in some cases confidentiality can be ethically and legally broken. For example, a client who sues a therapist for malpractice and claims to have suffered emotional damage because of the therapist's incompetence gives up privilege to communications from the therapy sessions. The therapist may use case notes to defend against the malpractice charge. A similar example in which a client would forfeit the protection of privilege is a case in which the client is attempting to prove emotional injury in a workers' compensation lawsuit.

The other exceptions to confidentiality fit under the adage "Privileged communication ends where public peril begins." This includes peril to clients if they endanger themselves because of a mental disorder. If clients are considered suicidal or gravely disabled and unable to care for themselves, helpers may breach confidentiality to protect them. The spirit of this allowance is that sharing information is meant to be among professionals, family, and friends, and not for frivolous purposes. Gravely disabled clients are those who, because of a mental disorder, cannot take care of their daily needs for food, shelter, medical care, clothing, and so on. Clearly, it is more important to break confidentiality to save someone with Alzheimer's disease from starving because he is delusional about having food in the house than it is to maintain confidentiality.

The other situations in which privileged communications should be broken involve trying to prevent clients from harming others. These conditions include elder abuse, child abuse, and the possibility that clients might cause different kinds of danger to others.

Elder Abuse Reporting Act

The department of social services in some states has an adult protective services program that responds to reports of abuse of the elderly (i.e., adults over 65 years old). Elder abuse refers to any of the following acts inflicted by other than accidental means on an elder by another person: physical abuse, fiduciary abuse (involves trust and money), and neglect or abandonment. In many states, knowledge of such abuse must be reported to social services, the police, or a nursing home ombudsman (governmental investigator). Some agencies have also begun taking reports of abuse of the disabled adult population. This could cover any adult who suffers from a mental or physical disability such as mental retardation or blindness.

Child Abuse Reporting Act

Since passage by Congress of the National Child Abuse Prevention and Treatment Act in 1974, many states have enacted laws requiring professionals to report child abuse. States differ on the indicators for reporting and whether sanctions will be imposed on individuals for not reporting. According to most professional associations, protecting children from harm is an ethical obligation, and there is a growing trend to ensure that reporting professionals are given immunity from suit if the suspicion proves to be false (Corey, 1996, p. 179). Child abuse reporting includes suspicions of physical abuse, sexual abuse, general neglect, and emotional abuse.

In many states, child abuse must be reported within 36 hours of its discovery to the department of social services or the police. The child protective services program will then investigate the suspicion. Remember that as a mental health provider, you are not required to have evidence of abuse before you report; you need only the suspicion that it exists. If you suspect abuse that is later proved and you failed to report it, you may be fined by the state.

On the other hand, more and more states are ensuring immunity from suit for false reports.

The Tarasoff Case   The consequences of failing to warn an individual of possible danger to her or him by another are dramatically illustrated in the Tarasoff case. In 1969, Prosenjit Poddar was seeing a therapist at the campus counseling center of the University of California, Berkeley. Poddar confided to the therapist that he intended to kill Tatiana Tarasoff when she returned from Brazil. The therapist considered Poddar dangerous and called campus police, requesting that Poddar be confined. He was not confined. To complicate matters, the therapist's supervisor ordered that all case notes be destroyed. Tarasoff was later killed by Poddar, and her parents filed suit against the California Board of Regents. The decision from this case requires a therapist to notify the police and the intended victim when possible if the therapist has reasonable belief that a client is dangerous toward others (**duty to warn**) (Corey, Corey, & Callanan, 1993, pp. 117–119).

INFORMED CONSENT

Informed consent is a way of "providing clients with information they need to become active participants in the therapeutic relationship" (Corey, Corey, & Callanan, 1993, p. 87). Although no specific rules exist governing how much information a therapist is to provide, three legal elements to informed consent do exist. First, clinicians must make sure clients have the ability to make rational decisions and, if not, must ensure that a parent or guardian takes responsibility for giving consent. Second, therapists must give clients information in a clear way and check their understanding of the risks and benefits of treatment and alternate procedures available. Third, clients must consent freely to treatment. The exceptions to these elements occur when clients are dangerous to themselves and others or are gravely disabled. Electroconvulsive shock treatments and psychosurgery (lobotomies) cannot be done without consent; however, there are times when medication is given without client consent.

SUPERVISION AND TRAINING

The ethical code requiring counselors to receive appropriate supervision and training must be followed for both the benefit of the client and the clinician's growth and confidence. Unless paraprofessionals are supervised by a licensed professional, most agencies—county, state, and nonprofit—do not let them provide crisis intervention and counseling. Even seasoned therapists should consult with colleagues about cases for which they have minimal training or experience. Referring a client to another helper is often done by crisis workers because the worker's duties mainly involve assessment and brokering out clients—tasks requiring a sound knowledge of community resources for a variety of problems.

Being able to make an assessment for organic illnesses and severe mental illness is especially important when a helper is conducting a crisis interview. Some cases require a multidisciplinary team approach with medical doctor involvement; they must be identified if the patient is to receive the total help needed. Even though making technical diagnoses is not usually considered appropriate for paraprofessionals, knowledge of the *Diagnostic and Statistical Manual of Mental Disorders* (American Psychiatric Association, 1994) is helpful in ensuring that clients receive services from the type of professional appropriate to their needs. This manual provides information about very serious mental disorders that require intervention by physicians. Crisis workers should review this manual when possible to gain a beginning understanding of the types of presenting complaints that usually necessitate physician involvement.

> **Example:** Suppose that a 45-year-old woman comes to a community center because her 70-year-old mother has been behaving strangely, does not recognize her family members, and leaves the gas stove burners on all day. Knowing that these symptoms are indicative of Alzheimer's disease or other organic brain disorders helps the crisis worker develop treatment strategies. Most important is having the woman examined neurologically to rule out any medical cause for her unusual behavior.

BURNOUT AND SECONDARY POSTTRAUMATIC STRESS DISORDER

People who regularly work with individuals in crisis situations may be prone to develop symptoms of burnout, or what can be referred to as secondary posttraumatic stress disorder (PTSD), which will be covered in detail in Chapter 11.

Burnout has been studied by many and has been seen in a variety of workers throughout the nation. Crisis workers should be informed about the possible symptoms and causes of burnout to be able to identify this state in themselves. The causes, definitions, and prevention of burnout are discussed. Secondary PTSD is then discussed in the context of a research study conducted by the author with 67 community workers who deal with crisis situations daily.

Definitions of Burnout

Maslach & Jackson (1986) have proposed three dimensions of burnout. Lack of personal accomplishment, emotional exhaustion, and depersonalization and deindividuation of clients are often the reactions of workers to chronic stress. Burnout can be thought of as a "syndrome of physical and emotional exhaustion involving the development of negative self-concept, negative job attitudes, and a loss of concern and feelings for clients" (Pines & Maslach, 1978, p. 224). When these reactions occur, individuals in the helping professions who are particularly susceptible to burnout may develop negative and cynical attitudes and feelings toward clients and may not be as supportive as needed (Vettor & Kosinski, 2000, p. 1).

Symptoms of Burnout

Researchers have described a variety of physical and emotional symptoms indicative of burnout. In the 1980s, hundreds of workers at an aircraft manufacturing facility developed symptoms of burnout that were referred to as **aerospace syndrome.** Most suffered from dizziness, nausea, headaches, fatigue, palpitations, shortness of breath, and cognitive impairment. Three-fourths of them also showed symptoms of major depression and panic disorder (Sparks et al., 1990).

Other common symptoms of burnout include psychosomatic illness, social withdrawal, substance abuse, and deterioration of family and social relationships (Freudenberger, 1975; Maslach & Jackson, 1986).

Causes of Burnout

Negative emotional and behavioral reactions on the job occur in many professions. Human service workers may be more prone to burnout as a result of conflicts between an idealistic "professional mystique" and the harsh realities of working in human services (Leiter, 1991). In addition, human services workers may find it emotionally taxing when consumers resent them, when they must work with consumers with limited capabilities to help themselves, when they must deal with tedious bureaucratic exercises daily, and when they receive little positive feedback from authority figures (Gomez & Michaelis, 1995). Lack of company support, poor relations among staff, lack of competence, and a perception that success is unlikely on the job are other general causes of burnout (Clarke, 2000).

In helping professions in which the professionals such as emergency medical technicians (EMTs) must deal with intense emotional arousal, depersonalization is used to minimize this arousal. Burnout may be seen as a coping strategy to ensure that performance is not affected in these crisis situations. Burnout may also occur as part of a tendency for helping professionals to evaluate themselves negatively when assessing their work with patients (Vettor & Kosinski, 2000). EMTs may be more susceptible to burnout because they are faced with human tragedies such as as injury, mutilation, and death on a daily basis. Services are often delivered in a hostile world of darkness, poor weather conditions, difficult terrain, and unpredictable dangers (Vettor & Kosinski, 2000). The technicians are at risk for developing secondary PTSD from exposure to critical incidents. (Effects of exposure to critical incidents are discussed in detail in Chapter 11.)

Negative emotional and behavioral reactions have also been observed in professionals who are not considered to be in the helping professions but who deal with crisis situations. Aerospace syndrome was determined to be caused by several psychosocial aspects in the workplace. Fear of chemicals, labeling of aerospace syndrome, fear of AIDS, mass hysteria crisis building, work intensity, mental strain, increased production pressure, tense labor-management relations, inadequate attention to safety, and reinforcement of fear by media and coworkers were all found to be causes of high work-stress burnout among aerospace workers (Vettor & Kosinski, 2000). The mass hysteria was so extreme that only 14 of the hundreds of workers observed showed no symptoms!

Prevention of Burnout

Several conditions may help prevent burnout and increase positive emotional reactions among workers. Kruger, Bernstein, and Botman (1995) suggest that having fun with team members, work discussions, peer cohesion, and social support, in which assistance is directed toward helping the worker cope with stressful circumstances, combine to reduce symptoms of burnout.

Human services workers who spend more time in direct contact with consumers and less time processing paperwork had higher scores on personal accomplishment assessments (Gomez & Michaelis, 1995). Reduced feelings of personal accomplishment have been associated with burnout, so it appears that one way to reduce burnout would be to spend more time with clients. However, because paperwork is often required in human services occupations, management would be wise to ensure that workers have enough client contact, as this seems to buffer workers against the worst effects of stress and is a valuable source of reward among staff. Other factors that may reduce burnout include workers feeling that they have some control over their time at work, some control over their workload, and an ability to organize their own work. Recognition of quality of care is also helpful in reducing burnout, as is clarity over one's role at work.

A Study of Community Crisis Workers

Sixty-seven community workers were surveyed in 2001 by the author with the assistance of several of her students who collected data by personally distributing questionnaires to various community workers who frequently work with crisis situations. These workers responded to questions regarding their emotional and behavioral reactions to working with people in crisis. Emergency room physicians and nurses, ambulance drivers, mental health workers, rape crisis counselors, firefighters, and police were included. The types of crisis situations they commonly work with were also identified.

Of the 67 workers surveyed, 21 identified themselves as counselors or therapists, 12 as police officers, 3 as physicians, 11 as nurses, 5 as emergency response workers, 7 as firefighters, and 8 as "other."

Table 3.1 shows the types of crises dealt with according to occupation.

The participants were asked several questions about their reactions to working with people in crisis. When asked if they felt anxiety when a client reports being suicidal, 23 (34%) of the crisis workers said yes. Only 12 (17%) reported being depressed after working with a person in crisis. However, when asked if there had ever been times when the worker was unable to stop thinking about clients in crisis, 41 (64%) said yes. These problems do not seem to prevent workers from going to work, though, as only 4 participants (all counselors) said they had missed work as a result of working with people in crisis. There was little increase in drug or alcohol use reported as a result of working

TABLE 3.1 | TYPES OF CRISES DEALT
WITH BY OCCUPATION

Type of Crisis Situation	Counselor	Police	Physician	Nurse	Emergency Response Worker	Firefighter	Other
	N = 21	N = 12	N = 3	N = 11	N = 5	N = 7	N = 8
Medical	4	12	3	11	4	3	0
Sexual assault	12	7	1	8	3	5	6
Spousal abuse	17	8	2	7	2	6	7
Child abuse	19	7	1	7	2	6	4
Victim of robbery or burglary	1	3	0	7	1	5	1
Victim of physical assault	14	7	2	10	4	6	5
Significant other of a murder victim	1	3	0	4	1	5	0
Victim of a natural disaster	1	2	0	7	3	4	0
Victim of a shooting spree	1	3	1	7	3	3	0
Substance abuse crisis	6	11	3	9	3	5	3
Sexually transmitted disease, HIV, AIDS crisis	5	6	2	9	2	3	1
Teen runaway, pregnancy, disobedience	16	4	2	2	1	4	6
Disability crisis	5	9	2	8	3	2	2
Illness crisis	8	11	3	9	4	2	2

with crises. Only 5 people stated that their use increased. This low number does not mean that the workers do not feel stress. In response to the question about feeling powerless after working with people in crisis, 23 (34%) answered that they did. This same percentage stated that they felt grouchy or agitated after dealing with people in crisis.

One common response of workers who deal with crises seems to be anger at the system. Thirty (45%) stated feeling angry at the system when working with someone in crisis. It is no wonder then that 35 (52%) of the workers stated that they think of quitting their job one to five times a month.

As to what these workers do when feeling emotionally stressed after working with people in crisis, the vast majority (80%) stated they talk with coworkers. Only 13 (19%) stated that they seek professional mental health services when feeling emotionally stressed.

The results of this study and previously discussed ones indicate that workers have many emotional, psychological, and behavioral reactions to stressful working conditions. In the case of crisis workers, many of the symptoms reported in this study are similar to the types of symptoms found in people going through a crisis. Symptoms of posttraumatic stress disorder included the inability to stop thinking about the client in crisis, agitation, irritability, anxiety, depression, and thoughts of wanting to quit the job. Because these symptoms are a result of working with people going through a crisis and not the result of the workers' own personal crises, it can be thought of as **secondary PTSD.**

The fact that these symptoms were reported to exist by so many of the crisis workers surveyed indicates a need for a strategy to reduce these symptoms. As was shown in many of the studies presented earlier as well as in the responses of this current study, maintaining ongoing communication with coworkers is essential in managing the symptoms. It is hoped that this will allow crisis workers to stay on the job at peak effectiveness.

KEY TERMS FOR STUDY

burnout: Feelings and behaviors that often result when a crisis worker feels powerless to help people in crisis. Symptoms of burnout include absenteeism, agitation, depression, anxiety, and anger.

child abuse reporting: Reporting required of anyone working with children as a counselor, doctor, teacher, or any other capacity since passage of the 1974 Child Abuse Prevention and Treatment Act by Congress. These people must report any suspicions of child abuse to the child protective services agency in their state. The requirement is mandatory and in many states overrides the client's right to confidentiality.

confidentiality: An ethical standard providing the client with the right for all disclosures in counseling to be kept private.

countertransference: A situation in a counseling relationship that arises from unresolved feelings experienced by a counselor in a session with a client. These feelings come out of the counselor's personal life and cause him or her to act out these feelings with a client, behavior that may cause emotional harm to the client.

danger to others: Condition in which a client is deemed to be a threat to others. At this time, the counselor must breach confidentiality and report his or her concerns to the police or the intended victim, or both. This is called the "duty to warn."

dual relationship: A relationship that a counselor engages in with the client outside the professional one—for example, a social, sexual, or business relationship.

elder abuse: Physical abuse, fiduciary abuse, neglect, or abandonment of someone 65 years old or older. In many states, anyone working with clients over 65 years of age must report suspected cases of elder abuse to the state's adult protective services agency. This reporting is often mandatory and grounds for breaching confidentiality.

exceptions to privilege and confidentiality: Situations in which communications between therapist and client can be legally and ethically shared with others. In the case of confidentiality, these include elder abuse and child abuse; when the client is gravely disabled; and when the client is a danger to self or others. In the case of privilege, these include voluntary waivers given by the client for information to be shared in a limited forum as well as some involuntary disclosure, as in certain court cases.

gravely disabled: Condition in which clients are psychotic or suffering from a severe organic brain disorder. People with such disorders are often incapable of meeting basic needs, such as obtaining food or shelter and managing finances. Being gravely disabled is often a reason for involuntary hospitalization of a person.

informed consent: Permission for treatment given by a client to a therapist after the client has been thoroughly informed about all aspects of the treatment. Anyone entering a counseling relationship has the right to understand the nature of therapy, give his or her consent for it, understand that it is voluntary, and be told the limits of confidentiality.

mental status exam: An examination used to rule out severe forms of mental illness and organic disorders. As part of their ethical responsibility, crisis interventionists must know when to refer a client to a physician. Use of this exam can help in making those determinations.

privilege: The legal counterpart of confidentiality. Clients may waive the right to privilege if they wish the counselor to share certain information in court or other limited venues.

4 | CHAPTER CULTURAL SENSITIVITY IN CRISIS INTERVENTION

Interest in the sensitivity of counselors and therapists to culturally diverse clients has been growing in the past few decades. It began in the 1960s when the civil rights and affirmative action movements emerged, and became a part of formal education in the late 1980s and 1990s. Arredondo and colleagues (1996, p. 43) describe specific behaviors and attitudes of culturally aware counselors: "Multicultural counseling refers to preparation and practices that integrate multicultural and culture-specific awareness, knowledge, and skills into counseling interactions." They suggest that **multicultural** refers to five major cultural groups in the United States: African Americans, Asian Americans, Caucasians, Latinos, and Native Americans. The reader is encouraged to obtain a copy of their article and keep it for reference. Although these groups have been the main focus of multicultural studies, other subgroups such as people with disabilities; gays, lesbians, bisexuals, and transgenders; and certain religious groups also have special needs.

This chapter explores the process of becoming a culturally sensitive counselor. Additionally, special issues and intervention strategies related to working with various ethnic groups, persons with disabilities, and gays and lesbians are discussed.

DEVELOPMENT OF CULTURALLY SENSITIVE PSYCHOTHERAPISTS

As part of a course in a doctoral program at the University of Southern California, seven students coauthored an article that describes the development of cultural sensitivity in therapists. The

TABLE 4.1 | **PROPOSED STAGES AND STATE-SPECIFIC CONSEQUENCES IN THERAPISTS' DEVELOPMENT OF CULTURAL SENSITIVITY**

Stage	Description	Consequence
Unawareness of cultural issues	Therapist does not consider a cultural hypothesis in diagnosis.	Therapist does not understand the significance of the clients' cultural background to their functioning.
Heightened awareness of culture	Therapist is aware that cultural factors are important in fully understanding clients.	Therapist feels unprepared to work with culturally different clients; frequently applies own perception of clients' cultural background and therefore fails to understand the cultural significance for a specific client; can at times accurately recognize the influence of clients' cultural background on their functioning.
Burden of considering culture	Therapist is hypervigilant in identifying cultural factors and is, at times, confused in determining the cultural significance of clients' actions.	Therapist believes that consideration of culture is perceived as detracting from his or her clinical effectiveness.
Movement toward cultural sensitivity	Therapist entertains cultural hypotheses and carefully tests these hypotheses from multiple sources before accepting cultural explanations.	Therapist has increased likelihood of accurately understanding the role of culture on clients' functioning.

Source: Lopez et al. (1989). ©1989 by the American Psychological Association. Adapted with permission.

students and their professor found similar patterns as all of them struggled with the gender and ethnic issues involved in diagnosing and treating various groups. Based on case vignettes and class discussion, a model of developmental stages was created and is shown in Table 4.1. Counselors do not have to be perfect models of cultural sensitivity, but they do need to be aware of cultural, ethnic, religious, and gender issues that may affect the crisis intervention process.

Knowing about various cultures before meeting with clients can be helpful. It is more important, however, to follow a client's lead in these matters, in order to help the client feel understood and validated. If a counselor fails to respect cultural differences, the crisis intervention may come to an end. In the following case example, the therapist did not show cultural sensitivity, with the consequence that the client dropped out of therapy prematurely.

> **Example:** A 41-year-old man requested an emergency session regarding his marriage. At his request, I saw him Saturday morning. The man spoke with an Asian accent and said that he was half-Chinese and half-Spanish and had been born in China. As we discussed his presenting problem, the client resisted any of my suggestions that part of his problem might be that his wife was Caucasian and her parents and siblings disapproved of him. He had come to my office to appease his wife, who said she would leave him unless he sought counseling. The couple had a poor sex life, but he resisted discussing this openly. He kept insisting that the problem was him, and he described himself as a cold person who did not like to be around people.
>
> I noticed myself becoming very frustrated. The client refused to accept the idea that he and his wife had a relationship problem. I guess the client sensed my frustration because he asked if I could refer him to another therapist. He had many demands regarding the times he was available for appointments. He refused marital therapy, which I recommended. I guessed that some of his issues were cultural in nature, but, unfortunately, I will not have the opportunity to explore these issues with him. (Lopez et al., 1989, p. 370)
>
> This vignette indicated that the therapist did not consider cultural factors in her work with this ethnic minority client. She appears to be defining the problem for the client without considering the client's definition of the problem and working from there. This is not to say that the therapist is wrong in her assessment; the client is likely having marital problems. However, her failure to validate his explanatory model or interpretation of the problem may have led to his request for another therapist. (Lopez et al., 1989, p. 371)

The intent of this chapter is to teach readers how to look at certain groups so they can form a working model that will help them understand the norms and family structures of the groups, crises that often arise, and interventions that will alleviate them.

LATINOS

The terms *Hispanic, Latino,* and *of Spanish descent* all refer to people whose culture was influenced by the Spanish conquerors of the 15th and 16th centuries. Most of these Spaniards settled in Central and South America. **Hispanic** is an umbrella term for descendants of the colonized natives, Hispanos, and descendants of foreigners and political and economic refugees. **Latino** refers to people from Latin America, which is actually Central and South America. Although there are differences between the various Latino groups, certain similarities exist as well. The most notable commonality is the Spanish language. Language influences thoughts and behaviors, and, therefore, many Latino groups have similar customs. The Spanish influence is also evident in many of their cultural patterns.

About 35.3 million Latinos reside in the United States. They are by far the largest minority group (U.S. Bureau of the Census, 2001). They range from Mexican Americans to Puerto Rican Americans to Cuban Americans to Central and South Americans. Over 10 million live in California, a state that borders Mexico and was at one time a territory of Mexico. Many Mexican traditions are alive and well in the coastal state. About 6.6 million Latinos live in Texas, and about 2.8 million in New York. Florida has 2.6 million, Illinois 1.5 million, and Arizona 1.2 million. New Mexico is home to 765,386, which is 42% of the total population of the state. Because Mexican Americans are the largest group of Latinos in the United States (about 58.5% of all Latinos), it is important to examine Mexican American culture. Counselors should use information about this culture when conducting crisis intervention. Despite differences in migration patterns and other historical events, most Latino individuals have been strongly influenced by their Spanish heritage, so the issues discussed are relevant for other Latinos as well as Mexican Americans.

Mexican American Families

Over 20.6 million Mexican Americans live in the United States. They often suffer discrimination in housing, employment, and education. Their school dropout rate is high, and they are often exploited by employers, who keep them in low-paying, low-prestige jobs. They often do not receive welfare benefits despite their high unemployment rate. The "oppressed servant mentality" that was forced on them after they were conquered by the Spaniards is still evident in their lives. Mexicans who emigrate to California or other states usually do so because they are poor. They want to earn enough money to survive and also support their families back in Mexico.

Most Mexicans are *mestizo* people, who have a mixed American Indian and Spanish heritage. From the 17th century to the 19th century, Spain extended its rule over the region that is now Mexico and moved into California and other southwestern states. The Spaniards and Indians shared much, but the Spaniards took Mexico's riches and kept the natives poor. Spanish priests taught Catholicism to the natives, who combined it with their own religions. From these interchanges, a new culture was created: the Mexican culture.

After the 1848 gold rush in California, settlers from the eastern part of the United States went west, and conflicts began to erupt between them and the Mexicans. The two groups lived separately. Eventually, Mexicans lost much of their property and many of their rights to the newcomers. The U.S. citizens were happy to settle in areas where gold could be mined and other natural resources such as agricultural land and water were available. The Mexicans were pushed far back into Mexico, where the land is arid and not suitable for agriculture. Industrial development has been slow in Mexico, and it has become a poor country (McGoldrick, Pearce, & Giordana, 1982).

Many Mexicans stayed in the United States. Areas in which they settled, creating pockets of their own subculture, are sometimes called **barrios.** Some Mexican Americans speak English and have adopted some mainstream values, but they still have certain distinctive values. Because the United States and

Mexico are so close to each other geographically, Mexicans continue to enter the United States illegally. The undocumented status of many Mexicans is an important factor in understanding their behavior. Sensitivity to the history of Mexican American clients can help crisis counselors approach them with empathy.

Mexican American Cultural Patterns

One Mexican cultural behavior that may differ from Anglo norms is child-rearing practices. In Anglo-American culture, autonomy is stressed; in Mexican culture, however, nurturance and obedience to authority are stressed. Mexican American children often appear to be delayed developmentally. For example, a 5-year-old may sit on his mother's lap; a 3-year-old may drink out of a bottle; and a 14-year-old may spend all her time with her mother. However, these behaviors are all considered normal in Mexican American culture.

Physical distance between people is another difference. By Anglo standards, Mexican Americans might seem overinvolved with, enmeshed with, or over-protective of one another. It is normal, however, for family members to sit close together or to assume that they are to be included in any individual family member's crisis (McGoldrick, Pearce, & Giordana, 1982, p. 151). Because family closeness is such an important part of Latino culture, crisis workers should keep systems theory in mind when working with Mexican American families.

> **Example:** If an 18-year-old daughter is raped or a 22-year-old daughter battered, it is likely that each young woman's family will become involved in helping her through the crisis. This is not to say they will tell her to leave her husband or go to trial for the rape. The daughter will most likely tell them of her distress, however. In many Anglo cultures, victims deal with these crises with the help of professionals and community support groups without telling their families about their problems.

Mexican American families sometimes do not seek help because they do not know about community resources (McGoldrick, Pearce, & Giordana, 1982, p. 154). Language barriers, racism, or lack of knowledge may keep them from using even the most basic services available. Workers should not try to conduct long-term introspective, psychodynamic psychotherapy (which, by the way, is counter to most Mexican American norms). Instead, workers should serve as "brokers" for services. This is often an extremely helpful role for a counselor who is working with a Mexican American family in crisis.

> **Example:** In some families, the children are bilingual but a parent speaks only Spanish. Children may not get the services they need because the parents feel embarrassed or frustrated when they try to explain their needs to professionals and agencies. Often, the job of a crisis worker is to make contact with a school official or a legal advocacy program and connect a family with these services.

Personalismo is a cultural pattern of relating to others in a manner that may include exaggerated warmth and emotions and a strong need for rapport in order to feel safe or trust others. It is particularly important for crisis workers to grasp this concept when working with Latinos because developing trust is a hallmark process in the helping relationship. Workers may have to spend time in seemingly idle chitchat. The Latino culture is much more relationship oriented than task oriented, unlike mainstream American culture.

One last characteristic of Latinos is their tendency toward emotionalism, even exaggerated expression that borders on the dramatic. If given the chance and if they feel safe, they often express their feelings openly in counseling. This expression of affect may allow them to master their feelings. Caplan discussed this process when he proposed seven characteristics of people coping effectively. At times, crisis workers may just want to allow clients to express their feelings and not pressure them to solve a problem.

Issues Related to Different Rates of Acculturation

Other crises that may emerge in Mexican American families may reflect patterns that developed and were functional when the family first immigrated to the United States but have since become restrictive for certain family members. For example, many parents depend on their children to be their intermediaries with the larger culture. When the children grow up and want to separate from their parents, the parents may find it difficult to let them go (McGoldrick, Pearce, & Giordana, 1982, p. 155).

Adolescents may adopt Anglo values that are contrary to traditional Mexican values. Rejection of parents' cultural values may precipitate a crisis between an adolescent and a Mexican American mother or father.

> **Example:** A 15-year-old girl may act out rebelliously by dating boys, staying out late, or dressing less than modestly. A crisis interventionist may suggest that the parents take a more active role in their daughter's growing up by structuring traditional activities for her, such as a *quincinera* (a party to announce entrance to womanhood). The girl's acting-out behavior can then be reframed as confusion about whether she is growing up. A structured ritual will help everyone to more easily accept role changes and should help reduce the family's distress. (McGoldrick, Pearce, & Giordana, 1982, p. 156)

A teenager who joins a gang is acting in a way that is related to different rates of acculturation. In order not to accept an "oppressed servant mentality," the adolescent engages in the power and control activities that are common in gangs, such as drug dealing, drug use, assault, and murder. Gang activity may be considered a sign of negative acculturation of teenage Mexican Americans.

Using negotiation skills and finding compromises is essential for the interventionist working with dual-culture families. Remember that the parents have chosen to live in the United States; this decision says something about their desire to be connected with some parts of American culture. A counselor can weave this idea into positive reframing, pointing out the opportunity afforded the family that adopts certain Anglo behavioral norms. Studies have shown that emotional distress is higher in Latinos who have either adopted American cultural norms in toto or have held onto traditional Mexican cultural norms in toto (Hovey, 2000; McQueen, Getz, & Bray, 2003). Maintaining a bicultural identity seems to be the healthiest mental position for Latinos, and it should be encouraged by mental health clinicians.

Comparison of Mainstream Cultural Values and Latino Resistance in the Mental Health Field

Most theories and techniques in the counseling profession developed within an Anglo-Saxon value system. The three major camps that have traditionally defined mental health and emotional dysfunction are the behavioral, psycho-analytic, and humanistic systems. If crisis workers depend on these tradition-al theories when working with Latinos, they may encounter much resistance. Table 4.2 presents traditional mainstream values as related to these traditional models and possible Latino resistance to them.

Although these traditional approaches do not appear to be applicable to the Latino population, approaches do exist that are more amenable to their needs. In a 2000 research study (Kanel), 268 Latinos were asked what type of mental health services they would prefer. Of the individuals surveyed, 163 were low-skilled factory workers, most of whom spoke little English. The other 105 individuals were students at a local community college who were learning English or fulfill-ing general education requirements. The vast majority said they would seek out a counselor if they had family problems (67.2%) or if they had their own emotion-al problems (63.1%). Depression and nervousness were the problems for which they would be most likely to seek help (26.9% and 24.3%, respectively). Other problems that would precipitate a visit to a counselor included "out-of-control anger" (17.2%); marriage problems (18.7%); disobedient children (16%); anxi-ety (15.3%); children's school issues (15.3%); and drug problems (15.4%).

When asked about the way they would want the counselor to relate to them, 35.8% said they would prefer to have the counselor give a lot of advice, 26.5% stated they wanted the counselor to ask a lot of questions; 21.6% pre-ferred the counselor to be personal; and 50.4% wanted the counselor to be very professional. Interestingly, although 63.8% believed that talking about their childhood would help resolve current problems, only 18.3% stated they would want to talk about their childhood; 66.4% preferred to talk about current problems. As for the use of medication, 59% did not believe it could help them with their problems, and only 7.8% preferred to take medication to resolve emotional problems.

The author simultaneously surveyed 43 Spanish-speaking therapists in southern California on their treatment of this population. When asked about the type of intervention they use with Spanish-speaking clients, 28% said cognitive-behavioral therapy, 26% said family counseling, 23% said psychoeducational therapy, and 23% said referrals to other agencies. These approaches in combi-nation are the same as the crisis intervention model presented in this book.

Based on these results and Latino cultural norms, it appears that two approaches would be most effective: the family system model and the crisis intervention model (which is heavily influenced by cognitive, behavioral, and psychoeducational models).

Ataque de Nervios

One Latino phenomenon that may come to the crisis worker's attention is *ataque de nervios (los nervios),* which literally means "attack of nerves." This is

TABLE 4.2 | COMPARISON OF MAINSTREAM AND LATINO VALUES IN THE MENTAL HEALTH FIELD

Mainstream Theoretical Model	Latino Resistance
Behavioral Approaches to Parenting	
Behavior modification:	
a. Positive reinforcement or rewards	*Respeto:* Children should do what parents tell them to just because they are children.
b. Response cost	Punishment is considered a form of love and a way to avoid spoiling children.
c. Active parenting approach	Indirect, guilt-inducing methods are commonly used with teens; parenting is not active but assumed.
d. Plan for future parenting	Deal with parenting when it comes; present orientation.
Psychoanalytic Approaches to Parenting	
Stages of development move from complete dependence to complete independence:	
a. Complete dependence	Complete dependence lasts as long as possible.
b. First independence, mobility, self-feeding, bowel control	Physically: Some children are bottle-fed or nursed until they are 5 years old; even preschoolers may be hand-fed.
c. Social independence	Socially: Children have few friends outside the home; they play with siblings and cousins. Children do not have sleepovers. Intrafamilial dependence is normal.
d. Moral independence	Morally: Law and order are valued; children should do what authority says; they are not encouraged to make decisions on their own.
e. Emotional independence	Emotionally: Interdependence with parents and enmeshed boundaries are normal; children are expected to meet their parents' needs.
Humanistic and Existential Approaches to Parenting	
a. Self-awareness	Denial of relational conflicts; anxiety with self-awareness
b. Confrontation in relational conflicts	Avoidance of confrontation
c. Genuine encounters and intimacy	Lack of intimacy and authentic relating; interactions are prescribed and based on hierarchy and gender roles.

This table is the original work of Kanel, 2003.

a culture-bound, self-labeled syndrome found only in Latinos. It is often a reaction to trauma, death, marital infidelity, or family conflict. A person suffering from this may seek help from a physician, counselor, or *curandero* (folk healer). Symptoms include panic attacks, fits of violent agitation with self-mutilation and suicidal behavior (Schechter et al., 2000, p. 530), shaking, heart palpitations, numbness, shouting, swearing, striking others, falling, convulsions (Liebowitz et al., 1994, p. 871), and signs of dissociation (Oquendo, 1995).

In 2004, the author conducted a study of 198 Latinos whose dominant language was Spanish and 37 mental health clinicians who treat Spanish-speaking clients to better understand *ataque de nervios* and treat it. Mental health counselors have been confused about how best to diagnose this disorder and how to intervene when it occurs. The two main symptoms reported by participants were screaming and despair. Being out of control, crying, and feeling irritable and anxious were mentioned frequently as well. Crisis workers may attribute these symptoms to panic disorder, generalized anxiety disorder, or depression. Of the Latinos surveyed, 76% reported symptoms of *ataque de nervios* that could fit more than two diagnoses or would not fit any diagnosis. Others have reported confusion in diagnosing *ataque de nervios* when using the universally accepted nomenclature of the DSM-IV, developed by the American Psychiatric Association in 1994. None of those studies resulted in an exact fit with traditional diagnoses, either, and most recommended further study to better understand the relationships between *ataque de nervios* and other disorders (Koss-Chioino, 1999; Liebowitz et al., 1994; Oquendo, 1995; Schechter et al., 2000).

What then are the implications for the crisis worker when a client presents with *ataque de nervios?* Both groups in the author's 2004 study overwhelmingly selected family conflicts (76% of Latinos and 82% of clinicians) as the number one cause. Emotional problems and work conflicts were mentioned as the next two causes by the Latino group. Clinicians reported that drug and alcohol abuse, childhood abuse, and intrapsychic conflict were also important causes. Only 26% of clinicians stated that the cause was a biochemical imbalance. This is important information because people suffering from *ataque de nervios* are usually diagnosed as having biochemical imbalances and given medication as the treatment of choice. According to the study, however, the causes are interpersonal and psychological and, therefore, need psychological treatment and family therapy. Although medication may help, it is not sufficient. In fact, *curanderos* may help clients more than therapists if clients believe in the power of herbal cleansing or faith healing.

When Latinos present with *ataque de nervios,* crisis workers would be wise to use the ABC model, giving the client plenty of time to express feelings. Helping the client feel understood is vital for him or her to overcome the sense of being out of control. Family sessions are helpful. The focus should be on developing new ways to cope with stress in relation to family members and co-workers. If the symptoms are extremely debilitating, referral to a physician may be warranted. In the study, 31% of Latinos stated that they talked to family and friends to overcome *ataque de nervios,* 21% saw a therapist, 21% received medication from a physician, 17% said the condition went away by itself, 12% received medication from a psychiatrist, 10% saw a *curandero,* and 14% used folk remedies such as smelling onions, prayer, and hands-on healing. Of the clinicians surveyed, 60% used cognitive therapy, 56% supportive therapy, and 48% family therapy; 43% recommended using medication; and only 0.08% used expressive or psychoanalytic therapy.

AFRICAN AMERICAN FAMILIES

In an ideal world, people would pay no attention to skin color. However, if mental health providers do not realize that African American culture differs in various ways from mainstream American culture, they may do a disservice to this group. Even if one is not a bigot or does not discriminate against African Americans, one must understand the ways in which an African American person in crisis may be affected by racial issues.

When one considers the history of African Americans, one can understand their family structure and value systems. African Americans who were raised in slavery learned to exist in settings where roles were flexible and families usually extended to several generations. These aspects can be readily seen in modern-day African American families. Elderly people as well as young adults "tend to be supported by the collective efforts of family members both within and outside the nuclear family" (McGoldrick, Pearce, & Giordana, 1982, p. 90). This history certainly has implications for the crisis interventionist. The worker should use naturally existing support systems for each individual. The worker should also explore the role norms of the person's family system so he or she does not see a problem when none exists.

> **Example:** A child may be brought in by his parents for misbehaving in school. You may discover that the parents do not understand his behavior and seem to be ineffective in eliminating it. Perhaps the child's grandmother is perceived by all to be the primary disciplinarian and nurturer. Instead of taking those responsibilities away from the grandmother and giving them to the parents (which would disengage the grandmother from the problem), you may want to bring the grandmother into the sessions and work with her alongside the parents. You would be culturally biased if you insisted that only the parents be involved in the child's therapy.

Role of Religion in African American Life

Slaves found solace in the view that God would provide a better world for them after they had left this world of suffering. This tradition of strong religious beliefs and practices has been passed down through the generations and must be kept in mind by the crisis worker.

The church has been a forum in which many African American women and men have expressed their talents and leadership skills (McGoldrick, Pearce, & Giordana, 1982, p. 96) and have found a kind of haven from a racist society. For the crisis interventionist, incorporating the church into therapy, either by seeking support from a minister or by encouraging the client to become involved in church activities, is valuable. Many African Americans do not place much trust in mainstream, middle-class mental health counselors. African American ministers, however, often do trust counselors and may be able to allay the fears of parishioners who would benefit from counseling.

Sometimes, appeals for help from the church are not productive. If clients are extremely mistrustful of counselors, workers should not try to convince them to change their views. Instead, counselors can empathize with the distrust and help clients engage with traditional cultural support systems that they do trust, such as family and friends. Unfair treatment of African Americans by the legal system is well documented; a disturbing encounter with the system is one event that may lead to a family crisis.

Problem-Solving Model for African Americans

Not all African American families in crisis need to be referred to traditional support systems. A growing number have adopted mainstream, middle-class values and will respond to crisis intervention. Focusing on the presenting problems and setting up goal-specific plans often work well. Some African Americans will seek out and accept insight-oriented therapy. The most important goal is to determine the needs of a particular client or family and meet these needs with cultural sensitivity. The worker must always acknowledge that racism is present in our society and must try to understand the world of a client who deals with racism every day.

Wright (1993) emphasizes the importance of cultural sensitivity when a worker has an African American male client who is dealing with issues of sexual behavior and the risk of HIV infection or AIDS. His research shows that African American men may have different views about sexual categories and behavior than mainstream white men. AIDS is widespread among African Americans and is primarily spread by men. Therefore, intervention strategies must be sensitive to the values and behaviors of African American men.

Wright suggests that current educational materials, health facilities, and community-based AIDS education and prevention programs are inadequate in their cultural and racial sensitivity. He states that "the AIDS epidemic is not merely a medical dilemma but is a socio-cultural medical dilemma. For African American men, AIDS has become an overwhelming and devastating blow that has torn away at their already threatened health and social status" (Wright, 1993, p. 430). Wright recommends that future policies should address cultural issues when programs are created to help prevent and reduce the risk of AIDS transmission among African Americans.

Although this research focuses on social policy, individual crisis workers can also benefit from these studies of the sexual behavior of African American men. Crisis workers must realize that for this group, a person's sexual behavior does not necessarily cause the person to be labeled a homosexual, heterosexual, or bisexual. Asking questions such as "Are you gay?" to see if a person is at risk for AIDS would be inappropriate, because even though a man may be engaging in homosexual behavior, he may not regard himself as a homosexual. (This is true for any client, not just African American clients.) It would be more suitable to identify specific behaviors that are associated with a high risk of AIDS and to provide information about such behaviors and about ways to prevent transmission of the HIV virus. (See Chapter 9 for more details.) Once a worker understands the client's perspective, the worker has accomplished the most important part of his or her task. Using this knowledge to help the person cope is the next challenge.

ASIAN AMERICAN FAMILIES

Asian American families have their roots in East Asia—China, Japan, and Korea—which is an area distinguished by having the oldest continually recorded civilization in the world. Its history gives it a background very different from that of the West in a variety of ways. For example, there are differences in philosophical approaches to life that are dictated in the East by Confucianism and Buddhism rather than Judeo-Christianity. Eastern systems do not stress independence and autonomy but rather emphasize the importance of the family and the specific hierarchical roles established for all members. Rules for behavior are extremely strong and more formalized than in other cultures. Because these people lived for years under oppressive dynastic rule and needed to maintain a large labor force capable of heavy manual and agricultural labor, male offspring became more valued than female offspring (McGoldrick, Pearce, & Giordana, 1982, pp. 208–210).

There are historical differences between the various Asian cultures. Language is one difference; another is the specific immigration problems and circumstances that each group experienced. Many Vietnamese people fled in boats to escape Communist rule. Many Japanese people came to America to take advantage of financial investments and employment opportunities.

Crisis Intervention Issues for Asian Americans

Although not all persons of Asian descent react the same, certain characteristics are commonly seen in people in crisis states and those using coping skills. The typical middle-class Judeo-Christian attitude of many mainstream training programs and work settings in the mental health field often does not address the special needs of Asian Americans.

The idea that the family should be placed ahead of individuals is one cultural difference that can definitely affect the counselor's work. Asian Americans are traditionally taught to respect family needs more than personal needs. Kashiwagi (1993, p. 46) states that "back in the old country the people had to band together, work together cooperatively, just to survive. I think because this value system worked then it was handed down." He further proposes that Asians who came to America felt the need to prove themselves, and this set up the "model minority" stereotype. This tradition of being overachieving, hardworking, and industrious may lead to stress and pressure to maintain the status quo inside and outside the Asian American community. The crisis worker should keep these characteristics in mind when working with this population.

Southeast Asians and Posttraumatic Stress Disorder

Kinzie and his colleagues (1984) have noted certain values held by Southeast Asian clients that affect the course of psychotherapy when they are treated for posttraumatic stress disorder (PTSD):

1. An orientation to the past, including great respect for ancestors
2. A primary reliance on the family as the basis of personal identity and self-esteem
3. The tolerance of multiple belief systems in regard to religion and cosmology and acceptance of life as it is rather than what it could be (pp. 645–646)

The mainstream-oriented crisis worker must consider these values when dealing with this Asian population so as not to force values on them that do not fit with their cultural norms. However, Boehnlein (1987, p. 525) believes that the mainstream cognitive psychotherapeutic approach does have relevance for Cambodian patients with PTSD:

> This approach facilitates an ongoing dialogue allowing the therapist to directly address issues in treatment that may relate to conflicting beliefs and values, along with doubts about one's personal and social identities that may affect interpersonal functioning. This is especially helpful in PTSD patients who have such profound doubts about their self-worth and their abilities to make effective changes in their lives based on personal traumatic histories and religious belief systems which often lead to a pessimistic view of fate.

Boehnlein (1987, p. 526) offers some specific questions a crisis worker might ask a Southeast Asian client with PTSD:

> "Do you have to attain perfection in order to not consider yourself a failure?" "Given the progress you have steadily been making, is your life still fated to be continuously and forever difficult?"
>   "You have been viewing yourself as a weak and ineffective person, yet you had the strength as an adolescent to survive years of starvation and brutality. There must be strengths that you and your family possess that you have not been aware of in recent years." [Note that these statements are examples of reframing.]

Boehnlein further notes that these patients tend to minimize outward emotional expression. Persons with PTSD who feel they must not display emotions can use up a lot of psychic energy. Therefore, when working with Asian patients with PTSD, crisis workers need to be aware of their own affective responses and the subtle cues of internal distress communicated by patients. These cues may be communicated through reports of dreams or perhaps behavioral signs of depression, such as somatic distress or sleep disturbance.

Finally, Boehnlein (p. 527) suggests that the

> therapist can communicate a sense of warmth, genuineness, and competence by being direct, yet compassionate; by being assertive in the recommendation of treatment approaches, yet responsive to possibly conflicting cultural concepts of illness and healing; and by allowing the patient to report difficult historical information or express intense emotion without a sense of shame. Explaining to patients in a matter-of-fact way that a number of their experiences and feelings are shared by many other Cambodians does not trivialize their personal situation but instead serves to minimize their fear of going crazy.

This is a good example of how educational comments and reframing can be used.

In his work with Asian Americans, Hong (1988) has found that mental health workers would do well to adopt a general family practice model whereby they maintain an ongoing interaction with the family and serve as a resource that the family can consult when they are in difficulty. A counselor should use knowledge of the client as well as knowledge of the client's family, community, and social environment. This approach seems particularly suitable for Asian Americans whose culture emphasizes the role of the family. It helps to minimize the client's inhibition against seeking mental health services, gives the client the advantage of having family support, and helps the client in therapy because there is less resistance from the family system.

Whenever possible, the crisis worker must take into consideration the effect any intervention will have on the client's family. The worker should bring in the family whenever possible. To suggest that a client focus exclusively on her or his own problems will undoubtedly wreak havoc on the family system.

> **Example:** A 26-year-old Vietnamese female came for crisis intervention because of her depression and the increasing tension in her house. She was a medical student and working full-time. Her father expected her to serve him, support the family financially, and stay at home when she was not at school or work. Her older brother was permitted to lie around the house, contributing nothing; the client was very angered by this inequality. She realized that she had become quite Anglicized in her value system and felt taken advantage of by her family. She was miserable and pondered suicide.

In analyzing this case, the helper realized that cultural sensitivity was vital. If the counselor thought only in terms of middle-class, Caucasian values, he would support the separation/individuation process and encourage the client to assert her own needs and rights. However, if this client were to go against the wishes of her father, she would be ostracized from her family. A few concepts can help explain this dilemma.

Asian American Family Structure

In most traditional Asian families, males are respected more than females. The oldest son has more privileges than his own mother, though he must respect her at certain levels. The mother plays the stereotypical role of nurturer, providing domestic structure, whereas the father dictates all family decisions. The daughter contributes to the household until she marries; then she belongs to her husband's household and family. The concept of individualism is not part of this culture.

Shame and Obligation in Asian American Culture

If the norms are not followed, an individual and the family will experience a sense of shame, not only for their own actions but for the entire family line. This factor makes it necessary at times to reject a family member completely so as not to bring shame on the family. Differentiation between the family as a whole and its members often does not exist as it does in European cultures. Obligation arises in any situation in which the rules of family structure come into play. The child is obligated to respect the structure. If the child does not, he or she will bring shame on the family. Having to choose between obligation and individual freedom often brings on feelings of depression and anxiety. The crisis worker needs to be sensitive to these struggles and search for ways to negotiate compromises when possible.

In the case of the young medical student, the counselor did not suggest that she move out and tell her father that she is an adult and does not have to support him. Instead, the counselor encouraged her to use the counseling sessions as times to vent her frustrations. The crisis worker let the young woman know that she understood her dilemma and that by choosing to maintain the status quo, the woman could continue to be a part of her family. The consequences for violating the system would be complete alienation from her mother and sisters as well as the men in her family. If she could learn to keep her focus on the value of family, perhaps she could learn to let go of her feelings of unfairness. In reframing the situation, the worker pointed out that although the client felt a lot of pressure to keep the family from being shamed, her father felt this obligation even more. In actuality, the father carried the burden of keeping his family in line. He would experience incredible shame if his daughter were to move out while she was unmarried and refuse to support his family financially.

Kashiwagi (1993, p. 46) provides another example of how "certain traditional Asian cultural influences, such as bringing shame to the family and losing face in the community," have an effect on mental health problems and intervention. He asserts that when an Asian American teenager has a drug or alcohol addiction, the family often denies the condition and perpetuates the problem. This denial results in large part from the lack of connection, communication, and understanding in the parent-child relationship. If the counselor recommends a tough love approach—that is, tells the parents to refuse to continue being enablers for the teenager's behavior and set standards that he must meet—the parents probably will not follow through adequately because of the cultural tendency to care for family members at a surface level.

Another example of the importance of avoiding family shame was presented by Carol Cole (1993). In her role as an emergency response worker with a county mental health unit, she received a call from neighbors, who complained of an awful stench coming from a house next door. When she arrived, she found a 40-year-old Asian American woman who was completely psychotic. She was delusional, disheveled, and disoriented, had no food in the house, and showed no signs of reality orientation. Her Asian family had immigrated to the United States 5 years earlier, and the parents had kept this 40-year-old daughter in the home with no treatment because acknowledging that a child was mentally ill would bring shame on the family. Two weeks earlier, the parents had been in a car wreck, and no one was at home to take care of the daughter. In this case, although the client was hospitalized involuntarily, the action was reframed as an opportunity to help stabilize the daughter and teach the family about available resources—in this case, resources in the Vietnamese community.

Strict approaches that require setting firm limits, such as making a child sleep outside or go to school in dirty clothes, bring shame to the whole family;

therefore, parents tend to enable irresponsible behaviors to avoid shame. To confront a child about how her or his behavior makes the family feel would be shameful, so parents' true feelings are often hidden. The child usually knows this, can take advantage of it, and can abuse the parents' acts of kindness. This situation is especially damaging when a child is addicted to drugs. Teenagers know that their parents will bail them out of jail if they are arrested or will always allow them to stay at home. Not to do so would bring shame to the family. Unfortunately, many parents of drug-addicted Asian American teenagers believe they are helping their children by taking care of their basic needs and buying them material things. This, however, reinforces the addicts' behaviors and enables further drug use. The crisis counselor must be sensitive to these cultural norms and slowly encourage open communication between generations rather than force them to take such actions as tough love.

Communication Process in Asian American Culture

Another area in which sensitivity is needed is communication style. Asian Americans have been conditioned to avoid eye contact and direct confrontations, especially with doctors and authority figures. This trait may create complications during an interview if the counselor is not aware of this cultural style. Whereas mainstream Americans may consider avoiding eye contact to be rude, Asians may feel that looking someone in the eye is rude. Also, Asian clients may feel that they cannot disagree with the counselor because of respect for the authority position. The counselor may have to encourage disagreement and define it as part of the interview process at times.

Also, if a crisis worker is working with a family, the tendency to ask family members to confront each other directly may be culturally insensitive. They will probably do best with more educational, problem-solving approaches that focus on a presenting problem. Reframing the solution as strengthening the family unit will probably be well received by Asian American clients. The crisis worker needs to be aware of the hierarchy in the family and include the most powerful family members in making decisions.

> **Example:** A 19-year-old Asian American youth was depressed about having received a C in a chemistry course. He felt ashamed and was sure his father would be angry with him for bringing disgrace on the family. He believed that his only solution was to kill himself by jumping off a tall building.

Instead of working only with this client, the counselor would be well advised to bring in the young man's parents. The client needs to be told that his suicide might bring more shame to the family than getting a C in chemistry. The worker can reframe the problem by pointing out that the lower grade in chemistry could be balanced by a high grade in another class. By asking his parents for their opinions and possible solutions, the client will feel more secure in the fact that he will not bring shame to them. Instead, the family may be brought closer together. The counselor should emphasize to the parents that their son cares so much about the family name that he was willing to sacrifice his own life for the family honor—another reframing of the situation.

TABLE 4.3 | SUMMARIZATION OF SPECIAL CONSIDERATIONS IN WORKING WITH MEXICAN AMERICANS, AFRICAN AMERICANS, AND ASIAN AMERICANS

Mexican Americans
- Enmeshed family structure
- Language barriers
- Different levels of acculturation
- Strong Catholic religious focus

African Americans
- History of racism dating back to era of slavery
- Group with the most salient differences from the mainstream group
- Distrust of mainstream institutions
- Clergy serve as traditional support system when crises arise

Asian Americans
- Shame and obligation
- Rigid family roles and structures
- Counseling should be problem focused and formal

Table 4.3 summarizes salient issues for the crisis worker to remember when working with the three ethnic groups just discussed. The worker should remember, however, that each person is unique and that these issues may not apply to everyone. Most importantly, the worker must remember to understand the crisis experience from the client's point of view. Other issues may be important.

PEOPLE WITH DISABILITIES AND CRISIS INTERVENTION

(THIS SECTION WAS WRITTEN PREDOMINANTLY BY JOHN DOYLE, PhD)

When compared with the general population, persons with disabilities are more prone to crises, and as such deserve particular attention from a crisis intervention perspective.

Example: Jack, a disabled police officer in his mid-30s, has been forced to resign his position because of a diagnosis of bipolar affective disorder. Like many with this condition, even when he takes his medications as prescribed, it is difficult for him to maintain his emotional equilibrium, to the point where he requires psychiatric hospitalization about twice a year. He is also alcohol dependent, which he controls by rigorous participation in the Alcoholics Anonymous 12-step program. With the benefit of vocational rehabilitation services, Jack has been relatively successful in maintaining part-time employment.

Example: Victor, a retired teacher in his mid-60s, has been enjoying his leisure years in a wide array of activities, including travel. Suddenly and unexpectedly, his vision has deteriorated; the cause is an eye condition that is progressive and irreversible. He is no longer allowed to drive, which is a severe blow to his sense of independence. But for both him and his family, the psychological impact of his disability has proved to be the more difficult adjustment.

Example: Debbie, age 39, has a diagnosis of mild to moderate cerebral palsy and is profoundly deaf. She has always resided with her mother, who has provided her with the necessary support to live a relatively normal and independent life. Debbie has an awkward gait, which gives the impression that she is intoxicated. This appearance has led to frequent arrests by the police as she walks to and from her place of part-time employment. Her hearing impairment limits her communication skills, further complicating her ability to communicate with the police and others. Her mother, now elderly and in deteriorating health, has been Debbie's lifetime advocate and care provider.

Responses to People with Disabilities

Disability, a broad concept, is physical or mental impairment that substantially prevents or restricts the ordinary course of human development and accomplishments. Disabilities are often present from birth but can develop at any time in the life cycle. They include such clearly recognizable conditions as blindness, deafness, mental retardation, and mental illness, but also conditions that are less obvious, such as learning disabilities, AIDS, heart disease, and cancer. Depending on the severity of the impairment, the functional level of the person is impaired to a lesser or greater degree. Some people have more than one disability or struggle with both physical and mental impairments. The level of impairment dictates the degree of support needed; not only is the disabled person challenged but so are his or her family members, caregivers, and society at large.

Throughout human history, society has frequently greeted disabled people with stigma, prejudice, mistreatment, discrimination, social isolation, inferior status, and inferior services. Changing the culture of disability is an ongoing challenge. Until relatively recent times, mentally retarded people were officially referred to as idiots, feeble-minded people, imbeciles, or morons. These terms, now obsolete in professional and clinical settings, survive in everyday language as powerful derogatory epithets. It is often easier to find agreement on terms that should not be used than on terms that are suitable to use. The term *mentally retarded* has negative connotations and is being replaced in some settings by the term *developmentally disabled* or *mentally challenged.* However, the terms *disability* and *disabled* are often seen to connote weakness, dependence, abnormality, and inferiority.

Even when people have the best of intentions, they often view persons with disabilities unrealistically. Disabled people may view themselves unrealistically. On the one hand, the disability can be overestimated to a point where the individual is sentimentalized and unnecessarily relegated to a position of overdependence. On the other hand, the disability can be underestimated to the point where the person and his or her family experience endless failure and emotional frustration. Achieving a realistic balance in which the functional strengths of the individual define him or her rather than the disability can be difficult; however, achieving that balance is important in preventing crises.

The Disabled Population and the ADA

Depending on the definition applied, the number of disabled individuals in American society varies. The legal journey defining persons with disabilities and articulating their rights reached a high point when Congress passed the **Americans with Disabilities Act (ADA) of 1990,** which broadly challenges discrimination against disabled people. The ADA went into effect in July 1992. It defines a person with a disability as having a physical or mental impairment that substantially limits one or more major life activities; has a record of such an impairment; or is regarded as having such an impairment. The intent of the legislation is to make society more accessible to people with disabilities, but its implementation continues to be a major challenge. According to Census 2000, 48.9 people who were 5 years old and over living in housing units had a disability, or 19.2% of the disabled population in the United States (Stern, 2001). Congress recognizes the historical and present tendency of society to discriminate against disabled people, and mandates remedies in such areas as employment, housing, public accommodations, education, transportation, communication, recreation, institutionalization, health services, voting rights, and access to public services. It also prohibits coercion of or retaliation against people with disabilities or those who advocate for rights for the disabled.

Not only are people with disabilities discriminated against, but they are frequently abused. Women with disabilities are more likely to experience abuse by a greater number of perpetrators and for longer periods than nondisabled women (Young et al., 1997). Unfortunately, many people with disabling conditions are especially vulnerable to victimization because of their real or perceived inability to fight or flee, notify others, or testify in court. Despite the advocacy of ADA workers, crime victims with disabilities are less likely than those without disabilities to reap the benefits of the criminal justice system. The reason is that crimes against disabled victims go unreported because of victims' mobility or communication barriers, social or physical isolation, or normal feelings of shame and self-blame, or because the perpetrator of the crime is the victim's caretaker (U.S. Department of Justice, 2001).

Once the ADA was passed, one could say that people with disabilities entered mainstream society. However, their challenges continue. The main controversy concerns the cost of changes for accommodating disabled people in both the public and private sectors of society. According to Title II of the ADA, discrimination of any kind on the basis of disability is prohibited. Community agencies, including the police force, firefighting force, state legislature, city councils, state courts, public schools, public recreation departments, and departments of motor vehicle licensing, must allow people with disabilities to participate fully in all of their services, programs, and activities. An example of the effect of the ADA on the police force can be seen in the **Police Executive Research Forum,** which provides a detailed training curriculum and model policy for responding to people with mental illness, developmental disabilities, and speech and hearing impairments.

Vulnerable Subgroups within the Disabled Population

Because the ADA has been passed, many people with disabilities can now live more as part of mainstream society. For instance, wheelchair-accessible buildings allow many with physical disabilities to enjoy social and vocational independence. However, some subgroups within the disabled population are particularly prone to crises, and there is no simple way to offset their vulnerability. The most vulnerable groups are fragile elderly people, mentally ill people, and developmentally disabled people.

Disabled Elderly People Elderly people are not automatically disabled. However, there is a greater risk of disability as a person ages. In 1994 and 1995, 52.5% of people over 65 years of age reported having at least one disability, and 33% reported having at least one severe disability. Over 6 million, or 21%, had difficulty in carrying out activities of daily living. As people grow older, there is a corresponding increase in disabilities. Walker (1994) argues that prevention of disabilities in older adults is a shared responsibility, involving the elderly individual, healthcare providers, and society at large. Individual choice is not sufficient; rather, there is a need for a broad social commitment to the promotion of health. However, diseases are significant risk factors for disability in elderly people, and age itself is a risk factor for those over 85 years of age. Hogan, Ebly, and Fung (1999) examined cognitively intact community resident seniors and found that age alone accounts for the fact that twice as many in the 85-plus age group are physically disabled compared with the 65- to 84-year-old age group. Hence, disease prevention will not necessarily impede disability in older seniors. Compared with the 65- to 80-year-old population, those over 80 are twice as likely to have difficulty with such activities as bathing, dressing, eating, preparing meals, shopping, managing money, and taking medication.

It is clear from the literature that intervention for elderly people with disabilities must be holistic in nature, involving a network of community resources. In a study of the characteristics of older adults with intellectual disabilities who required crisis intervention, Davidson and colleagues (1995) concluded that intellectually disabled adults require comprehensive age-span community mental health and behavioral supports. The severity of the behavioral crises decreases over the life cycle, but the need for intervention remains constant. The need for intervention is not limited to elderly persons with a disability. Altman, Cooper, and Cunningham (1999) described the struggles of a family with a disabled elder. Families experience an increased number of emotional, financial, and health crises. Alzheimer's dementia and senile dementia are particularly stressful for the family. Graham (1989) points out that as these diseases and disabilities progress, day-care placement may be necessary; even with day care, the stress level does not necessarily decrease for family caregivers. Frail elderly people are the most vulnerable to neglect and abuse by caregivers, both professionals and family members.

Talecxih (2001) reports that by 2050 the number of elderly people requiring institutional care will likely more than double, from 5 million to 11 million. The elderly population will be more diverse, so the long-term care workforce will have to be more culturally competent. Human service workers generally will need more training in dealing with the problems of an aging population (Rosen & Zlotnik, 2001).

Mentally Disabled People   Although it is more difficult to define and measure mental disabilities, the debilitating nature of emotional and psychological problems is quite clear. Under the ADA, a mental impairment includes any "mental or psychological disorder, such as . . . emotional or mental illness." Among the examples cited are "major depression, bipolar disorder, anxiety disorders (which include panic disorder, obsessive disorder, and PTSD), schizophrenia, and personality disorders." Comer (1995) gives the following statistics on mental illness in the United States: 13% have significant anxiety disorders; 6% have serious depression; 5% have debilitating personality disorders; 1% has schizophrenia; 1% has Alzheimer's disease; and 10% are suffering from drug and alcohol difficulties.

With the introduction of the major tranquilizer medications in the 1950s, psychotic behaviors could be controlled, and the treatment of people with serious mental illnesses changed significantly. Before this new treatment mode, those with serious mental illness were confined to psychiatric hospitals, which were locked facilities. The major tranquilizers made deinstitutionalization possible. Treatment is now community based; and hospitalizations, especially long-term stays, are avoided as much as possible. Further goals of deinstitutionalization are the promotion of the rights and independence of mentally ill people and a more cost-effective delivery of services. The **National Institute of Mental Health** indicates that the number of institutionalized mental health patients decreased from a high of 559,000 in 1955 to 69,000 in 1995.

The **Community Mental Health Act of 1963** set goals for the provision of community-based services for the mentally disabled. These services include inpatient care for seriously ill patients, with the goal of returning them to the community as soon as possible; outpatient clinics for ongoing care; partial hospitalization, where patients can go home at night and on weekends; 24-hour crisis centers; and consultation, education, and information services for those who regularly interact with these disabled people in the community. Unfortunately, the provision of these community-based services has lagged, making deinstitutionalization, at best, a measured success. Although the major tranquilizers work well for seriously mentally ill people when they are in the hospital setting and help them return to the community, individuals who do not have the support of friends, are unemployed, or do not have access to ongoing mental health services are destined for failure in community-based living. Some observers feel that the deinstitutionalization policy for the mentally ill has been a dismal failure. Others see it as a success in that it promotes civil liberties for those with serious mental illness. Johnson (1990) points out that with certain supports in place, such as housing, outreach by human service workers, independent living skills support, and occasional hospitalizations for stabilization of their condition, community-based placement is appropriate. Without the necessary supports, seriously mentally ill people in the community are in a permanent state of crisis. Unfortunately, people in the community often see these people as a public nuisance that should be controlled by the criminal justice system; this is an inappropriate and highly unfair assessment.

It can be argued that institutionalization in the absence of proper community support is more humane for seriously mentally ill people because they do not fall victim to homelessness, hunger, abuse, or the criminal justice system and because, with their limited coping skills, they avoid living in a permanent state of crisis. It is also clear that because of the number of community support services needed to help some of these people, community placement is not necessarily less costly than institutionalization.

Developmentally Disabled People   The developmentally disabled population includes those with mental retardation, cerebral palsy, epilepsy, autism, and other neurological disorders. In particular, mentally retarded people have been unnecessarily institutionalized and subject to involuntary sterilization. The deinstitutionalization movement of the 1970s reflected a concern for the civil rights of the developmentally disabled; today, very few are institutionalized. The guiding principle is that they have the right to develop as fully as they can and live as normally and independently as possible. Most now live more independently with their families or in group homes. The movement of developmentally disabled people into the community means that crises that once occurred behind the walls of state institutions now are seen in every community. There is an ongoing need to meet this inevitable problem. Community-based living places more demands on the limited coping skills of the developmentally disabled, making them even more prone to crises.

Shoham-Vardi and his colleagues (1996, p. 109) report that up to 60% of persons with developmental disabilities have behavioral and psychiatric disorders; the recidivism rate is 88% in 2 years. As reported by these authors, for developmentally disabled persons under age 30 years, the strongest predictors of recidivism are living apart from the family and an initial diagnosis of self-injurious behavior; for those over age 30 years, a history of aggression is the strongest predictor of recidivism. This population places special demands on the community with regard to creating and maintaining appropriate resources to meet their complex needs.

Like the mentally ill population, newly independent developmentally disabled people can fall victim—some say unfairly—to the criminal justice system. For example, a 23-year-old person with mental retardation from Tulare, California, is serving a third-strike prison sentence of 28 years to life for stealing a VCR and some jewelry from a residence. His previous "strikes" were for arson: The first time, he set fire to a trash can, and the second time, a fire began in a truck where it appeared he had been playing with matches. It could be argued that under the old system, this individual would have resided in the protective environment of a state institution and would not have become involved in the state criminal justice system. Others argue that there is a price for independence that cannot be measured by the mistakes of a few.

Like the general population generally, more developmentally disabled people are living to be elderly. Advances in medicine have helped these people, just as they have helped nondisabled people. The longer life span means that developmentally disabled people need more extensive and complex interventions over the life cycle. For the first time in history, these people are outliving their parents (Ansello, 1988). Estimates of the number of elderly developmentally disabled people vary from at least 4 in every 1,000 older persons (Janicki, 1991) to as many as 1 in every 100 older persons (Ansello & Eustis, 1992). To prevent or delay institutionalization, strengthen independence, and enhance daily functioning of the older population with developmental disabilities, a new emphasis on service needs must emerge. Collaboration is critical between service providers and family caregivers in serving the needs of the developmentally disabled elderly.

Coogle and his colleagues (1995) argue for resource sharing and collaboration among the developmentally disabled providers and other human service networks, and also for a managed approach to intervention in order to avoid costly duplication of services. They further argue for education of the public and community leaders about those with lifelong disabilities and their families; increased funding for supportive housing and independent living centers; advocacy for older adults with developmental disabilities and their families so they can secure community-based long-term care; respite care and income support; and an increase in federal and state resources for continued community living. Zola (1988) believes that the aged and disabled populations should be served together because of their similar conditions, the technical and medical requirements of their care, and the full implications of the home care revolution. The traditional approach of dividing them into two opposing entities is a form of unnecessary segregation.

Crisis Intervention Strategies for Persons with Disabilities

Effective intervention for people with disabilities requires detailed knowledge of this population, information on their civil and legal rights, a willingness to advocate for those rights, and comprehensive knowledge of available sources of support and intervention.

Crises do not occur in a vacuum. For disabled people, crises often occur because helpers do not have adequate knowledge and understanding of a particular disability and fail to establish the necessary support systems. For instance, a high-functioning autistic person who works in a predictable environment with structured supervision can be extremely productive and successful. However, because such an individual typically has great difficulty with social and environmental transitions, any change in work routine or personnel can provoke a major crisis. To decrease the likelihood of such a crisis requires not only the maintenance of a predictable work routine but ongoing education for other employees and the management staff on how to successfully interact with this individual. This requires a considerable commitment on the part of all concerned. Depending on the disability and circumstances, similar preventive strategies need to be employed.

Case management is one of the most important developments in human services in the past half century. Schneider (1988) emphasizes the importance of case management as an intervention strategy. It is consumer centered; embraces the elements of screening, assessment, specific goals, interdisciplinary and interagency cooperation, and measurable outcomes; and is subject to monitoring and evaluation. Case management is a proactive, positive way of intervening with regularity with the chronically disabled, a way of anticipating situations before they become full-blown crises.

Effective crisis intervention and prevention are rooted in a system of comprehensive collaboration. Knowledge of available services and the ways in which they can be accessed is essential. For example, the 1975 federal **Education for All Handicapped Children Act** (Public Law 94-142), updated in 1997 as the **Individuals with Disabilities Education Act (IDEA),** is just one of many federal programs for the disabled. It mandates free, appropriate, individualized public education for handicapped children—those with learning handicaps, developmental disabilities, orthopedic conditions, and mental illness. Local school districts play a major role in the lives of disabled children from the time they are 3 years of age until they reach 22 years of age, so an important intervention is assisting the disabled and their families in using this resource.

People who are not disabled, even human service workers, react differently to disabled people. Some common reactions are fear, repulsion, anxiety about loss and dependence, embarrassment, and avoidance of social contact. Working with disabled people may be perceived as less prestigious than working with other types of people. Legislation mandating full inclusion of the disabled population is one thing; implementation of the legislation is another. Both physical and psychological obstacles to inclusion remain, including the cost of services, competing interests, and discrimination, as well as the self-limiting roles of disabled people themselves. This population requires meaningful intervention and attention, not stigmatization or sentimentalization.

THE SUBCULTURE OF GAYS, LESBIANS, BISEXUALS, AND TRANSGENDERS

Terms that are commonly used in discussions of the gay, lesbian, bisexual, and transgender population are listed below. These individuals are sometimes referred to as the g/l/b/t population. The definitions may be helpful to the reader.

bisexual: A person who experiences social and romantic attraction to both genders.

closet gay: A person who is unaware of his or her homosexuality or is unwilling to publicly acknowledge it; such a person may be described as "being in the closet."

coming out: The process of identifying and coming to terms with one's homosexuality. The term is also used to describe a homosexual person who is telling another person that he or she is gay.

gay: A man that is mostly sexually attracted to men.

heterosexism: The attitude of overt or covert bias against homosexuals based on the belief that heterosexuality is superior.

homophobia: Unreasonable fear or hatred of a homosexual.

homosexuality: Sexual desires primarily for a person of the same sex.

lesbian: A woman who feels sexual desire predominantly for other women.

transgender: A person who has experienced himself or herself socially, emotionally, and psychologically as male if the person was born female, or female if the person was born male.

There seems to be a trend among adults toward more acceptance of gays and lesbians in society (Yang, 1999). This is evident in the ratings of television shows that have been nominated for and won Emmy awards, such as *Queer Eye for the Straight Guy* and *Will and Grace*, and in the open disclosure by some celebrities of their homosexual identity. However, many people still have negative feelings toward individuals who live openly gay and lesbian lifestyles. Adults who present themselves to the world as gay make themselves open to criticism and rejection by family, friends, and co-workers. Recent political discussions have highlighted the ongoing debate about whether gays should be allowed to be legally married with the same rights as heterosexual married couples. Proponents of gay marriage believe that not allowing gay marriage is a form of discrimination. This is such an important issue that it has become a platform upon which certain major political parties run.

Keeping one's homosexuality hidden can lead to mental health problems such as anxiety and depression. The closet gay must always worry about keeping his or her true sexual orientation concealed. Often these people must lie to those they care about, and this duplicity leads to negative feelings.

Crisis hot lines and centers have been established to help this population live healthy gay and lesbian lifestyles, disclose their orientation to others, and learn how to handle rejection from society. A counselor must be sensitive to the special issues faced by both the closet gay and the openly gay person. It is best to find out how each individual perceives his or her situation and continue with the interview following the ABC model. Knowing about community resources is a big help.

Typical Issues Facing G/L/B/T Persons in Crisis

Unlike other minority groups, when an individual accepts the fact that he or she is gay, lesbian, bisexual, or transgender, he or she usually feels isolated from family and friends. Many times the child grows up in a home where he or she receives messages full of heterosexism (i.e., that the only proper sexual relations are between females and males) and homophobia (i.e., the fear of homosexuality). When individuals begin to recognize themselves as being gay or lesbian, they must also contend with their own homophobia. They often prefer to deny the possibility of being gay or lesbian.

Families of these individuals also experience crises. Parents are not prepared to raise or be involved in the life of a gay child. They often feel like failures and feel guilty about their resentment of their child's sexual orientation. Many parents believe that being gay is an illness and seek treatment for their child's homosexuality, despite the fact that, since 1974, psychiatrists have not considered homosexuality to be a mental disorder.

Suicide is a big risk for individuals in the beginning stages of discovering their gay sexual orientation as well as for gay persons who experience societal discrimination. The news media often has reports of hate crimes against gays. Gay persons have been socialized in a culture that fears homosexuality on moral grounds. Judeo-Christian culture has emphasized that sodomy is a sin. Therefore, gay individuals often experience self-loathing for a time until they can come to terms with the reality of their sexuality.

Although certain sexual acts, such as sodomy and oral sex, are illegal in some states, being gay is not illegal. In fact, being gay is much more than a sexual act. People who are gay build lives together, build friendship networks, work in many fields, and live productive lives.

Coming Out

Coming out does not happen overnight; it is a process that happens over time. The phrase usually refers to telling someone of one's gay sexual orientation. It is often done in stages rather than as a single event. This process of accepting one's gay sexuality usually begins deep within a person's psyche as he or she experiences feelings, thoughts, and desires related to his or her sexuality. There may be an inner battle as the person fights with cultural homophobic norms. When an individual is socialized to believe that gays are deviants, it is difficult to come to terms with one's own feelings of homosexuality without believing that one is deviant.

The person coming out often contends with shame that he or she imposes on himself or herself or that society imposes on him or her. Fear is a big factor as well. Some of this fear is realistic, as rejection from family and friends is a common consequence of coming out. Each time an individual informs someone that he is gay, he must face the fear of the unknown. Because of societal discrimination, the person may fear losing a job, losing a home (or not being allowed to purchase a home), or losing respect from others. The decision to come out, then, must not be an impulsive act but rather one that is well thought out and strategic. A crisis counselor can assist persons as they move slowly through this process to help reduce negative consequences.

Once there is an internal acceptance of being homosexual, individuals begin the process of reprogramming their ideas about being gay and turn the shame into pride. There may be a phase of experimentation with their new identity when they tell friends and family or connect with the gay community through nightclubs and community centers.

The age of an individual who is coming out makes a difference in the consequences in his or her life. For example, a middle-aged woman who had been married for 15 years and has children will need to think carefully before coming out. It could take several years for her to make the decision to live as a lesbian, even though she clearly experiences her sexuality that way. She must proceed slowly and deal with all the members of her family so as to decrease trauma for everyone. The crisis worker should not encourage people to come out immediately but rather guide clients into their own coming-out process. The counselor may even play devil's advocate and help clients question whether the gay feelings are real. This does not mean that the counselor discourages a person from being gay. It is not a disorder that needs to be fixed but, rather, an identity with social consequences. This fact must be part of crisis intervention.

A 25-year-old woman who lives on her own, has good self-esteem, and can rely on a good support system might have an easier time coming out. However, keep in mind that coming out is probably never easy because of societal taboos, parental reactions, and reactions of friends and co-workers who did not know about the person's gay sexuality. Some people believe that being gay is fine until one of their own loved ones comes out as gay. Family members might go into a state of shock when they find out that a child is gay.

> **Example:** A 17-year-old girl had been struggling with her sexuality for 2 years. She had engaged in moderate lesbian sexual activities with a girl on her basketball team. She kept the truth about this relationship from her parents and said the other girl was just a good friend. The girl finally told her mother that she was bisexual and wanted to date males and females. The mother became hysterical and said that the girl was just confused and would eventually realize she was totally straight. Soon, the girl met another female who was a lesbian. The girl became very involved with her and realized that she was a lesbian herself, not bisexual. She told her mother, who went into shock. All the mother's hopes and dreams about having a big wedding for her daughter and future son-in-law and having grandchildren were lost. The mother could not see that there could still be a future with her daughter. The father disowned the daughter.

During the coming-out process, there is an increased risk of suicidal thinking and attempts. The individual may feel hopeless about the future, helpless, and worthless, and may experience many painful feelings. Add to these feelings increased social isolation, and the risk of suicide can be quite high. The crisis worker should evaluate suicide regularly when a client is experiencing this type of crisis, particularly when disclosures are being made and rejection by loved ones is possible.

Remember that there will be consequences when a person comes out. The counselor must not make the decision about when to come out for a client. Instead, the crisis worker should help client make his or her own decision by using empowering and support statements. By discussing the consequences of not coming out, such as emotional repression, unhappiness in relationships, and pervasive guilt and shame, persons considering coming out might be helped to see that the immediate consequences of possible rejection are better than a life of permanent dissatisfaction.

The crisis counselor can say that although friends and family may be rejecting at first, attitudes change over time. Just as clients may not have been able to accept their gay sexuality at first, loved ones may not be accepting, either. Time is an important factor. Support groups are useful. The crisis worker should refer clients to a group in which others can relate to the dilemma first-hand. Being reassured by educational statements that homosexuality is not a disease can often help the client feel better as well. Many communities have gay/lesbian/bisexual/transgender centers that provide services for the many issues facing the gay population. Most colleges have special centers for gay people. Even some high schools have gay and lesbian associations. Crisis workers may also provide family counseling to mediate between children and parents or between spouses. Of course, suicide assessment should be done when clients are depressed.

Transgender people are usually men. They have experienced themselves emotionally, psychologically, and socially as females since childhood, despite having a male body. As an adult, a transgender may choose to change his physiology by taking female hormones to enlarge his breasts or by undergoing major reconstructive surgery to create a completely female body. He may then choose to identify himself as a "she" in society and even on legal documents. The process of becoming a transgender may take years. Many "sex-change" surgeons require that patients receive psychological assessment prior to this dramatic life change. Some transgenders do not undergo full sex-change surgery, as it is expensive. Instead, they live as women by dressing and grooming themselves as women and by taking hormones. Because this procedure is not common, most people in society have had little contact with transgenders. Most stereotypes about transgenders probably have to do with them being gay "drag queens" or "freaks." Human service workers will find transgenders to be fairly normal except that they are not happy living as the biological gender with which they were born. Some may be gay (attracted to men after sex-change surgery), and others may be attracted to women.

Case Vignettes

The following case vignettes may be useful to practice once you have studied the ABC model presented in the next chapter. Come back to these cases when you are ready to practice role-playing.

Case 1 A Mexican American woman comes to see you because she has been depressed since her last child entered kindergarten. She does not sleep well, is nervous, and fights to get her child to obey her.

What cultural issues are at stake here? How would you proceed?

Hint: Offer psychoeducational information regarding child development.

Hint: Offer supportive statements about letting go of her child.

Hint: Reframe the child's rebelliousness as a sign that the mother has raised a secure child who can function in school.

Hint: Empower the mother by pointing out how her role as a mother has just changed, not been eliminated. She has new tasks to master now, which will be even more challenging than when her child was younger.

Hint: Offer educational information about the possibility of different rates of acculturation as a child enters school.

Case 2   A 19-year-old Vietnamese female college student is distressed because she has fallen in love with an American boy. She wants to spend time with him, but her parents expect her to stay at home when she is not at school. She wants to kill herself because she is so depressed.

How can you help her? What must you keep in mind?

Hint: Offer supportive statements about how difficult it is to respect one's parents and still have one's own life.

Hint: Educate her about the different rates of acculturation of her and her parents.

Hint: Empower her by focusing on what she can do to feel better; talk about ways that she can show respect to her parents and perhaps still see the boy at school.

Hint: Conduct a suicide assessment and discuss the fact that if she killed herself, she would bring more shame on her family than she would by dating a boy.

Hint: Offer to speak with her parents about the situation and let them know how much their daughter respects them—so much that she would rather kill herself than shame them. They would not want her to kill herself over this situation.

Case 3   A 14-year-old African American boy is sent for counseling by his school counselor because he has not been coming to school and is not performing when he is in school. His mother brings him to the appointment. She is in a hurry because she is on her lunch break from her full-time job. His father does not live with them, though he comes around frequently.

Who might be available for support? What biases must you avoid?

Hint: Find out who the teen and his mother live with, and if is there a grandmother available to help out.

Hint: Educate the boy about the need to finish high school and the special importance of this for African Americans because discrimination is bad enough, even when one has a diploma.

Hint: Encourage the father to be involved in the situation and be a good role model.

Hint: Empathize with the teen about the fact that school is not always easy or fun.

Hint: Assess the teen's level of depression and ask about what has been happening in his life recently.

Case 4   A man is in a wheelchair because his legs were paralyzed in a surfboard accident a year ago. He comes to you because he is lonely. Last weekend at a party he talked with a woman that he had met once before, prior to his accident. He wants to date her but is afraid she will not want to date him because of his disability.

Hint: Offer support statements about how difficult it is to be disabled and have to change one's lifestyle.

Hint: Empower him by helping him focus on what he can do. Maybe this girl will not be his lover, but she may want to hang out with him.

Hint: Reframe the situation as a chance to find out how females will react to his advances. Because he had met the woman before, she may be willing to be honest with him. He needs to find out how women feel about a man in a wheelchair.

Hint: Educate him about the fact that many men in wheelchairs are married and that people can be sexual without having sexual intercourse.

Case 5   A 17-year-old girl comes in because she is depressed and her mother is worried about her. The girl has begun a sexual relationship with a female basketball teammate, but claims that she still likes boys. The mother insists that her daughter is not a lesbian. The father will not have anything to do with his daughter if she chooses to date girls.

Hint: Empathize with all about how difficult it is to deal with sexuality issues.

Hint: Educate about the fact that a 17-year-old has not completely formed her identity.

Hint: Educate about homosexuality, bisexuality, and heterosexuality (you may need to read up on these subjects).

Hint: Focus on the cognitions underlying the mother's distress and the father's rejection.

Hint: Talk with the daughter alone about the coming-out process.

KEY TERMS FOR STUDY

African Americans: As seen by the crisis worker, a minority group that does not use the mental health system often. The historical roots of this group help explain why its members tend to resolve crises through the extended family and clergy rather than through governmental or other mainstream agencies. Racism and discrimination are still common problems for this group and must be kept in mind by crisis workers. Religion has historically been important in helping this group to get through the many daily stressors they encounter in America.

Alzheimer's dementia: A progressive disease that usually begins in elderly people. There is deterioration of mental functioning, particularly short-term memory. When the brain loses its ability to maintain regulatory functions such as breathing and eating, the person may die.

American with Disabilities Act of 1990: The intent of this legislation is to make society more accessible to people with disabilities. It defines disabilities and challenges the discrimination associated with disabilities.

Asian Americans: As seen by the crisis worker, a minority group whose members may seek the services of mental health workers in crises, but who prefer a problem-solving approach similar to that used by a family doctor to treat physical illnesses. The crisis worker must be aware of issues of shame and obligation because they may come into play when a family member is in crisis. Crisis workers must also respect the family structure to prevent resistance to proposed coping alternatives.

case management: An effective approach to working with individuals and families in which a disability is a factor. It includes such elements as screening, assessment, setting goals, interagency and interdisciplinary cooperation, and measurable outcomes. It is a proactive way to regularly intervene with the high-risk disabled population in order to prevent full-blown crises.

development of cultural sensitivity: A four-stage process during which counselors learn to consider cultural factors when they are conducting counseling sessions. The stages are (1) lack of awareness of cultural issues; (2) heightened awareness of culture; (3) realization of the burden of considering culture; and (4) beginnings of cultural sensitivity.

developmental disabilities: Neurological disorders such as mental retardation, cerebral palsy, epilepsy, and autism.

disability: Physical or mental impairment that substantially prevents or restricts the ordinary course of human development and accomplishments.

mainstreamed: People with disabilities who function in society with as much independence as possible both socially and vocationally.

Mexican Americans: As seen by the crisis worker, a cultural group whose members seek mental health services more often than African Americans or Asian Americans. Mexican Americans suffer crises related to language barriers, religious differences, and cultural differences in child rearing. Families tend to be enmeshed, and children are encouraged to be dependent.

role of systems theory: An important element in working with clients from minority groups. The crisis worker must identify family roles and allowable behavior for a particular cultural group; these may be different from mainstream roles and behaviors. Imposing mainstream psychological theories on other cultures is often counterproductive.

senile dementia: Deterioration in mental faculties found in some elderly people. It might include poor memory, delusions, confabulations (making up memories to fill in gaps), and socially inappropriate behaviors.

THE ABC MODEL OF CRISIS INTERVENTION

The ABC model of crisis intervention is a method for conducting very brief mental health interviews with clients whose functioning level has decreased following a psychosocial stressor. This model follows the formula presented in Chapter 1 regarding the process of crisis formation. It is a problem-focused approach and is most effectively applied within 4 to 6 weeks of the stressor. Identifying the cognitions of the client as they relate to the precipitating event and then altering them to help decrease unmanageable feelings is the central focus of the method. In addition, providing community referrals and other resources such as reading material is also essential in applying this model.

Caplan and Lindemann first conceptualized the crisis intervention approach in the 1940s (Caplan, 1964; Lindemann, 1944); others have since developed models that use the principles and techniques of these founders. The ABC model of crisis intervention presented in this text has its origins in a variety of sources. It is loosely based on Jones's (1968) A-B-C method of crisis management, with its three-stage process: A, achieving contact; B, boiling the problem down to basics; and C, coping. Moline (1986), a former professor at California State University, Fullerton, developed a course called Crisis Intervention, in which she used a modified version of Jones's model. From her lecture notes and from discussions with her about how she organized the course, the author developed, as noted in Chapter 2, the ABC model of crisis intervention discussed in this book. Over a period of 20 years, the author has expanded and revised the ABC model. Revisions are based on current information from experts in the community who provide crisis intervention for a variety of populations, the author's experiences in teaching the model to students and community counselors and receiving feedback from these students, and the author's experiences as a counselor in public, private, and nonprofit agency settings.

Other models have also influenced the ABC model of crisis intervention in terms of the particular structure and stages. Structuring the counseling process around certain phases or stages is not a new phenomenon. It has been done by mental health practitioners since the days of such founding theorists as Sullivan (1954) and Adler (Corey, 1996, p. 143). The phases are not linear but, like those of the ABC model, are best "understood as a weaving that leads to a tapestry" (Corey, 1996, p. 143). Adler developed a four-phase model for the therapeutic process: phase 1, establishing the relationship; phase 2, exploring the individual's dynamics; phase 3, encouraging insight; and phase 4, helping with reorientation (Corey, 1996, pp. 143–150). These four phases are similar to those of the ABC model:

A: Developing and maintaining contact (corresponds with Adler's phase 1)
B: Identifying the problem and providing therapeutic interaction (corresponds with Adler's phase 2 and phase 3)
C: Coping (corresponds with Adler's phase 4)

Sullivan (1954) also used a phase model to structure psychiatric interviews. His stages can be seen to correspond with the stages of the ABC model: phase 1, the formal inception (analogous to A of the ABC model); phase 2, the reconnaissance, and phase 3, the detailed inquiry (analogous to B); and phase 4, termination (analogous to C).

Although the ABC model of crisis intervention has a three-stage approach, in an actual interview the components of any one stage could be used at any time. Readers should keep this thought in mind during the discussion of each stage that follows. The crisis worker will learn how to integrate the stages through practice and experience.

A: DEVELOPING AND MAINTAINING RAPPORT

The foundation of crisis intervention is the development of rapport—a state of understanding and comfort—between client and counselor. As the client begins to feel rapport, trust and openness follow, allowing the interview to proceed. Before delving into the client's personal world, the counselor must achieve this personal contact. The counseling relationship is unique in this regard; before any work can be done, the client must feel understood and accepted by the counselor. A student of the author summed up this need quite appropriately: "People don't care what you know, until they know that you care."

By learning several basic attending skills, the beginning crisis counselor can develop the self-confidence needed to make contact with someone in crisis. Use of these basic rapport-building communication skills invites the client to talk, brings calm control to the situation, allows the client to talk about the facts of the situation and the counselor to hear and empathize with the client's feelings, and lets the client know that the counselor is concerned and respectful.

Remember that the interview process does not proceed in a linear fashion; the various attending skills can be interwoven as appropriate. For example, the counselor may ask a question before reflecting or may reflect before asking a question.

Unlike other approaches to counseling, crisis intervention does not typically include the use of such techniques as interpretation or direct advice giving. These techniques generally require a therapeutic relationship of long duration before they are effective; in crisis intervention, developing such a relationship is not practical. Although it may be tempting to jump in and tell clients what is wrong with them and what to do about it, the crisis interventionist is encouraged not to do this. The basic attending skills are a useful alternative to the sometimes rote practice of asking routine questions and giving routine advice and interpretations. Sometimes, clients are just not routine!

The primary purpose of using the basic attending skills is to gain a clear understanding of the internal experience of the crisis as the client sees it. Only when the counselor truly understands can he or she help to bring change to the client's subjective distress and assist the client in improving his or her functioning.

Table 5.1 can be used as a guide for the beginning counselor. It is not meant to be followed as a linear script but rather as a reminder of the skills the counselor is to use throughout the interview. Skill proficiency columns are built into the table to allow evaluation of student performance by the course instructor.

Attending Behavior

The most basic skill of helping is listening. Appropriate verbal and nonverbal behavior—that is, attending behavior—is the hallmark of a helping interview. Good eye contact, attentive body language, expressive vocal style, and verbal following are valuable listening tools, but they are not always present. The next time you carry on a conversation with a friend, observe whether these behaviors are in evidence. Using a soft, soothing voice, showing an interested face, having relaxed posture, leaning toward the client, making direct eye contact, and maintaining close physical proximity (Cormier et al., 1986, p. 30) are all ways to convey warmth and are part of active listening. These attending behaviors "demonstrate to the client that you are with him or her and indeed are listening," enabling the client to talk more freely (Ivey, Gluckstern, & Ivey, 1997, p. 19).

Active listening requires being able to observe the client and at the same time pay attention to how one should best react to the client. Try the following exercise.

Exercise

Break into groups of three or four. Using the basic attending skills evaluation sheet in Table 5.1, rate each other on attending behaviors. One person can play the client and another can be a crisis worker. A third can be the rater. If there is a fourth, that person can be an observer. The rater also enhances her or his skills of observation while giving feedback to the counselor. After this exercise, have

TABLE 5.1 | BASIC ATTENDING SKILLS

	Skill Proficiency		
	Good	Fair	Poor
Attending behavior			
Eye contact			
Warmth			
Body posture			
Vocal style			
Verbal following			
Overall empathy (focus on client)			
Questioning			
Open-ended			
Close-ended			
Paraphrasing			
Restating in own words			
Clarifying			
Reflection			
Painful feelings			
Positive feelings			
Ambivalent feelings			
Nonverbal feelings			
Summarization			
Tying together precipitating event, subjective distress, and cognitive elements			

Source: From Basic Attending Skills, Third Edition, by A. E. Ivey, N. B. Gluckstern, and M. B. Ivey, pp. 19, 20–21, 35, 56, and 92. Copyright © 1997 Microtaining Associates. Reprinted with permission.

some fun exaggerating an interview in which the crisis worker does not employ these behaviors (i.e., has poor eye contact, is cold, keeps arms folded, does not pay attention verbally). This behavior will impress on everyone what not to do!

Crisis workers must remember that the attending behavior of different cultural and ethnic groups may vary in style, and these helpers may need to adapt when working with the groups discussed earlier. Ivey and colleagues (1997, pp. 20–21) have summarized typical variations:

- *Eye Contact:* African Americans, Latin Americans, and Native Americans may avoid eye contact as a sign of respect. With Latinos, direct sustained eye contact can represent a challenge to authority. A bowed head may be a sign of respect from Native Americans.

- *Body Language:* The public behavior of African Americans may seem emotionally intense and demonstrative to European Americans. A slap on the back may be insulting to an Asian American or a Latin American.
- *Vocal Style:* Latin Americans often begin meetings with lengthy greetings and pleasant talk before addressing key issues. European Americans tend to value a quiet, controlled vocal style; other groups may see this as manipulative or cold.
- *Verbal Following:* Asian Americans may prefer a more indirect and subtle communication and consider the African American or European American style too direct and confrontational. Personal questions may be especially offensive to Native Americans. (Reprinted with permission from Ivey, A. E., Gluckstern, N. B., & Ivey, M. B. *Basic Attending Skills,* 3rd ed. Pp. 19, 20–21, 35, 56, and 92. © 1997 by Microtraining Associates.)

Questioning

Asking clients pertinent questions is an invitation to them to talk. Open-ended questions provide room for clients to express their real selves without categories imposed by the interviewer. They allow clients an opportunity to explore their thoughts and feelings with the support of the interviewer. Close-ended questions can help the interviewer gather factual information such as age or marital status. However, clients frequently feel attacked or defensive with certain close-ended questions (such as "why" questions), which should be used sparingly if at all (Ivey et al., 1997, p. 35).

Beginning counseling students tend to ask "do you, have you, could you, and would you" questions. These types of close-ended questions can be answered with a "yes" or "no" by clients, with the result that an interview bogs down. Counselors should avoid these types of close-ended questions, asking more specific open-ended questions instead.

Try to tie your open-ended questions to what the client has just said. Questions that begin with "what" and "how" are very effective in allowing the client to explore his or her ideas and feelings. When the question is posed effectively, it helps move the interview along and allows gathering essential information about the nature of the crisis. Remember, it is all right to ask pointed open-ended questions when they relate to what the client has just said, and, hence, verbal following is extremely important to proper questioning. Whenever a client offers a new word or expresses energy behind what he or she says, the counselor should ask a question that helps him or her to better understand the meaning of the word or the energy. Never assume that you know what the client means. Inquire!

The following dialogue between a client and a crisis worker shows an appropriate use of questions.

CLIENT: "I am so angry at my husband. He won't talk to me anymore and we just don't communicate at all."

CRISIS WORKER: "What do you mean by communicate?"

CLIENT: "He refuses to sit down and listen to me. I have no idea what his problem is. I can't get him to tell me anything. He obviously doesn't want to be around, but I don't know why."

CRISIS WORKER: "What makes you think he doesn't want to be around?"

CLIENT: "He is never home. He stays late at work, out with his friends every night, and is gone on the weekends. I don't know how long I can stand it."

CRISIS WORKER: "What do you mean by you don't know how long you can stand it?"

CLIENT: "Well, I am crying every night, my kids wonder where their dad is, and I am miserable and don't want to live like this."

(At this point, a reflection of feelings would be helpful, as would some close-ended questions about the kids' ages.)

Of course, these are not the only questions that could be asked. But notice that each question relates to what the client has just said, which has the effect of unrolling the client's cognitive and emotional experience. A useful metaphor is to think of the client's cognitive schema as a tree. The client presents the counselor with the trunk in the beginning. As the interview progresses, there is movement up the trunk and onto the branches. Each question allows movement onto the smaller branches and twigs, until the entire tree has been explored and is viewed in its totality. All branches, twigs, and leaves are connected to the trunk, whether directly or indirectly. When the counselor can see the tree fully, the nature of the crisis can be fully understood, and movement into offering coping strategies and altering cognitions can be accomplished.

Below are some examples of poorly worded questions and appropriately worded questions.

Poorly Worded Counselor Questions	Appropriately Worded Counselor Questions
Do you feel sad about losing your husband?	How do you feel about losing your husband?
Have you tried to talk to your father?	What have you done?
Could you tell me more about your sadness?	What is your sadness like for you?

Providing information in response to open-ended questions is generally more comfortable for clients than giving answers to 20 close-ended intake questions. There is a time and place for close-ended questions, usually when a fact is needed and during suicide assessments. Although it is true that many counselors must complete forms for their agencies, this does not mean that the interview should be a series of close-ended questions. Interweaving close-ended questions with open-ended questions, reflection, and paraphrasing should allow a counselor to complete the intake forms in most agencies. This takes practice, but clients benefit from this style.

Following are some examples of effective open-ended and close-ended questions. Included are suggestions for changing "why" questions into open-ended questions. Role-play these questions with friends.

Effective Open-Ended Questions	Appropriate Close-Ended Questions
How have you been feeling?	How long have you been married?
What is the worst part for you of being raped?	Have you been checked by a doctor yet?
What is it like for you to be diagnosed with AIDS?	Are you taking any medications?
How are you doing at work lately?	How old are your children?
What are your thoughts about death?	Has your husband ever abused the kids?
	Are you thinking of hurting yourself?

"Why" Questions	Open-Ended Questions That Replace "Why" Questions
Why did you ask him into your apartment?	How did things get out of control in your apartment?
Why did you smoke crack?	What was it like to decide to smoke crack?
Why did you try to kill yourself?	What was going through your mind when you took the pills?
How do these questions make you feel?	

Paraphrasing

Paraphrasing by the counselor can be done in two ways. Counselors can either restate in their own words what they thought they heard clients say, or they can clarify what was said in a questioning manner. The clarifying technique is used to clear up confusion or ambiguity and thus avoid misunderstanding and confirm the accuracy of what counselors heard. Clients are asked to rephrase or restate a previous message. This type of question is used for verification (i.e., making sure that what the crisis worker heard is what the client intended to say). The question is not meant to encourage clients to explore more of what was said, but simply to help counselors make sure that they understood what was said. Sometimes, clients talk in such a fragmented manner or so rapidly that important facts and ideas may not be heard accurately, and clarifying aids counselors in clearly understanding what was said.

Restating back to the client what the counselor heard is essential in building rapport and empathy. The crisis worker should not parrot or simply repeat exactly what the client said, but instead the goal is to share with the client what was heard by the counselor. The focus is on the cognitive and factual part of the client's message. The intent is to encourage elaboration of the statements to let the client know that you, the counselor, have understood or heard the message; to help the client focus on a specific situation, idea, or action; and to highlight content when attention to affect would be premature or inappropriate (Slaikeu, 1990, p. 38).

Exercise

Choose a partner, and ask a third person to be an observer. One person plays the crisis interviewer, and one plays a client in crisis. After the client tells the counselor about the crisis, the counselor is to restate in her own words what was heard. Do not parrot or repeat exactly what was said. Sometimes it is helpful for the counselor to break out of character and tell the observer, in the third person, what she heard the client say. The counselor can then go back into character and talk directly to the client, paraphrasing what she heard the client say. The dialogue shows how this might work:

> CLIENT: "I've been depressed since I had to have my dog put to sleep last week. I can't sleep or concentrate at work and everyone thinks I'm a big baby."

> CRISIS WORKER: "Are you saying that you have felt very bad since your dog died and aren't receiving any support from your coworkers?" (Clarifying)

> CRISIS WORKER: "I hear you saying that since putting your dog to sleep last week, you've been unable to sleep and feel depressed, and no one at work seems to understand your feelings." (Restatement)

Reflection of Feelings

Empathy is integral to achieving and maintaining contact with clients. This means being able to let clients know you understand their feelings. The technique of reflection, which is a statement that reflects the affective part or emotional tone of the client's message, whether verbal or nonverbal, is a powerful tool in creating an empathic environment. Not only does it help clarify the client's feelings in a particular situation, but it also helps the client feel understood. Clients can then express their own feelings about a situation; learn to manage their feelings, especially negative ones; and express their feelings toward the mental health care provider and agency. As we saw in Chapter 1, Caplan proposed that one characteristic of people who are coping effectively is their ability to express feelings freely and master them. Reflection of feelings allows such a process to occur.

Therapists from Freud to Rogers have believed that catharsis and experiential awareness of feelings are the curative factors in therapy. The crisis interview might be the only time the client has ever felt validated in her or his feelings, and that is a good experience!

Exercise

In pairs or in a group, have someone role-play a client in crisis, who will tell the others of his or her problem and feelings. Each student counselor then restates just the feelings to the client. Listen to the emotional tone and look for nonverbal cues, such as eyes watering or a fist pounding. Try using these openings: "You seem to feel . . . ," "Sounds as though you feel . . . ," "I sense you are . . . ." Look for ambivalent and contradictory feelings as well as positive feelings.

Here are some examples:

Painful feelings: "Sounds like you are furious with your wife."

Positive feelings: "You seem to be happiest when you don't drink."

Ambivalent feelings: "Although you say you hate your husband, you also seem to pity him."

Nonverbal feelings: "I can see by the tears in your eyes how painful this loss is."

Summarization

The key purpose of summarization is to help another individual pull his or her thoughts together. A secondary purpose is to check on whether you as a helper have distorted the client's frame of reference. Summarization may be helpful in beginning an interview if you've seen the client previously; it may help to bring together threads of data over several interviews or simply clarify what has gone on in the present interview (Ivey et al., 1997, p. 92). This is an example of a summarization: "So, your husband beat you last night and this time hit your daughter. You are scared and lonely and don't know where to turn."

The next section of the ABC model shows that summarization can help make a smooth transition from identifying the problem to finding coping strategies. Usually the cognitive and affective content are restated as well as the precipitating events and coping efforts. These aspects are easy to remember if you keep in mind the three aspects of any crisis: (1) the precipitating event; (2) the perception of the event by the client, which leads to subjective distress; and (3) failure of the client to cope successfully with the distress.

Now that you've learned the basic attending skills, practice them in 7- to 10-minute role-plays using the evaluation sheet in Table 5.1. Once you have mastered these skills, you are ready to move on to more advanced communication skills. The basic attending skills will be used throughout every session. They help counselors maintain rapport and allow them access to delicate information about the client. Counselors must use these basic attending skills during both the "B" and "C" stages of the ABC Model.

B: IDENTIFYING THE PROBLEM

After demographic information has been gathered and as rapport is developing, the crisis worker starts to focus on the client's presenting crisis. Identifying the problem is the second step in the ABC method and the most crucial one. Refer to the ABC Model of Crisis Intervention outline in Table 5.2 for a look at the interview process. Each aspect is examined individually as well as in the context of the others in the process. Beginning counselors should become so well-versed

TABLE 5.2 | ABC MODEL OF CRISIS INTERVENTION

	Skill Proficiency		
A: Developing and Maintaining Contact	Good	Fair	Poor
1. Attending behavior	____	____	____
2. Questions	____	____	____
3. Paraphrasing	____	____	____
4. Reflection	____	____	____
5. Summarization	____	____	____
B. Identifying the Problem and Therapeutic Interaction	Assessed	Not Assessed	N/A
Identify the precipitating event	____	____	____
Explore cognitions	____	____	____
Identify emotional distress	____	____	____
Identify impairments in functioning			
1. Behavioral	____	____	____
2. Social	____	____	____
3. Academic	____	____	____
4. Occupational	____	____	____
	Done	Not Done	N/A
Identify precrisis level of functioning	____	____	____
Identify ethical issues			
1. Suicide assessment	____	____	____
2. Child abuse, elder abuse, danger to others	____	____	____
3. Organic or other medical concerns	____	____	____
Identify substance abuse issues	____	____	____
Use therapeutic interactions			
1. Educational comments	____	____	____
2. Empowerment comments	____	____	____
3. Validation and supportive comments	____	____	____
4. Reframes	____	____	____
C. Coping			
Identify client's current coping attempts	____	____	____
Encourage client to think of other coping strategies	____	____	____

TABLE 5.2 | **CONTINUED**

Present alternative coping ideas

1. Refer to support groups,
   12-step groups   _____   _____   _____

2. Refer to long-term therapy, family
   therapy   _____   _____   _____

3. Refer to medical doctor   _____   _____   _____

4. Refer to lawyer   _____   _____   _____

5. Refer to agency   _____   _____   _____

6. Suggest bibliotherapy, journaling,
   "reel" therapy   _____   _____   _____

7. Suggest other behavioral activities

Follow-up

in the various aspects of this model that they do not appear mechanical to the client. Keeping in mind the definition of crisis helps counselors remember what to identify: precipitating events, perceptions, subjective distress, and functioning.

Although the model is presented in a linear outline form, interviews do not have to be conducted in a linear fashion. Unfortunately for beginning counselors, having a script for each crisis situation is just not practical. However, the examples presented can be used in conjunction with the counselors' creative processes and intuition. This outline will be useful for you as you practice each type of crisis in subsequent chapters. In each of those chapters, examples are given for practice in role-playing. Do not be restricted to using only the ideas given. Create your own ideas whenever possible. The outline can be used for a 10-minute phone call, a 50-minute session, or a 6-week (or longer) series of crisis intervention sessions. Each week, new issues can be addressed and new coping strategies sought; also, changes in functioning can be assessed from week to week. Notice that the model has several areas to assess. This does not mean that on every visit the counselor must make an assessment for each area. Rather, each area should be addressed at least on the first or second visit and then reassessed thereafter as necessary to evaluate the client's progress.

Of particular importance in crisis intervention and in brief therapy is the ability to explore the client's perceptions. Most sessions will be spent in this process; and through these explorations clients gain knowledge of the source of their pain. Once clients' perceptions and frame of reference regarding various situations are understood, the crisis worker is in a position to guide clients into new ways of thinking and experiencing themselves and the world. Also, once clients' cognitions are changed, subjective distress will be reduced, coping skills can be implemented, and functioning will be increased. This, as you will recall, is the goal of crisis intervention.

The interview process can be thought of as climbing a tree with the client (see figure 5.1). The client will usually present with the precipitating event or subjective distress such as emotional pain or impairment in functioning. The

FIGURE 5.1 | THE COGNITION TREE

Cognition 1 Is a Branch
[Twigs and leaves explore this cognition—leaves are brown (cognitive key)]

Cognition 2 Is a Branch
[Twigs and leaves explore this cognition—leaves are brown (cognitive key)]

Cognition 3 Is a Branch
[Twigs and leaves explore this cognition—leaves are brown (cognitive key)]

Clients present a trunk: a precipitating event, emotions, or impairments in functioning

goal of the B section is to "climb the tree" to explore how all the components are related to the cognitions.

The counselor climbs up the trunk with the client by asking what the client's thoughts are about the trunk. These thoughts are explored by asking the client to further explain what the client means. Open-ended questions are used to help the client explore all related thoughts and perceptions until the leaves are understood—they are the cognitive key. The counselor can help change the leaves from brown to green with therapeutic interaction comments. Examples of therapeutic interaction comments can be found in many sections of subsequent chapters and will be defined clearly later in this chapter. Many times, several important cognitions are presented. Each one will have to be explored and new therapeutic comments then provided. Identifying cognitions and offering new ways of thinking about the situation is the main focus of any crisis intervention session.

By exploring the many limbs and twigs of the initial perception presented, the counselor and client gain a deeper understanding of what is really bothering the client most about the precipitating event. It often takes as many as six questions before the cognitive key can be established and therapeutic statements offered. If the counselor attempts to provide an educational statement, a reframe, a support statement, or an empowerment statement too soon, the client often resists. The client probably just needed more time to fully explain his or her cognitive tree. Below is a sample dialogue in which therapist and client climb the tree:

CLIENT: "My husband left me." (Presents a precipitating event)

COUNSELOR: "What does that mean to you?" (Asks open-ended question to explore perception)

CLIENT: "I will be alone forever." (First cognition presented; client thinks she'll be alone forever)

COUNSELOR: "In what way alone?" (Counselor tries to understand exactly what client means by "alone")

CLIENT: "No one will ever love me again." (New cognitive statement)

COUNSELOR: "What makes you think that?"

CLIENT: "He told me that he's the only one who could ever love me because I'm so ugly and stupid." (More new information about the original cognition)

COUNSELOR: "What are your thoughts about the idea of your being ugly and stupid?"

CLIENT: "Well, I don't think I'm really that stupid."

COUNSELOR: "What do you think?'

CLIENT: "I'm afraid to be alone and start all over."

COUNSELOR: "What is most scary for you about this?"

CLIENT: "I'm afraid to get close to someone else and feel hurt."

COUNSELOR: "It is often scary to start over." (Support statement that validates client's feelings and thoughts) "This scary feeling may at some point turn into excitement at the opportunity to have a more rewarding relationship." (A brief reframe of the scariness possibly being excitement)

At this point, the client may feel some hope and her cognitions will probably have changed to some extent. Notice how many questions were necessary to reach the deeper meanings behind her initial cognition.

Probably the most important reason for exploring the client's internal frame of reference is that changing internal perceptions is easier than changing external situations. If the crisis worker spends too much time focusing on the significant others and the details of the situation—elements that generally cannot be changed—the client may experience increased frustration.

At the end of this chapter, a "script" using the ABC model of crisis intervention is presented. It offers specific questions and statements a crisis worker might use. It is presented after readers have had a chance to learn about each section of the model individually. Then they should be able to understand how to integrate all the sections in a typical interview.

Identifying the Precipitating Event

Shortly after the interview begins, the counselor should begin to ask about the precipitating event. To ask, "What happened that made you call for an appointment?" is appropriate. It is an opening for clients to tell what is going on with them. If clients cannot think of any particular event that brought them to counseling, the crisis worker must probe further, explaining that understanding the trigger of a client's crisis aids in relieving the crisis state.

The precipitating event may have happened yesterday or 6 weeks ago. A helpful strategy is learning when the client started to feel bad, which helps pinpoint the triggering event. "The straw that broke the camel's back" is a common expression that can help clients focus on the beginning of the crisis.

Another reason for specifying the precipitating event is to be able, later on, to explore how the client has been trying to cope since it happened. When the client's denial is strong, the crisis worker must confront the client about why exactly the client decided to come for counseling. The reason is usually because of difficulty in coping with a precipitating event. If the event is not clearly defined, the counselor will have problems presenting alternative coping strategies to deal with the event. Last, identification of the precipitating event is vital because the crisis worker must identify the client's perceptions about the episode. If these cognitions are not identified properly, there can be no therapeutic interactive comments related to them. Remember, change in the way the event is perceived is essential to increasing the functioning level of clients. In Chapter 1, two formulas were presented and are repeated here. Refer to them as you practice using the ABC model.

Formula for Understanding the Process of Crisis Formation

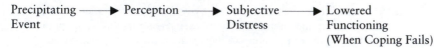

Precipitating ⟶ Perception ⟶ Subjective ⟶ Lowered
Event   Distress   Functioning
                                                (When Coping Fails)

If the goal of crisis work is to increase clients' functioning, the following formula aids crisis workers in understanding how to move clients out of a crisis.

Formula to Increase Functioning

Change in Perception ⟶ Decrease in ⟶ Increase
of the Precipitating Event   Subjective Distress   in Functioning
and Acquiring New Coping Skills

No matter how much clients profess that "nothing has happened, really," something drove them to seek help. Squeeze it out of them! They need to see that their current state of subjective distress is tied to an actual event or fact.

Recognizing the Meaning or Perception of the Precipitating Event

In addition to identifying precipitating events, crisis workers need to actively explore the meaning clients ascribe to these events. It is clients' perceptions of stressful situations that cause them to be in a crisis state as well as the inability to cope with the stress. Usually, stress originates from one of four areas: loss of control, loss of self-esteem, loss of nurturance, or forced adjustment to a change in life or role. The meaning behind these losses is helpful to explore.

All aspects of the situation should be examined. For example, suppose a woman is raped. Not only does the actual rape cause stress, but her perception of how her husband will react also contributes to her stress as she struggles with her perceived new role with him.

Some questions the crisis worker may ask to elicit the client's frame of reference regarding the crisis situation include these: "How do you put it together in your head?" "What do you think about this?" "What does it mean to you that . . . ?" "What are you telling yourself about . . . ?" "What assumptions are you making about . . . ?"

Cognitive restructuring or reframing is a valuable tool for the counselor but can be done only if the client's current cognitions are known. It is impossible to develop a coping plan for clients without examining the cognitive and perceptual experience. Think of yourself as a mechanic who needs to analyze and experience the trouble firsthand before tinkering with the engine.

Assessing the client's perception of the precipitating event is the most important part of the interview and must be done thoroughly on every visit to check for changing views as well as long-standing views on a variety of issues.

Identifying Subjective Distress and Functioning Level

In addition to exploring stressors and clients' perceptions of them, counselors must inquire about clients' functioning and how the precipitating events are affecting it. Clients seem to benefit from expressing painful feelings and sharing other symptoms—symptoms that may impair clients' occupational, academic, behavioral, social, interpersonal, or family functioning. Counselors should ask how clients' perceptions about the precipitating event are affecting their functioning in each area.

Often each area in which the person is suffering distress is dealt with separately because a specific perception may be associated with that area and not another. The crisis worker is advised to explore each area affected during the crisis state in as much detail as possible. This probing gives the counselor a feel for the degree of impairment the client is experiencing and can be used later to help select coping strategies. When clients discuss their symptoms and impairments in functioning, they can receive feedback, education, and support from the counselor. Often, understanding one's feelings and behaviors is the first step in coping with them.

> **Example:** A battered woman might be experiencing much anxiety at work because she believes that her husband will come there and cause a scene, which would probably result in her being fired. This perception might be dealt with by letting her know that bosses can often be sympathetic and helpful, and that her boss might even provide her with support and initiate legal action for her.

In addition to identifying the client's current level of functioning, the crisis worker needs to assess the client's precrisis level of functioning in order to compare the two. This will help the counselor determine the level of coping the client can realistically achieve; it also gives the counselor an idea of the severity of the crisis for the person. The comparison serves as a basis for evaluating the outcome of crisis intervention. Remember that the goal of crisis intervention is to bring the client back to the precrisis level of functioning.

> **Example:** If a woman was getting straight As in college before being raped, and afterward her grades went down to Cs and Ds, her crisis was worse for her than for a woman who was raped but showed only minimal disturbance at work or school. In these cases, it is probable that the first woman's perception of the rape was more drastic than the second woman's. Maybe she told herself that she was at fault, that she is dirty, and that no one will ever love her again. The second woman might have a more realistic view of the rape and be able to tell herself that it was the rapist's fault and that no one is going to hold her responsible or think differently about her.

Most intake forms ask for a comparison between current and previous functioning on a regular basis. It is important to include this information as part of any crisis assessment procedure.

Making Ethical Checks

Several other areas need identification at this stage of the interview. These have ethical implications and must be assessed either directly or indirectly with every client. However, in order not to behave like a prosecuting attorney, the crisis worker is encouraged to extract this information in a fluid, relevant manner. Rather than going down a list and asking one question after another, the counselor should weave the questions in as the issues arise in the normal flow of the conversation.

Suicide Check   Because people in crisis are vulnerable and often confused and overwhelmed, suicide sometimes becomes an alternative for them. Every crisis worker must assess for suicidality, particularly when the client is depressed or impulsive. Suicide assessment and prevention are discussed in detail in Chapter 6.

Homicidal/Abuse Issues   As discussed in the ethics chapter, mental health workers in many states are required to report child and elder abuse and any suspicion that a client may harm someone. Assessment of these issues must be done during the course of an interview. Often, the counselor's intuition will provide the basis for detailed inquiry. Child abuse and elder abuse are dealt with in subsequent chapters; working with clients who are a danger to others is examined in Chapter 6.

> **Example:** A 43-year-old male may say that he hates his father for having beaten his mother and can see himself smashing the father's face. This statement alone does not warrant an attempt to take the client into custody. However, I would inquire how he deals with this anger, especially toward his wife and children. It is important for counselors to know that suspected abuse of children must be assessed in all cases. Sometimes, turning away and collaborating in denial with an abusive family is easier than facing the issue, but doing so is never in the best interest of the child. Such action is unethical and might be illegal, depending on the laws of the state where the action occurs.

> **Example:** The mother of a 15-year-old boy and a 16-year-old girl is in a crisis state and seeks help from a counselor. Two weeks earlier, the husband whipped the boy

with a belt and left welts on his back. The father also slapped the girl across the face. When the mother was informed by the crisis worker that a child abuse report would have to be made, she was very upset and pleaded with the therapist not to make the report. She thought that it would affect her getting a high-security job for which she was applying; would make the husband angry; and would cause anxiety for her son, who was worried that his dad would take his car away. The counselor explained that a report was mandatory in this situation. To alleviate the mother's concern, the counselor made the report in the presence of the clients, so they would know what would most likely happen according to the social worker taking the call.

Making clients part of the reporting process helped them deal with it in a less fearful manner. The counselor had no choice but to make the report, even though the clients did not want her to.

Organic or Other Concerns   If clients state that they suffer from serious depression, bipolar disorder, obsessive-compulsive disorder, or schizophrenia, they should already be receiving medication. Crisis workers should assess for medication compliance for these cases and encourage noncompliant clients to continue with prescribed medication until they can schedule an appointment with their physician. In these situations, crisis workers may want to consult with the physician by phone to ensure that clients receive the most effective treatment. When clients describe or exhibit behaviors, symptoms, or complaints that may be due to biological factors such as Alzheimer's disease or attention deficit disorder with hyperactivity (ADHD) but have not yet been formally diagnosed with a serious disorder, crisis workers should refer them to a physician or psychiatrist for further assessment.

Substance Abuse Issues

Checking for substance abuse on a regular basis is a good idea and is often part of the intake form in most agencies. Because clients involved with substance use and abuse often deny and minimize their use, the crisis worker needs to be somewhat assertive in gathering information about drug use. Following are some examples showing how to extract this information without offending clients:

"Tell me about your past and present drug and alcohol use."

This statement assumes that use exists or existed and is stated matter-of-factly, as if you won't be shocked to hear of it. The person who has not used drugs can simply say "None."

"How much alcohol do you use a week?"

"What other drugs besides cocaine do you use or have you used?"

These questions do not seem to be as judgmental or grilling as the following do:

"Do you use alcohol? Do you use cocaine? Do you smoke pot? Do you drink daily?"

Using general, open-ended questions will save time and reduce defensiveness in clients.

Therapeutic Interaction

The main part of the session, and probably the most therapeutic part, will be spent in identifying the client's beliefs and feelings, and then providing supportive statements, educational information, empowering statements, and reframing statements that will aid the client in thinking differently about the situation and assist them in coping with it. Of course, active listening skills remain important, but once these are mastered, the counselor is ready to use the more advanced skills discussed next to help clients improve their coping ability.

Validation and Support Statements   The counselor may, from time to time, tell clients that their feelings are normal or suggest there is hope that things will get better. In response to a woman who has just found out that her husband has been molesting their daughter and feels as though the world has come to an end, a crisis worker might respond supportively by saying, "I know that right now you feel that everything is falling apart, but many people have gone through the same situation and have survived. You have every reason to believe you can survive, too."

Support statements are not false hopes or words like "It'll be OK," "Don't worry," or "Forget about it." These comments are typical of family and friends who mean well; however, they are not very useful. As crisis workers, we need to say things to people that others do not say. Also, because clients see counselors as experts in crisis situations, they will tend to take comfort in supportive comments from these helpers, often adopting a more optimistic attitude. Receiving validation from a counselor about one's feelings can help clients not see themselves as sick, weak, or bad.

Educational Statements   Providing factual information, whether developmental or situational, is vital in every crisis. Clients often suffer merely because they lack, or have incorrect, knowledge about the precipitating event and aspects associated with it. Thus, it is imperative for crisis workers to gather as much information as possible about each crisis situation. Whether this is done through formal academic courses, books, experience, or supervision, it gives counselors an edge in helping clients work through their issues.

Educational statements may include psychological, social, and interpersonal dynamics, or they may provide statistics or frequency of the problem. In any case, when a counselor helps people in a crisis state increase their knowledge of facts, the clients will have stronger coping skills for the current crisis and future crises. You will remember from Chapter 1 that seeking reality and information was one of Caplan's characteristics of effective coping behavior.

Picture a woman who has been completely isolated from others because she is in an ongoing battering relationship. She will most likely perceive herself as abnormal and bizarre. When she learns that about 30 percent of women live in such relationships, she may feel differently about herself and the abnormality of the situation. Without this issue to deal with, the counselor is now free to process other issues.

Empowering Statements   Clients who are in certain crisis situations in which they feel violated, victimized, or helpless respond well to empowering statements. Clients are presented with choices and are encouraged to take back personal power by making good choices. Battered women, rape survivors, and survivors of child abuse often suffer from learned helplessness stemming from the abuse. They feel that they cannot prevent bad things from happening because, in the past, they could not prevent abuse by a physically stronger (or in some other way stronger) perpetrator. This perception often motivates them to survive abuse rather than try and escape from it. A useful strategy is to let clients know that they may not have had the choice to stop the abuse from happening at an earlier time but that now they certainly can make choices to do something about the abuse (e.g., press charges, confront the perpetrator, talk about it). Also, the crisis worker can point out that they do not have to choose certain behaviors. It is important that they move from a position of feeling powerless to feeling that they have some control and choice in their life now.

> **Example:** A rape victim might be told, "You didn't have a choice in being raped, but now you do have a choice of what to do. You can call the police, go to counseling, tell a friend, or not do any of these things. Let's talk about your feelings and thoughts on each of these choices."

Reframing Statements   In its simplest form, reframing is defining a situation differently from the way the client is defining it. It is a cognitive restructuring tactic that aims at changing the crisis from danger to opportunity. American clichés such as "Every cloud has a silver lining" and "When life gives you lemons, make lemonade" convey this idea quite clearly.

Reframing may seem like rationalizing away a problem to some. However, it is probably one of the strongest healing skills available to the crisis worker and for people in general. It allows us to acknowledge that life is a struggle, that we aren't perfect, and that dwelling on our failings is not necessary or helpful. Instead, if we can believe that something positive or beneficial will be an outcome or result of the problem, we can usually integrate the difficult episode more easily. The crisis worker's responsibility is to be creative in finding the right reframe, which means actively searching for the positive. Reframing is an advanced technique that puts problems in a solvable form by changing the meanings of behaviors and situations and providing a new perspective that opens up new possibilities for change.

> **Example:** The author worked with a woman whose rape case was rejected by the district attorney after she had hoped for a year that it would go to court. The rapist was free, and her victimization had not been acknowledged because of a legal technicality. The counselor and client could have both thrown up their hands, called the judicial system names, and seethed internally. Alternatively, the counselor pointed out to the client that the rape prodded her to seek counseling that allowed her not only to work through the rape issues but also to identify her codependency and its effects on her relationships. This knowledge led the way to better family relations and intimacy with her boyfriend. The reframe was that the rape, although terrifying, had been survived and indirectly allowed for an opportunity

to gain self-understanding and growth. This client could tolerate this reframe because she had undergone one year of intensive therapy and had strong rapport with the counselor, who truly understood the client's frame of reference.

Reframing is possible only if the counselor first understands fully the client's current frame of reference. Otherwise, the counselor would not know what should be reframed. Counselors can learn the client's frame of reference by asking direct questions: "How do you perceive the situation?" "What does it mean to you?" "What runs through your head about it?" Reframing is not a technique to be taken lightly, and careful supervision is necessary in learning its effective use. Sometimes reframing is associated with a cold, strategic approach, but it can be done in an authentic, caring manner. The counselor does not deny the seriousness of the problem but instead offers a way out of a problem that allows the person to preserve the integrity of the self and often the family unit as well. Because reframes are usually offered with the person's self-identity in mind, shame is reduced and self-integrity is preserved. The examples of reframes provided in each of the following sections show this principle of self-preservation clearly.

In summary, the B section of the ABC model can be thought of as identifying issues one at a time and providing various forms of feedback as the process moves forward to a place where the client can accept coping as viable behavior. Periodically, the crisis worker should summarize the precipitating events, the client's perceptions of them, the client's functioning in several areas of life, and any major symptoms of concern.

C: COPING

The last step of the ABC model is concerned with the client's coping behavior—past, present, and future. Past coping success can be built on to help the person weather the present and future difficulties.

Exploring the Client's Own Attempts at Coping

Toward the conclusion of an interview, counselors should begin summing up the problem and moving clients into a coping mode. To do this, crisis workers ask clients how they have managed crises in the past. All coping, whether it is helpful or not, should be examined. In this way, clients can make a mental list of what works and what does not.

If the client cannot think of any past coping behavior, the crisis worker should be very encouraging. The counselor might say, "Well, you must have done something or you would not have made it this far." Remember that even sleeping and social withdrawal are coping strategies, and the counselor and client should talk about their helpfulness or unhelpfulness. Eliciting unhealthy attempts at coping is especially valuable as it helps the client see what has not worked in the past. The client will generally be more open to alternatives once the ineffectiveness of his or her current behavior is made evident.

Encouraging the Development of New Coping Behaviors

After current coping attempts have been discussed, the counselor can prod clients to ponder other possible ways of coping. The crisis worker can ask clients how they think they can proceed at this point to begin to get out of the crisis state. Remember that clients have already been presented with educational information, reframes, supportive comments, and empowerment statements. It is time for clients to do some of their own thinking. Clients are more likely to follow through with a plan they have developed themselves than with one suggested by the counselor. It is appropriate for a counselor to be challenging and persistent in getting clients to think of ways they could begin to cope better. This approach helps clients get in touch with their problem-solving abilities.

Presenting Alternative Coping Behaviors

Clients should be allowed first to propose their own methods for coping with their problems. When they have reached the end of the resources they know, however, the counselor should suggest other options. Many of these may be completely new to clients, offering them fresh insights. The suggestions offered by the counselor should be based on previous discussions with the client. The client will often provide the counselor with the best alternative for that particular client. For example, a client might have said that one of the things that made her feel better was talking to her girlfriends about her divorce. But now, she says, they are tired of listening. This should trigger in the counselor the idea that this client feels better talking to a group of women about her problem. Getting the client to accept a referral to a support group should not be difficult, because the client herself has said that doing this type of thing has already made her feel better!

Support Groups and 12-Step Groups   If support systems haven't already been discussed, now is a good time to identify some existing natural support, such as coworkers, supervisors, relatives, friends, schoolmates, or church members. Clients may not have considered any of these people as helpers in getting through the crisis. With a little encouragement, they may be persuaded to reach out to others. This is not to suggest that crisis workers should avoid giving support to clients. However, it is often more comfortable for clients to receive help from natural support systems than to rely on mental health professionals during crises. As Caplan (1964) suggested earlier, people who are coping effectively with a situation will actively ask others for help, not necessarily mental health workers. The idea of encouraging clients to help themselves parallels the adage of teaching a man to fish versus just giving him fish. Self-sufficiency is more economical in the long run. I have often felt that as a crisis interventionist, my job is to put myself out of a job by encouraging clients to function on their own and with the support of others in their life. A crisis worker is merely a beacon shedding light on these resources.

Some clients may need referrals to 12-step groups such as Alcoholics Anonymous (AA), Al-Anon, Co-Dependents Anonymous, Cocaine Anonymous, or others. These mutual self-help groups are free and have no time limits for attendance; sessions can be found in every city at various hours of the day. The trend now is for insurance companies to pay for only 6–12 sessions of therapy, so 12-step groups are a lifesaver for many people who cannot afford to pay for therapy out of their own pockets.

Long-Term Therapy, Marital Therapy, and Family Therapy   Some clients' problems have been going on for so long that crisis intervention cannot resolve them. Perhaps because of a personality disorder or other chronic emotional disorder, clients need ongoing therapy with a trained professional. This might be individual therapy or marital or family therapy. Often, a crisis is an opportunity for clients to resolve long-term problems that have been hidden for many years.

Shelters and Other Agencies   To address other problems, crisis workers need to be knowledgeable about community agencies and resources. Clients who are anxious and feeling overwhelmed are more likely to follow through with a referral when it is presented in written form with choices, addresses, phone numbers, and fees. Providing written information is much more effective than telling clients to look for certain services in the Yellow Pages. Even if you are conducting a phone interview, having these resources in hand, separated by the type of crisis, certainly aids the expediency of referral. Also, crisis workers will know whether an agency can actually help a client at an affordable rate if workers have recently updated their information about the agency.

Most communities have community resource directories that list various agencies, and local libraries also have listings available. One of the best ways to get names of agencies is by contacting an agency that has similar services. Most mental health and social service agencies are familiar with agencies in the community.

A useful assignment for beginning crisis intervention students is to do research on various community agencies and resources that regularly intervene in crisis situations. It is amazing to learn how many resources are available in most communities for almost any crisis situation. Community resources were developed during the grassroots era of the 1960s, and they have evolved over the years into an elaborate networking system of many different agencies. Large organizations often have nationwide toll-free phone numbers that workers can call to get information about many agencies. The organizations serve as clearinghouses for a variety of resources. Some examples of community resources include local churches, local community colleges, county mental health agencies, local AA groups, and private clubs such as the Sierra Club.

Some resources are more appropriate for certain crises than others. Suicidal clients should be given a list of hotlines to call, if necessary, between sessions. Persons suffering a loss from divorce might be referred to a divorce recovery workshop through a church or support group. Clients dealing with issues related to HIV or AIDS should be referred to a local AIDS services foundation for support groups. It is widely known that substance abusers and their significant others benefit from 12-step groups such as AA or Al-Anon. Sexual assault victims and battered women benefit from a referral to shelters or specialized support groups.

At times, crisis workers may want to contact an agency and let someone there know about a referral. It is quite reasonable to ask for a follow-up call or note about whether the client used the resource. In other instances, a client may return to a crisis worker for another individual session and the crisis worker at that time can ask whether the client attended the support group or used the service recommended.

Medical and Legal Referrals   In some cases, medical or legal referrals are necessary. Even crisis workers who are considered paraprofessionals should have an understanding of the legal, political, and medical systems and how they will make an impact on various types of crises. For instance, workers should know the conditions under which a police officer may arrest a battering spouse. Also, they should have knowledge of restraining orders, which may be useful for a victim of abuse. How the court system generally deals with rape or child abuse is useful information as well. Though they are not expected to be lawyers, crisis workers need to keep abreast of recent laws that affect clients in crisis.

Similarly, though they are not expected or allowed to be physicians, crisis workers need to be able to refer someone to a doctor for an evaluation when medication or other treatment might be useful. Learning to consult and work with medical doctors is a skill worth developing, and knowing when to make a referral to a physician is vital.

Bibliotherapy, Journaling, and Reel Therapy   Every crisis worker needs to have some knowledge of reading material for clients in a variety of crisis situations. Using these materials with clients is called bibliotherapy. Reading often provides a new way of looking at the crisis (reframing) and gives the client information and support—especially books written by a person who has gone through a similar crisis. For example, reading a book by a woman who was raped will help the recently raped woman see that her feelings are normal; this knowledge should have a calming effect. Also, reading helps people think rather than feel, encouraging more productive problem-solving activity. Having clients keep a journal of their thoughts is also quite helpful; the clients may discover new feelings and thoughts as they jot them down on paper. The journal may be shared with the counselor or remain private.

Many therapists are also using movies to help move their clients toward breakthroughs more quickly. Viewing movies allows clients to "grow" in their own "free" time. For example, Nielsen (quoted in Hesley, 2000, pp. 55–57) has used the movie *Distant Thunder* for clients experiencing posttraumatic stress disorder. He states that many of his clients find it easier to explain their own "flashbacks" and "social phobia" after viewing this film. The use of films—so-called reel therapy—is likely to become more common because many future therapists watch films as part of their graduate school studies. Films do have limitations and should not take the place of personal discussion with the counselor. Movies should be selected carefully and thoughtfully (Hesley, 2000, pp. 55–57).

Other Behavioral Activities   Some clients may benefit from assertiveness training, in which the counselor teaches them how to ask for what they want, express feelings and needs to others, or set boundaries with others. Other tasks may include having clients exercise, visit friends and family, or engage in a recreational activity such as going to the beach.

All of these types of coping referrals provide ways for the client to cope and think differently about the precipitating event.

Commitment and Follow-Up

Part of making any referral or suggestion is commitment and follow-up, that is, counselors get a commitment from clients that they will indeed follow through with recommendations. This explains why it is best for clients to develop their own coping plans; they are more likely to follow through with a plan they have formulated themselves. In some cases, as with highly suicidal clients, a written contract may be prudent. The no-suicide contract is a useful intervention that will be discussed in a later chapter. Written contracts are often used with clients who need to control their impulses or with acting-out teenagers. Both the therapist and the client keep a copy of the contract and discuss it at the next session.

In sum, the C part of the ABC model first asks clients to explore current, past, and possibly new coping strategies to deal with the crisis at hand. Then the crisis worker offers alternative ideas, makes referrals, and asks clients for a commitment to follow through on the plan. The worker's hope is that clients will move from a dysfunctional state to a higher level of functioning and perceived control over the precipitating event. At each visit, the crisis worker can verify and suggest connecting with these various coping aids, which gives clients something concrete to take home.

KEY TERMS FOR STUDY

attending behavior: Behavior that has to do with following the client's lead, actively listening, and demonstrating presence.

bibliotherapy: The use of books as an alternative coping strategy.

bipolar disorder: A condition in which states of manic behavior (i.e., out-of-control, hyper, grandiose behavior) fluctuate with states of extreme depression. It is sometimes known as manic-depression.

close-ended question: A type of question that can be answered with a "yes" or a "no" or some other one-word answer. Its best use is for obtaining facts such as age, number of children, or number of years married. Forced-choice questions, or "do you, have you" questions, are generally not effective. These types of questions can bring the interview to a dead end or sound like an interrogation.

commitment and follow-up: Verbal agreement given by client to a crisis worker at the end of a crisis intervention session. Specifically, it is what the client is going to do after leaving the session to deal with the crisis. It may include returning to see the same counselor or going elsewhere. Remember that the person in crisis is vulnerable and needs direction.

depression: A state of being in which the client is sad, low in energy, and suicidal; he or she feels worthless, helpless, and hopeless; the person lacks desire, is socially withdrawn, and is slowed in processes such as thinking and concentrating. This person should be referred to a physician for an evaluation.

educational statements: Types of therapeutic comments in which facts, statistics, and theories are presented to clients in an attempt to normalize their experience and change their misconceptions.

empowering statements: Therapeutic comments that help clients feel more in control and see choices they have. They are especially useful for clients who have been victimized.

hallucinations: False sensory perceptions. Auditory hallucinations are associated with schizophrenia; visual and tactile ones with substance abuse withdrawal; and gustatory and olfactory ones with organic brain disorders. Any hallucination is indicative of severe illness; when hallucinations are present, a doctor should be consulted.

legal or medical referrals: Referrals made by the crisis worker if the client needs the services of other professionals, as when a person has been arrested, wants a restraining order, or has a severe mental or other illness.

organic brain disorder: A condition resulting from a neurological disturbance, genetic abnormality, or tumor.

paraphrasing: A basic attending skill, or clarifying technique, in which counselors restate in their own words what was just said by the client.

rapport: A special type of bonding that a counselor seeks with a client. The more rapport there is between client and counselor, the greater the client's sense of trust and security.

reel therapy: The use of movies to aid clients in understanding and resolving their own issues.

reflection: The best way to show emotional empathy for a client; the counselor points out the client's emotions by stating them as either seen or heard.

reframing: A therapeutic restatement of a problem that helps the client see the situation differently, usually in a way that makes it easier to solve.

resources: Sources of help in the community. A crisis worker must be knowledgeable about community resources to be able to connect a client in crisis with the appropriate support group or other service.

schizophrenia: A disorder usually requiring the attention of a psychiatrist and characterized by the following symptoms: hallucinations, delusions, loose associations, blunt affect, and poor appearance.

support statements: Therapeutic statements that make clients feel validated and that the counselor truly understands and empathizes with their situation.

support systems: Networks of helping individuals and agencies. A crisis worker uses the client's natural support systems, such as family and friends, and also helps the client build new support systems.

summarization: A skill useful in tying ideas together, wrapping up a session, or moving from the B phase of the ABC model to the C phase; the skill is also useful when the counselor does not know where to go next. It is a statement that pulls together the various facts and feelings discussed in the session.

To sum up the ABC model, a sample script is presented in Table 5.3. This gives readers an idea of the types of questions to ask and statements to make when using the ABC model. The steps of the model are repeated in the table. In each section, please note the specific words (italicized) that a counselor might say to a client.

TABLE 5.3 | ABC MODEL OF CRISIS INTERVENTION (SAMPLE SCRIPT)

A: BASIC ATTENDING SKILLS

What brings you in today? You seem to be having a little trouble getting started. So your girlfriend told you she wants to break up last week and things haven't been going too well lately. You look like you are very sad.

B: IDENTIFYING THE PROBLEM AND THERAPEUTIC INTERACTION

Identify the Precipitating Event:

What specifically brought you in today? Did something happen recently, something different?

Explore Meanings, Cognitions, and Perceptions:

How do you think about it? What does it mean to you? What thoughts go through your mind when you picture the event? How do you put it together in your head? What is it like for you? What specifically do you mean? What are your perceptions about it (the precipitating event)?

Identify Subjective Distress (Emotional Distress):

How do you feel? What emotions are going on inside you? You seem sad, angry, ambivalent, in pain. How have you been feeling since (the precipitating event)?

Identify Impairments in Functioning in the Following Areas:

1. Behavioral
How have you been doing in your life? How are you sleeping? How is your appetite? Have you been carrying on with your normal activities?

2. Social
How are your relationships with your friends and family? Have you been seeing anyone socially since (the precipitating event)? How do you feel or act around people?

3. Academic
Are you going to school? How are your grades lately? Have you been able to study and concentrate in classes? How are you getting along with classmates?

4. Occupational
How are you doing at work? Has your work performance changed since (the precipitating event)? Have you been able to function adequately at work?

Identify Precrisis Level of Functioning in 1–4 above.

How has your ability to function socially, at school, and at work changed since (the precipitating event)? What was it like for you before (the precipitating event)? What/how were your relationships before (the precipitating event)?

TABLE 5.3 | **CONTINUED**

Identify Any Ethical Concerns:

1. Suicide assessment

Have you been thinking about hurting yourself? Have you attempted to kill yourself? Do you want to commit suicide? Do you have a plan? Do you have the means? What is stopping you from killing yourself?

2. Child abuse, elder abuse, homicide

Are your children in danger? Have you or your husband ever caused physical harm to your children? How hard do you hit your kids? How often do you leave your child alone? Have your kids gone without food for an entire day? Has your elderly parent been hurt by the retirement home? When did you first learn that your sister was stealing from your father? How often do you have thoughts about killing your wife? Have you ever hurt someone in the past? How strong are your feelings of murder?

3. Organic or other medical concerns

Are you able to get up in the morning and feed yourself? How many hours do you sleep? Can you dress yourself every day? Do you ever hear voices? Does it ever feel like the phone wires are talking to you? Do you have special powers? Can people read your mind or put thoughts into your head? Do you think people are out to get you? Do you smell or taste things that are unusual?

Identify Substance Abuse Issues:

What kinds of drugs have you used in the past? How much alcohol do you drink per week/month/day? What drugs do you use recreationally?

Use Therapeutic Interactions:

1. Educational comments

- *Although you feel as though you are the only woman who stays in a battering relationship, it is estimated that about 30 percent of women in the United States live in ongoing battering relationships. Going through a period of intense anger is quite normal and to be expected after the death of a loved one.*
- *Actually, it is not uncommon to be raped by someone you know. Date rape is extremely common for women ages 15–24.*
- *Studies to date do not show that one can catch HIV by shaking hands.*
- *It is not uncommon for the spouse of an alcoholic to be highly anxious about the spouse's drinking.*

2. Empowerment statements

- *It is true that you did not have a choice about being raped, but you do have choices now, including whether to press charges, get a medical exam, or drop the whole matter.*
- *Unfortunately, you cannot control your wife's drug use, but you can control your own behavior with her.*
- *True, you are HIV infected and cannot change that. You can, however, choose how to live the rest of your life.*

3. Support statements

- *This is an extremely difficult situation, and I don't take it lightly. I can only imagine the pain you are going through. I am so sorry this happened to you.*
- *Please, let me be there for you; I care. It must feel pretty bad if you want to kill yourself. These kinds of traumas often make people feel like giving up.*

TABLE 5.3 | CONTINUED

4. Reframes

I think it takes a lot of strength to cry, and I don't see crying as a sign of weakness. Although you see suicide as a sign of strength, it is actually the easy way out of a life filled with difficulties for us all. Staying with a batterer for the sake of your children is evidence of your strength, not a sign of weakness. (Please see each chapter for more examples of reframing.)

C: COPING

Identify Client's Current Coping Attempts:

What have you done to try to feel better? What else have you done? Anything else?

Encourage Client to Think of Other Coping Strategies:

What else can you think of to try to get through this? What have you done in the past to get through difficult times? What would you tell a friend to do in this case?

Present Alternative Coping Ideas:

1. Refer to support groups, 12-step groups
You said you feel better when you talk to friends; how would you feel about attending a support group with other people in your situation? I know of a very special group where people going through what you are going through meet to learn ways to deal with it. Will you give it a try? You can go for as long as you need to, and it is free.

2. Refer to long-term therapy, family therapy
I believe you could benefit most by going to a family therapist/marital therapist. Would you consider this? It appears that your problems are longstanding. I think longer-term therapy would be really good for you. I know several great counselors. I'll give you a list.

3. Refer to medical doctor or psychiatrist
I would feel most comfortable if you would see a physician. Your symptoms seem serious, and you may need medication or a physical. Do you know of a doctor, or shall I refer you to one that I really respect and work with on other cases?

4. Legal referral
I think you should get legal advice from an attorney. These matters are beyond my scope of expertise. Please go to the public defender today or tomorrow. Are you aware of restraining orders? You can find out about them at the district attorney's office.

5. Refer to shelter, other agency
How would you feel about going to a battered woman's/homeless shelter? You will be safe there.

6. Recommend books and keeping a journal
Do you like to read? I know of some really good books that help explain more about what you are going through. Here is a list of books I recommend for you to read. You said you like to write and have kept a diary before. Many clients feel more under control if they keep a journal while going through difficult times.

Obtain Commitment; Do Follow-up:

When can you make another appointment with me? Call me when you set up your appointment with Dr. Jones. I am going to call you tomorrow. Will you promise not to hurt yourself until you at least speak to me first?

WHEN CRISIS IS A DANGER

The responsibility of protecting society and its individuals from harm done by someone with a mental disorder has been delegated to the mental health community. Although law enforcement agencies, such as police and sheriff departments, may be called on at times to assist crisis counselors, it is the mental health worker who typically intervenes to manage life-threatening behavior. Frequently, persons with a mental disorder may pose a danger to themselves or others. In fact, threatening suicide, posing a danger to others, and being gravely disabled (which is often the result of a severe active psychosis) are often the grounds for involuntary hospitalization. Each state legislates the parameters of the duty to protect clients and potential victims. Guidelines are usually created to inform practitioners of ways to manage dangerous clients. Civil suits have been brought against therapists who failed to prevent suicide or homicide. It is essential for crisis workers to be familiar with the laws of the state in which they practice (Corey, 1998). Not all people who are suicidal, psychotic, or homicidal are detained in hospitals, however. Other interventions can be less costly and equally effective in managing these conditions. The first crisis to be examined is suicide.

SUICIDE

Suicidal ideation often results when a client feels totally overwhelmed because of his or her perception of a variety of precipitating events (see Chapter 1). Understanding suicidal thinking and intervention

97

strategies is essential for counselors working with the situational crises presented in subsequent chapters. The crisis worker must be aware that suicide assessment will be a part of all crisis intervention interviews, even if suicidal ideation is not the presenting problem. The possibility that a suicidal person will kill himself or herself is quite high, and the threat must be taken seriously. Often, the media give more attention to homicide, but, in actuality, more people die from suicide than murder. Factors often associated with a risk of suicide include unemployment, illness, impulsivity, rigid thinking (black and white, all or nothing), several stressful events, and release from hospitalization.

The burden caused by suicide and threats of suicide falls not only on suicidal persons and those closest to them but also on crisis workers. It has been estimated that 1 out of 59 individuals in the United States has been affected by the suicide of someone close to them (Westefeld et al., 2000). The effects spill over to crisis workers, also. Responding to a suicidal client can be intimidating for a counselor and is often a source of personal stress. When dealing with this population, crisis workers must seek and accept emotional support from colleagues, supervisors, and family. In a sample of 241 counselors, 71% reported that they had worked with persons who had attempted suicide, and 28% had worked with at least one client who had actually completed the suicide attempt (Rogers et al., 2001).

Rogers (2001) states that despite suicide prevention and intervention efforts over the past 40 years, suicide rates have remained relatively stable. One study indicates that 39,545 individuals in the United States committed suicide in 1997 and 765,000 individuals attempted suicide (American Association of Suicidology, 1999).

Stephen Wyman, a medical doctor, offers additional statistics:

- In the 15- to 19-year-old age group, suicide is the second highest cause of death; car accidents are the main cause.
- Three males to one female successfully complete suicide attempts.
- Three females to one male attempt suicide but are not successful.
- Of all professions, psychiatrists have the highest suicide rate and pediatricians the lowest.
- In patients with psychiatric disorders, most suicides occur within the first 3 months of a patient's improvement following an episode of depression.
- Of those diagnosed with affective disorders (major depression or bipolar disorder), 45% will attempt suicide and 15% will die.
- Among schizophrenics, 25% will attempt suicide; paranoid schizophrenics are at highest risk.
- Suicide will be attempted by 25% of those diagnosed with dysthymic disorder; 12 of 100,000 will succeed.
- Among alcoholics, 25–30% will attempt suicide. (Wyman, 1982)

Symptoms and Clues

Suicide is usually preceded by a warning. Almost always, persons considering it show symptoms of or provide clues to their intent. It is important for crisis workers to know how to read these signs and be able to distinguish between myth and reality. Some common myths that beginning counselors often hold about suicide and the corresponding facts are as follows:

1. If I discuss suicide with a client, that client is more likely to attempt suicide. *In reality, it will be a relief for this individual to talk about it with an accepting person. For thoughts about suicide to be eliminated, they must be discussed. If the person is not really suicidal, the conversation will not cause harm.*

2. Suicide threats don't need to be taken seriously. If someone were going to do it, why would that person announce it? *People who kill themselves have often disclosed their intent to others. Unfortunately, many significant others either don't believe that the person will actually follow through with it, don't care, or don't know what to do to help. The person who was told may feel guilty for not having stopped the suicide and may need crisis work for himself or herself.*

3. Suicide is a completely irrational act. *Suicide often makes sense when viewed from the perspective of the person doing it.*

4. Only insane people commit suicide. *Only a small percentage of suicides are psychotic or "crazy." Most are depressed normal people who are grieving, lonely, and feeling hopeless.*

5. The tendency to attempt suicide is inherited. *So far, there is no evidence to support a genetic tendency to attempt suicide. However, it can be learned from a family member or be the result of an intolerable family life.*

6. Once one ponders suicide, the thought never goes away. *Many people contemplate suicide but recover from the painful feelings that lead to the thought.*

7. Suicide is always impulsive. *Some suicidal acts are very deliberate.*

Suicidal individuals do not always tell a crisis worker about their intent directly. Prudent workers learn to read between the lines when dealing with possible suicide risks in clients. The following signs are typical:

- Giving things away
- Putting things in order
- Writing a will
- Withdrawing from usual activities
- Being preoccupied with death
- Experiencing the recent death of a friend or relative
- Feeling hopeless, helpless, or worthless
- Increasing drug and alcohol use
- Displaying psychotic behavior
- Giving verbal hints such as, "I'm no use to anyone anymore"
- Showing agitated depression
- Living alone and being isolated
  (Aguilera, 1990, p. 174; Gilliland & James, 1988, p. 81; Wyman, 1982)

A person displaying only one or two of these behaviors may not be suicidal. A crisis worker must take into consideration a number of factors. Remember, however, that counselors don't need to wait until they observe these clues before they assess for suicidality. No matter what the presenting problem, a crisis worker should ask every client the following question in one way or another: "Do you have or have you ever had thoughts about hurting yourself?" If the answer is yes, the crisis worker must follow up with a detailed suicide risk assessment (Wyman, 1982).

Suicide Assessment

At the present time, there is no psychological test, such as the Minnesota Multiphasic Personality Inventory (MMPI), that can predict suicide in a particular client. Suicide assessment is largely a judgment call on the counselor's part (Wyman, 1982). Hence, being sensitive to risk factors and asking appropriate questions are vital strategies. Depending on the client's responses to questions, the worker can introduce various intervention strategies to reduce the risk of lethal behavior by the client.

Steiner has developed an outline for assessing a person's potential for suicide (1990):

1. *Ask if the person has thought of killing himself or herself.*
   How often?
   How badly does the person want to die (on a scale from 1 to 3)?
   Does the person see suicide as a good solution or bad solution?
   Does the person perceive suicide as weak or strong?
   (A person is at high risk if he or she thinks about suicide often, has a score of 3, sees suicide as a good solution, and perceives suicide as a strong act.)
2. *Ask family members if they are concerned that the person will commit suicide.*
   (A person is a high risk if his or her family members say they don't believe it would happen and believe that the person is just acting.)
3. *Check the person's plan for suicide.*
   Is it detailed? General?
   Does the person have materials to carry it out?
   Does the person intend to do it soon?
   Has the person given away possessions or said good-bye, or both?
4. *Check the person's mental status.*
   Is the person confused? Intoxicated? Using street drugs? Hallucinating?
   Is the person in control of his or her faculties? Impulsive? Clinically depressed? Emerging from clinical depression?
5. *Check the history of suicide in a person's life.*
   Has the person made other attempts?
   Does the person have friends or family who killed themselves?
6. *Find out what the individual's support system is like by asking these questions:*
   "What friends or relatives have you told about your intent?"

"Who do you talk with when you are down?"

"How does your family respond to your concerns?"

7. *Find out how much control the person has by asking these questions:*
"Can anyone or anything stop you?"

"What has been stopping you?"

"What made you come for help?"

8. *Ask the person for a commitment to talk with you, to see you in 2 days, to give up all rights to suicide for a set period of time. Have the person tell you how he or she will do that.*

A Phenomenological Look at Suicide

Once an objective assessment of suicide risk is fairly well completed, the crisis worker needs to understand the phenomenological aspects (i.e., the subjective, unique view) of the client's suicidal thoughts and behaviors, past and present. This, of course, is part of the B section in the ABC model of crisis intervention. Remember that these assessments do not necessarily flow in a linear order. Counselors usually gather objective information and explore subjective perceptions of the client at the same time. This approach is presented in outline only to make clear what information needs to be extracted in the B part.

Steiner (1990), who counsels largely in a phenomenological style within the strategic systems model, has presented case examples and several ideas that clearly demonstrate the value of taking this position. By reviewing certain statistics, she theorizes that the reason teen suicide rates have increased is perhaps because teenagers' suicides in the past may have been mislabeled. It may have been too painful for parents to admit that their child had killed himself or herself. She suggests that today there are fewer taboos about dealing with pain and family problems; therefore, more teen suicides are labeled correctly.

Based on interviews with adult suicidal clients, Steiner proposes that suicide might seem to some troubled individuals to be a more viable alternative in times when the economy is slow, making jobs harder to find and creating confused roles in the family and society. As she says, the American dream is no longer achievable for many people.

Two case examples presented by Steiner demonstrate her use of the systems model when teenagers' perceptions of their families have led to suicidal ideation. In general, Steiner has found that many teens consider suicide because of chronic family fighting. The teen is often made to feel responsible for the arguments and tensions. Some conflict is inevitable with a teenager in the home. If this conflict is not dealt with well, the family may exist in a crisis state for 5–8 years. Teenagers who believe they alone are responsible for family conflicts may feel overwhelmed by the constant stress and may perceive suicide as the best solution for everyone. This is especially likely when parents blatantly tell the adolescent that family problems are completely the fault of the teenager. Of course, parents don't say this to encourage teens to kill themselves; the parents are in a crisis state and are ignorant about how to cope with the new demands of having an adolescent in the home.

Reframing a situation like this often helps everyone see the family differently and ease the tension. Some people need to be educated about the normal conflicts in families and shown that these are not one particular person's fault. Rather, they are the motivation that helps the family grow and adjust to the maturing child.

> **Example 1:** For an English assignment, a 16-year-old girl wrote a poem describing her thoughts of suicide. After reading it, the English teacher sent her to see Steiner for counseling. Steiner interviewed the girl alone, and then asked the girl's mother to come to a counseling session. The mother complained about the daughter's disobedience and defiant behaviors. The parents were divorced, and the mother had threatened to send the daughter to live with her father if she didn't change her behavior. The daughter was frightened of her father. She interpreted this threat as complete rejection by her mother. She responded by entertaining thoughts of suicide. Steiner saw the daughter's oppositional behavior as symbolic of the ongoing conflict between her parents.

Steiner reframed the situation by stating that the suicidal behavior was evidence of the daughter's love for her mother and fear of her father. The intervention used by Steiner was an agreement in which the mother would give up the right to send her daughter to her father.

Steiner is a firm believer in allowing clients to maintain the perspective that suicide is their right. She avoids the conflicts that can result from telling a client, "You have no right to kill yourself." She interprets Nietzsche's words, "Suicide has saved many lives," to mean that sometimes clients' only control over themselves and their lives is the option of suicide. Simply having this option is often enough to reduce the pressure they feel to the point that it is bearable.

> **Example 2:** A teenage boy felt lonely. People did not really know him and he did not express his feelings often. His parents had aspirations for him that he simply could not meet. They had filtered out his feelings of failure and had an unrealistic picture of what he could do. This boy was at high risk for suicide because he perceived his life as being very bleak and hopeless.

Including his parents in treatment was essential. Their expectations would have to be reframed as their own projections of what they expected of themselves, and the focus would be on them instead of the boy. This shift in attention would help release the tension in the teenager. His feelings of failure could be reframed as his unconscious identification with his parents' feelings of failure. Family therapy could focus on each member's realistic hopes for himself or herself instead of projected and introjected expectations.

Suicide Prevention

Although most mental health professionals assume it is their duty to prevent suicide, Thomas Szasz (1986) believes differently. Before examining mainstream suicide interventions, the reader may find it interesting to look at Szasz's somewhat radical perspective on suicide. Common sense suggests that suicide is a mental health problem, and that mental health practitioners have a duty to try to prevent it. Szasz (1986) believes that each individual is ultimately responsible for herself or himself and that the nation's mental health policy on suicide "undermines the ethic of self-responsibility" (p. 806). Also, if this policy regarding the duty to prevent suicide were changed, it would reduce the number of malpractice suits against mental health professionals, because failure to prevent suicide is one of the leading reasons for successful lawsuits against these professionals.

Another interesting point made by Szasz concerns using the word *prevention* to describe a mental health worker's duty to suicidal clients. He asserts that this term is synonymous with coercion; it implies a paternalistic attitude toward the client and gives certain people (mental health professionals) privileges and powers to protect the suicidal individual. As an example, in California a counselor can breach the confidentiality of a suicidal client without the client's consent. Also, persons can be involuntarily detained in a psychiatric hospital for up to 72 hours if they are deemed uncontrollably suicidal; the detention is to prevent people from killing themselves. Szasz suggests that these acts of prevention undermine each individual's right to suicide. Szasz would not encourage suicide, but he believes that the decision not to take one's life is the client's responsibility, not the mental health worker's responsibility.

Szasz concludes his message by comparing suicide with other moral decisions such as abortion or marriage. Why, he asks, are mental health professionals held liable for a successful suicide but not for an abortion or a divorce? Part of the reason has to do with the philosophy that suicide is an insane behavior and that if the mental disorder were treated, suicidality would cease to exist. In other words, suicide is never "desirable enough to justify it" (p. 811). This does not mean that Szasz accepts suicide as a legitimate option. Rather, Szasz believes that mental health professionals should be allowed to "treat it as an act that they may approve or disapprove in general and may choose to counsel for or against in any particular case" (p. 811), as they often do for clients who are considering having an abortion or getting a divorce. This philosophy would eliminate making counselors responsible and greatly reduce lawsuits. Most importantly, it places responsibility on the individual in a society that views doctors as having the wisdom of God.

Many examples exist that demonstrate sane suicidality. People with painful diseases or terminal illnesses (e.g., AIDS or cancer), or those who have suffered dishonor (in certain cultures), who feel that life is not worth living, point to suicide as a viable option. The Hemlock Society was created in support of situations in which individuals are seen as having the right to choose their own death.

Szasz and the Hemlock Society are in the minority, however, when it comes to suicide prevention. Most crisis workers with all types of licenses and in most agencies agree that it is their duty to prevent people from killing themselves. Szasz wonders about this, though, questioning whether this attitude would be so prevalent if suicide were not illegal and if a worker were not liable to be sued for failing to prevent a client from killing himself or herself.

Taking an opposing view, Steiner (1990) claims that although she sometimes can understand how suicide might be better than living for some people, she would still try to prevent it. She states her overall attitude clearly when she tells clients that she's in the business of helping people who will commit to being alive. These words tell clients that she opposes suicide and that she would not help them do it. When asked how she would deal with a dying AIDS patient who truly believed killing himself painlessly would be a better choice than dying in pain, Steiner suggested interesting questions to ask the patient: "What kind of example would you be for others who have AIDS or are just HIV positive? Can we find any meaning in your living it out until the end?" These questions may help the individual die in dignity through knowing he or she had contributed positively to others. Certainly, Magic Johnson's attitude about his HIV infection is considered exemplary because he is basically saying that whatever time a person has left on earth is valuable, and each person should make the balance of that life productive.

Steiner also suggests asking clients to think of reasons for not killing themselves. Usually, the most severely depressed person can think of one or two reasons to live. In my own practice, I worked with a very suicidal client who was ready to be hospitalized by her psychiatrist. When I asked her for reasons to continue living, she said she loved her 4-year-old grandson and enjoyed taking him to the park. By exploring this with her, I was able to join her phenomenological world and use this knowledge to show her that suicide might not be her only option and certainly not the best one if she wanted to continue going to the park with her grandson.

Interventions

After a client has been assessed as suicidal, the crisis worker must determine the likelihood that the client will actually kill himself or herself. Some clients can be treated as outpatients while they are dealing with active suicidal feelings. Others may need to be hospitalized until the level of risk is lower. Whatever the risk level, the crisis worker must be willing to devote more energy and time than usual to a suicidal client. This extra attention is often what the hopeless client needs to feel cared about, and the crisis worker must give evidence of genuine caring. This means that keeping the client alive must be a priority for the helper.

The key is to act quickly and decisively in a suicidal crisis. At times, the client must discard any potentially lethal instruments and amount of drugs. Counselors should not act surprised by the suicidal urge but instead indicate that there is hope. Treating the client's depression or other emotional disorders is the only way to prevent suicide, so the sooner the counselor can assess the client for these disorders, the sooner and more effectively suicide can be prevented (Harvard Mental Health Letter, 1996). Table 6.1 provides information about assessment, risk level, and interventions.

Low-Risk Suicidal Clients   Low-risk suicidal clients are those who have never tried suicide, have adequate support systems, and make comments such as, "I thought about it, but I'm not sure. It scares me to have feelings like these, and I need someone to talk to." These clients can usually be treated as outpatients and should be encouraged to make an appointment with a therapist if the crisis

TABLE 6.1 | SUICIDE ASSESSMENT, RISK LEVEL, AND INTERVENTION

Factor	Client response	Level	Intervention
Ideation	No	Low	Supportive crisis intervention
	Yes		(Go to next factor to decide)
Plan	No	Low	Crisis intervention
			Verbal no-suicide contract
	Yes		(Go to next factor to decide)
Means	No	Low	Maintain regular contact throughout the crisis intervention.
	Yes	Medium	Written no-suicide contract; increase contact; family watch; give the means to counselor.
What has stopped you?	Gives a specific reason.	Middle	Encourage clients to live for the reasons given. If very depressed, possible involuntary hospitalization.
Can anything stop you now?	No	High	Involuntary hospitalization

counselor cannot continue to see them (Wyman, 1982). They probably will respond well to educational interventions, such as reading books by others who have attempted suicide. Reframing the situation is also helpful. A crisis worker might say, "The fact that you are here is evidence you don't truly want to kill yourself. People who truly want to die usually don't go to a mental health worker, because they know we have an obligation to prevent suicide."

An empowering supportive comment might go like this: "The part of you that sought help is obviously very strong, and you can take comfort in knowing you have this inner strength that helps you choose to cope with your problems actively."

A client might be comforted to know that pondering suicide when things look bleak or stressful is a common human experience; it has been written about by the greatest novelists and philosophers from ancient to modern times. A helper can point out that pondering one's own death is not the equivalent of creating it and that the client appears to be in good control of this. Such thoughts will usually be a relief to low-risk suicidal clients.

Cole (1993) describes another type of low-risk suicidal case. Elderly people often consider suicide after the death of a spouse. Cole does not deny that this is a sad situation, but if the client can be brought to the clinic and stabilized on medication or if other resources can be mobilized, the client can often be supported through outpatient services rather than hospitalization. Her goal is to empower clients and preserve their dignity by connecting them with medical services and other resources such as senior citizen centers or in-home support services provided by most county governments. The counselor should try to get at least a verbal agreement from clients that they won't harm themselves without first speaking to the helper. This informal, no-suicide contract can be very effective psychologically with low-risk clients.

Middle-Risk Suicidal Clients   The most common suicidal clients a crisis worker will probably see are middle-risk clients. These individuals can still function at work but are not feeling well and are often difficult to evaluate. They feel there is no way out of their situation. Often, in the hearing of family members, they threaten to kill themselves. Unfortunately, these threats are ignored or not taken seriously. When this is the case, clients may need to be seen every day or hospitalized because they may carry out the threat just to get a reaction from the family. An intervention commonly used with middle-risk clients is a no-suicide contract. Clients agree that for 2 or 3 days they will give up the right to kill themselves while they see the crisis worker. Box 6.1 shows a sample pact.

B O X 6 . 1 *Sample No-Suicide Contract*

I _____ agree not to harm myself for the next week. I promise to contact
(Client's name)

_____ when my suicidal feelings get too strong to control.
(Crisis worker's name)

_____   _____   _____
(Client's signature)   (Date)   (Crisis worker's signature)

Shaking hands to seal the pact is a good idea. A no-suicide contract should not be used with a client who lives alone and has no support system because the client might not abide by it. This type of client should be monitored with a daily phone call. Most clients appreciate this type of concern. If possible, enlist family members to conduct a suicide watch. Family members accept a certain amount of responsibility for monitoring the suicidal person and commit to staying close to the person. In this way, the family helps assume some of the responsibility for the client's well-being. This behavior can show clients that family members do care enough about them to invest energy in helping them overcome their destructive feelings.

Hospitalizing the middle-risk client should be done only as a last resort. According to family systems theory, keeping the family involved makes more sense than reinforcing a family myth that the client is an identified, sick person. Suicide says much about the family, and the most effective treatment includes the entire family. When a family member is hospitalized, that person loses credibility in the family, and family members begin to treat her or him differently.

In a crisis intervention session, the crisis worker has several options for working with middle-risk clients. Besides a no-suicide contract and suicide watch, the counselor should ask the client to bring in items that the client has planned to use for committing suicide and give them to the counselor. The counselor must destroy or lock these items away so no one can be injured with them.

It is helpful for the counselor to address himself or herself to the ambivalence of the client and focus on the part that wants to live. Try to elicit from the client ideas for future plans and explore the things that have happened to make life no longer worth living.

High-Risk Suicidal Clients   High-risk suicidal clients say such things as, "I'm going to kill myself and you can't stop me." They are usually very depressed and angry, have tried suicide before, and lack support from loved ones. If pressed, they will admit to having a viable plan and the means for killing themselves. Crisis workers should be familiar with the laws in their state that apply to the hospitalization of suicidal clients. If clients are hospitalized, crisis workers must see that they are admitted to a psychiatric hospital rather than a general acute hospital, because staffpersons of a psychiatric unit are trained differently (Wyman, 1982).

If possible, crisis workers should convince clients to admit themselves voluntarily to a hospital. This empowers clients and reduces conflict. At times, however, calling the local police or psychiatric emergency team (PET) to request involuntary hospitalization becomes necessary. Doing this often causes unpleasant scenes and can be embarrassing, but it must be done, according to mental health ethics, if it is legal under state law. When considering hospitalization for a high-risk suicidal client, the mental health worker should explore the benefits and drawbacks. Current economic trends do not encourage hospitalization if maintaining someone out of the hospital is at all possible. Partial hospitalization is becoming popular, as it provides safety for the client and is less costly than round-the-clock hospitalization. The following example clarifies a situation requiring immediate drastic intervention.

> **Example:** Cole (1993) received a call from the sister of a 22-year-old man who had doused himself with gasoline and was looking for matches. He wasn't doing well in college and couldn't get a job, and his fiancée had broken up with him recently. In this case, the police and ambulance were called immediately, and an involuntary 72-hour hold was placed on this man so he could be cared for in a hospital.

Another instance requiring hospitalization is when schizophrenic clients are actively hearing voices telling them to hurt themselves. In this type of case, the individual needs to be medicated to control the hallucinations; this action should have the effect of removing the suicidal tendency.

SELF-MUTILATIVE BEHAVIORS (SMB)

Some people who visit counselors for crisis-related problems engage in self-injurious behaviors without the intent of killing themselves. Deliberately damaging one's own body tissue without suicidal intent is referred to as self-mutilative behavior (SMB) (Nock & Prinstein, 2004). SMB is seen in about 4% of the general adult population and 21% of adult psychiatric inpatient populations (Briere & Gil, 1998). Adolescents may be at increased risk for SMB; this behavior has been seen in 40–61% of adolescents in psychiatric inpatient settings (Darche, 1990; Diclemente, Ponton, & Hartley, 1991) and 14–39% of adolescents in the community (Lloyd, 1998; Ross & Heath, 2002).

In a recent study of adolescent psychiatric inpatients, Nock & Prinstein, (2004) examined the most common methods of SMB and self-reported reasons for engaging in SMB. The top five methods of SMB were cutting or carving one's skin, picking at a wound, hitting oneself, scraping one's skin to draw blood, and biting oneself. The top six reasons for engaging in SMB were to stop bad feelings, to feel something even if it was pain, to punish oneself, to relieve feelings of numbness or emptiness, to feel relaxed, and to give oneself something to do when alone. These results indicate that the primary purpose of most adolescent SMB is regulation of emotional or physiological experiences.

Interventions for SMB might focus on identifying the function of the particular client's SMB and teach the client functionally equivalent behaviors. This means helping the client to improve his or her emotional regulation and increase behavioral ways to relax and involve oneself in the world.

MANAGING A CLIENT WHO IS A DANGER TO OTHERS

Periodically, a crisis worker may come across a person who is homicidal or somehow a danger to others. As mentioned earlier, the crisis worker has the duty to warn the intended victim when possible and to contact the police. Sometimes a person may be a threat to the public because of a psychosis (e.g., an individual hears the voice of God telling him to pour poison into the town water supply). Individuals who are angry and lacking impulse control may also be threats.

The following six questions can be used to assess a person's potential for harming others:

1. Is the subject actively or passively engaged in violent or dangerous behavior?
2. Does the subject state that he or she is going to carry out violent or dangerous behavior?
3. Does the subject have a plan to follow through with this behavior?
4. Does the subject have the means to follow through with this plan?
5. Does the subject have a background of violent or dangerous behavior?
6. Has the subject acted on plans for violence in the past?

Answers to these questions can be obtained from an interview with either the client or relatives of the client. Try to get the client or relative to be as specific as possible about what the person has said or done and who the victims might be.

If the counselor believes the person is a threat and cannot comfortably end the session, the counselor must call for assistance. If permissible according to state law, the client should be involuntarily hospitalized until the client's violent impulses have been controlled either by medication or other forms of therapy.

In less volatile situations, crisis workers can try to help clients contain their violent urges by teaching them ways to manage their anger or referring them to a daily support group. If clients agree to refrain from acting out and intended victims have been warned, clients can be treated on an outpatient basis as long as any psychotic symptoms are controlled.

Certain psychotic states (e.g., mania or paranoia) may require clients to spend several days in a hospital receiving medication to control the delusions that lead to dangerous behaviors. Once individuals have been medicated and stabilized, they can often function appropriately with just a few counseling sessions to help them make the transition from hospital to outpatient living.

Some clients who are a danger to others may not be manic or psychotic but may have an impulse-control problem (e.g., spouse batterers and child abusers). These people seem to function normally in the larger society, but in close interpersonal relationships they control by acting out violently. In most states, crisis workers have a legal obligation to report suspected child abuse to the proper authorities. If the client has not abused a child but tells the crisis worker that he or she is on the verge of doing so, the crisis worker can suggest that the client call a child abuse hot line, go for a walk, count to 10, or temporarily move out of the house until he or she has cooled off.

Telling the client that counselors are required by state law to report violence against a child can be helpful in deterring this behavior. Impulsive people often need external controls because they feel so out of control internally. This holds true for spouse batterers as well. Crisis workers are not required to report battering of another adult; however, if the batterer feels the police will be called in, this possibility will often act as a curb on the person's potentially violent behavior. Even so, the person may continue to verbally and emotionally abuse others.

Some people are a danger to others because of antisocial tendencies and anger. In certain cases, the police should be involved, especially when the person has no history of being mentally ill. Cole (1993) tells of an ex-convict who came to a psychiatrist at the mental health clinic saying he was mentally disabled and needed medication. When the doctor evaluated him and asked about his history, he discovered that the patient had no history of mental health treatment and was not mentally ill, so he prescribed no medication. The man pulled out a knife, held it to the doctor's throat, and forced him to write a prescription. As soon as the man left, the police were called, and the man was arrested and put in jail rather than being hospitalized under provisions for involuntary commitment of the mentally ill. Another example of danger to others is what Cole (1993) calls the "fatal attraction case."

Example: A 23-year-old woman came to the mental health clinic complaining of being stressed out because her boyfriend had just broken up with her and was now with another woman. She was extremely angry and planned to wait until the man was asleep in his house and then pour gasoline all around the house and set fire to it. In evaluating the reality of such a plan, the mental health worker asked the client if she had any history of another man breaking up with her and what had happened at that time. The woman said that when her last boyfriend broke up with her, his car was wired so that it blew up when he got into it. In addition, she was discovered to have a history of mental health treatment going back 10 years. The worker also observed that the woman had a row of safety pins in her ear as earrings. By combining all this information, the worker decided that the woman was a danger to her former boyfriend. The client was involuntarily hospitalized, and the intended victim and the police were made aware of the situation.

PSYCHOTIC BREAKDOWNS AND GRAVELY DISABLED MENTALLY ILL PERSONS

Periodically, a crisis worker will come across a client suffering a **psychotic decompensation,** or "nervous breakdown" in lay terms. In essence, it is a state of florid, active delusions and hallucinations during which the person is out of touch with reality. This condition causes extreme personality disorganization and heightened states of anxiety; and the person cannot function in any way. People in this state cannot look after even their basic needs. They cannot provide themselves with food or water or keep themselves clean and therefore need someone to take care of them.

The term *gravely disabled* (see Chapter 3) applies here. This condition may be grounds for involuntary hospitalization, depending on the laws of the state. While these clients are in the hospital, they usually can be stabilized on medication and become able to function more realistically within a few days. For some, however, the stabilization period may take up to 2 weeks or 6 months, depending on the severity of the psychosocial stressor, the person's premorbid functioning (i.e., before the breakdown), and the available support systems. Clients experiencing this type of distress can be diagnosed as schizophrenic, being in a paranoid state, or having an organic brain disorder such as Alzheimer's disease.

> **Example 1:** A 17-year-old boy has become increasingly withdrawn and guarded at home. He no longer sees his friends, and his grades have dropped over the past year. He seems distant and shows little emotion (blunted affect). His mother brings him to a crisis counseling center because he has been suffering anxiety spells and believes extraterrestrials are watching him at night. When he is interviewed, he tells the counselor that he's been pacing at night and is afraid to sleep because he hears a strange whisper saying, "We're watching you."

This is a typical case of initial psychotic break. The young man will most likely be diagnosed as paranoid schizophrenic, hospitalized, and given antipsychotic medication that will reduce, if not eliminate, his symptoms. Unfortunately, he will probably have another breakdown at some time in the future.

> **Example 2:** A man who has become belligerent on the job is sent to a counselor by his boss. During the interview, the counselor finds that he believes a white van is following him and tracking him with ultrared sonar equipment. He brings in a magazine about hi-tech weapons and electrical devices to show the counselor. He is preoccupied with the information in the magazine and believes the equipment it describes is the type that is being used to spy on him. He seems connected to his family and friends, has a clear grasp of current events, and can still perform his job duties.

This man's condition may be diagnosed as a paranoid state; he might require hospitalization if it gets worse. Medication may or may not be effective in eliminating his delusions.

Example 3: A 70-year-old woman is brought to the mental health center by her 30-year-old granddaughter. The granddaughter found her sitting nude at home surrounded by newspapers and unopened Social Security checks. The woman had not eaten in several days because she believed the food was poisoned. She does not know what day it is, thinks she's still living in 1955, and believes that her granddaughter is her daughter.

The woman is probably suffering from Alzheimer's disease or senility. She is gravely disabled and needs someone to be her conservator (i.e., guardian of her finances).

In some cases, people's psychotic thoughts leave them both gravely disabled and a danger to themselves or others. Cole (1993) tells of a 25-year-old man who had been completely catatonic (immobile and mute) for 3 days. His legs were turning purple because of poor circulation from lack of activity, and he was dehydrated. When he was informed by the mental health worker that he was going to be involuntarily hospitalized, he ran to the roof and threatened to jump off. Eventually, someone was able to coax him off the roof, and he was hospitalized as both gravely disabled and a danger to himself. In emergencies such as suicide and psychosis, family members need to be involved. In cases where there is no family, board and care homes and case managers serve as support systems for clients. The crisis worker must remain calm and not be afraid when working with these people. As pointed out previously, the worker may have to be the client's ego strength until he or she returns to a realistic state of functioning.

Exercises

Practice conducting a suicide assessment and intervention for the following clients. Use the ABC model of crisis intervention to identify the precipitating event, cognitions, subjective distress, and impairments in functioning. The person who is role-playing the client should be creative and embellish the situation based on knowledge of the emotional and cognitive elements typically found in suicidal people. The practicing counselor should use the suggested therapeutic comments included at the end of the case description.

Case 1   A 19-year-old Asian boy has received two Ds on his college report card and feels he has shamed his family. He plans to kill himself by jumping off the highest building on campus. He knows that six other people have successfully ended their lives in this way over the past 10 years.

Reframe: Point out the shame the family will suffer if he kills himself in such a public display.

Support: Tell him how proud he can make his family by improving his grades. Focus on ways he can enhance his good qualities and point these out to his parents. Ask his parents to maintain a suicide watch. Have the client make a no-suicide pact that will obligate him not to harm himself.

Case 2 A 45-year-old woman is very depressed. All of her children are grown and married; she has been divorced for 20 years; and she is dissatisfied with her job. She sees no reason to live but has no specific plan to kill herself. She feels like a burden to her children.

> *Reframe:* Show her that killing herself would be an even bigger burden on her children. Does she really want to traumatize them in this way?

> *Support:* Help her think about her grandchildren, who will need a grandmother. Focus on volunteer work, adult education, and clubs. A no-suicide contract is needed here. Suggest that her children become more involved with their mother.

Case 3 A 68-year-old man whose wife died 6 months ago is very depressed and wants to shoot himself. He has a loaded gun at home. His dog has just died.

> *Reframe:* Does he believe his wife will rest in peace if he kills himself?

> *Support:* Let him know that you understand his loneliness and that there are groups and other involvements he can focus on, though his life will probably never be the same.

This man probably needs to be hospitalized unless his children will take care of him. His gun needs to be confiscated; perhaps he can move in with his children temporarily.

Case 4 A 30-year-old woman feels hopeless and despondent. She thinks she is a bad mother and wife and can't manage her household. She has no appetite and can't sleep. She has little involvement with her children. She spends her days crying while the children are left to look after themselves.

> *Reframe:* A bad mother wouldn't care if her children weren't being cared for. This mother is not bad; she is just depressed.

> *Support:* Let her know that being a mother is hard. Also, let her know that she feels this way because she is depressed; when the depression lifts, she won't be so miserable. There is hope! Refer this woman to a medical doctor to see if he will prescribe antidepressant medication for her. She might also need hospitalization.

KEY TERMS FOR STUDY

danger to others: Condition in which a client is deemed to be a threat to others. At this time, counselors must breach confidentiality and report their concerns to the police and/or the intended victim. This is called the "duty to warn."

high-risk suicidal clients: Clients who have a plan, the means, and the intent to commit suicide; they cannot be talked out of harming themselves. Hospitalization is often indicated for such clients.

involuntary hospitalization: Detaining clients against their will in a psychiatric facility for evaluation and observation when they have been deemed a danger to themselves or others, or are gravely disabled because of a mental disorder.

low-risk suicidal clients: Clients who have pondered but never attempted suicide. These clients have adequate support systems and can usually be treated as outpatients. Therapy and educational interventions are encouraged.

means: The actual physical implement, pills, or action that a suicidal person uses to kill himself or herself.

middle-risk suicidal clients: Clients who have been thinking about suicide and feel depressed. These clients probably still have some hope, but they might also have a suicide plan. A no-suicide contract works as well for such persons as does a suicide watch. Crisis intervention should be intense and frequent.

no-suicide contract: A formal written or verbal contract between the client and the crisis worker in which the client makes a commitment to speak to the counselor before harming himself or herself. It is considered an effective intervention for low- and middle-risk clients.

plan: A blueprint for action that clients have devised for killing themselves.

psychotic decompensation: A state in which the client is out of touch with reality and shows symptoms such as delusions and hallucinations. This often happens when a schizophrenic patient stops taking medication or at the beginning of a person's first schizophrenic episode. The state can also be associated with bipolar disorder and paranoid disorders. This person usually requires involuntary hospitalization.

suicidal ideation: The cognition component of suicide, the thinking involved.

suicide assessment: A process in which the crisis worker asks a series of directive questions to ascertain the seriousness of a client's suicidal intent and ideation. It includes identifying various risk factors, a means for suicide, a plan for suicide, and reasons for wanting to harm oneself.

suicide watch: Observation by family or friends of those who are at middle risk of hurting themselves. Someone stays by the client's side 24 hours a day to ensure that the person does no harm to himself or herself. Suicide watches are also conducted in psychiatric facilities for high-risk clients.

7 | CHAPTER DEVELOPMENTAL CRISES

The idea of developmental crises, first proposed by Erik Erikson, is well documented and almost universally accepted by social scientists. Erikson spoke of developmental crises induced by special tasks and role changes required by each new stage in the sequence of psychosocial maturation. People are more vulnerable to crises at these stages in life. This normal process of growth and development is gradual as a person moves from one stage of psychological, biological, and social development to another. The short periods of psychological upset that occur during a critical transition point in the normal development of a person from birth to old age are often major focuses for the crisis worker.

In working with developmental crises, the crisis interventionist must acknowledge that role development does not exist in a vacuum. If one person's role in the family changes, the roles of other family members change as well. Because of the involvement of the family in the completion of a role change, these crises can take years to complete.

Having a baby is an example of a psychosocial stage that creates the need for accomplishing various tasks. The first year of a child's life creates many stresses in the home, and these often lead parents to seek out the services of a mental health provider. The baby needs unconditional love, attention, and nurturance. These traits do not come naturally to all parents. The addition of a baby definitely upsets the steady state that existed when the family consisted only of a husband and wife. If the mother is not married or is a teenager, other crises may occur. Providing the nurturance necessary for an infant to grow up trusting that all of his or her needs will be met is quite a task. Parenting education may prove to be helpful during this first year because most parents have not been systematically trained to take care of a baby. Many hospitals and health maintenance organizations offer classes on parenting in addition to the more traditional "birthing" classes. Most bookstores have an abundance of "how to" books for parents needing suggestions and knowledge. Parents also need support and encouragement to take care of themselves as a marital unit. New parents might benefit from the common-sense advice of counselors, nurses, social workers, or other professionals. For example, they need to take time to go out on a date or ask grandparents to baby-sit so they can have a break from child care. Empathizing with parents on how difficult it is to be a good parent may help a couple during this stage of family development.

The next stage of parenting also brings many families in for counseling. Helping toddlers work through their power needs to reach a balance in independence and dependence is quite a challenge. Parents often need structured behavior modification strategies to get through this transitional process. The crisis worker should teach parents how to set boundaries and limits without shaming the child. It can be quite scary for a 2-year-old to be in charge of a home. Parents need to take control without being tyrants.

Once children enter school, social acceptance, assertion, self-esteem, and identity become the tasks they must master. Children of school age often experience crises related to social rejection. The crisis worker can help by exploring suitable alternatives by which children can get their needs met. Parents should be involved in these sessions and can be of great support to their children.

Crises during adolescence are so challenging that a separate section is devoted to this topic later in this chapter.

As individuals enter adulthood, new tasks arise. First, young adults must gain a sense of being responsible for themselves economically and socially. Young adults eventually seek partners to fulfill their emotional needs as they move away from their parents. Making the transition from parental affection to partner intimacy is no easy task. Generally, a decade is needed for young people to work through this stage. Relationship breakups are common during this period as young adults begin to engage in intimate relationships. Not only will crisis workers be dealing with young adults trying to find intimacy with peers but also with those who are trying to separate emotionally from their parents.

Another typical developmental crisis is often referred to as the midlife crisis. It can occur over a period of several years as the individual's life becomes routine. At this point, people usually have a stable career, their children are grown and independent, for the most part, and their marriage has lost its fire. To bring themselves out of this rut and reduce their feelings of boredom, many create circumstances that renew their youth, such as getting a sports car, having an affair, searching for a new job, or enrolling in college. The counselor can aid individuals at this time by showing them that their feelings are normal and helping them focus on productive ways to eliminate their depression. Marital counseling can be very useful at this point to help spouses grow together and create a relationship that does not depend on raising children but incorporates new activities into their lifestyle.

The last psychosocial stage is often referred to as integrity versus despair. This is the time when older adults begin accepting the knowledge that life is approaching its climax. Retirement, illness, and death are some of the stressors normally found during this time. The crisis worker needs to help this age group adjust to a new way of life. Retirees can be encouraged to play golf, volunteer at charity organizations, or take classes at a senior center. Also, couples may need marital therapy to help them find a new love for one another. They can then be at peace during their twilight years.

In Table 7.1, the author has used Erikson's eight stages of development as a beginning point, showing the particular changes occurring at each stage as well as interventions that can be helpful to clients experiencing crises at each stage.

EVOLUTIONAL CRISES

Another way to understand crisis states is to look at the normal passages, or evolutional crises, through which typical families go as the years pass. This model is helpful for crisis workers, who can explain it to clients when a crisis is clearly due to problems in adjusting to the growing family unit.

First Stage of a Family: Creating a Marital Subsystem

A typical nuclear family will be discussed here because Minuchin's (1974) original theoretical model was based on this type of family. This does not mean that other family structures are inadequate. This model does suggest that families, whatever their structure, evolve based on the growing and changing needs of all of their members. This model may also explain why certain family structures might be more difficult or easier for children and other family members. Many of the problems that people face in a nonnuclear family are the result of societal values suggesting that being raised with one's biological mother and father who are married is best. This view is obviously biased. It still may cause discomfort and difficulties for people living in other types of families. Of course, people living in different family structures (e.g., lesbians or gay men raising adopted children, couples living together without being married, single-parent families) may experience structural difficulties in the same way that nuclear families do. Crisis workers dealing with these issues must challenge themselves to apply the theoretical models in ways that are relevant for their clients. At times, crisis workers must be creative and offer interventions based on pure caring, intuition, and listening without judgment.

In a traditional nuclear family, the first adjustment must be made when a man and a woman decide to get married or move in together. Both the couple and their respective parents must change. Each member of the couple comes from a family in which certain values and behaviors are accepted and practiced. The new husband and wife need to create their own behavior patterns for their new home and their own marital subsystem. They will adjust to each other, try to change each another, and adapt. Sometimes conflicts occur because of the

TABLE 7.1 | CRISIS INTERVENTION AS RELATED TO ERIKSON'S PSYCHOSOCIAL STAGES OF DEVELOPMENT

Stage	Crisis	Possible Problematic Social Role Changes	Interventions
Infancy	Trust Versus Mistrust	Mother fails to bond/nurture infant	Teach mother proper parenting skills; discuss fears about intimacy
		Father fails to join in as a nurturer; father unable to maintain sense of belonging to family unit	Encourage communication and expression of sense of being left out with no function; educate mother on the need for father's involvement with infant
Toddler Years	Autonomy Versus Shame and Self-Doubt	Parents fail to allow independence and are overcontrolling	Educate parents about the needs of toddler to feel powerful over self
		Parents fail to set appropriate boundaries and limits	Educate parents about ways to set limits without creating uncontrollable power struggles
Preschool Years	Initiative Versus Guilt	Child is unable to interact with children and initiate play	Support parents in their efforts to role model proper assertive behavior for their child within the family and with extrafamilial relationships
		Child is overly competitive and aggressive and unable to share or cooperate	Teach parents how to help child submit without feeling completely worthless
Childhood Years	Industry Versus Inferiority	Child fails to master skills at school, either academic, physical, or social	Encourage child to develop competence at some task or game
		Child fails to demonstrate competence in areas parents perceive as appropriate	Teach parents about the need for child to develop an identity and skills appropriate for the child rather than expecting behaviors that meet the parents' emotional needs and desires

TABLE 7.1 | CONTINUED

Stage	Crisis	Possible Problematic Social Role Changes	Interventions
Adolescence	Identity Versus Role Confusion	Parents fail to allow child freedoms and responsibilities	Introduce family therapy that focuses on negotiation and compromise
		Parents fail to listen and understand the needs of the child	Teach parents active listening and empathetic understanding skills
		Child fails to transfer emotional need fulfillment to peers	Support child to interact with peers and encourage social involvement
		Child fails to manage increased responsibilities and stress of growing up	Support child to accept reality of growing up, pointing out the advantages that go along with stress and responsibility
Young Adult Years	Intimacy Versus Isolation	Young adult fails to form intimate relationships; experiences loneliness	Teach healthy social interaction skills; help work through grief and depression
		Young adult fails to experience independence from parents emotionally, financially, or physically	Educate young adult about normalcy of fears regarding independence, life cycle; give practical suggestions on how to manage daily stresses and let go of parents
		Parents fail to let go of young adult, attempt to control his or her life	Help parents grieve loss and focus on new involvements

Middle Adult Years	Generativity Versus Stagnation	Spouses fail to rekindle marital bond after children move out	Suggest marital counseling to address feelings of loss, increase marital interactions and activities
		Adult fails to involve self in new and fulfilling activities	Encourage career change, enrolling in college, starting a hobby, doing volunteer work
		Adult fails to adapt to grandparental role appropriately	Teach appropriate role behaviors and boundaries for grandparents
		Parents fail to let go of adult children; experience profound depression because of their loss	Help parents grieve loss and work through depression
Mature Adult Years	Ego Integrity Versus Despair	Older adult fails to continue participation in life	Encourage involvement in senior centers and support groups
		Older person experiences depression about his or her life	Provide supportive counseling focusing on positives in life
		Older person experiences anger and shame about dependence on family	Use family therapy to address feelings and communicate needs

Source: Adapted from Erikson, 1953; expanded by author.

inability to adjust. Sometimes this conflict results from the interference of in-laws who discourage adjustment, albeit in subtle ways. Power struggles are common during this time. The parents still want to control their adult child, and the adult child wants to assert independence without totally alienating the parents, a definite setup for a crisis.

Education and reframing are helpful here. The couple needs to be encouraged to set up their own home without completely negating their parents' wishes. Compromise is helpful when possible. Also, cultural considerations need to be explored.

The couple needs to decide how each set of parents is going to influence their marriage. Also, they need to set boundaries that say "We are united for each other" as opposed to "We are united against you." One way to prove to one's parents that one is truly an adult worthy of respect is to approach one's parents as an assertive, respectful adult. When a member of a newly formed couple wishes to behave in ways outside the norms of his or her family of origin, he or she can be encouraged to speak directly and lovingly to his or her parents. This can be done by reminding one's parents how scary and difficult it is to venture in adulthood and create a close, secure relationship with a mate. It may help ease tension if the young adult asks his or her own parents for tips on how to succeed. Of course, if someone has been brought up by parents who have been abusive, have substance abuse problems, or have other types of mental illness, this may not be the best strategy. The young adult may have to start understanding the emotional pain of the parents and deal with them as people. It would be unrealistic for the young adult to pretend that the parents know everything and do not have any problems. The author has found that teaching clients to empathize with the issues of their parents goes a long way in helping to relieve the fear, anger, and guilt that clients often feel toward their parents when they first become intimately involved with a mate.

Some parents will be more accepting of their child's choice of a mate than others. When there is lack of acceptance, young adults may need encouragement to take care of their own emotional needs, and, if possible, still maintain some involvement with the parents. Sadly, some parents are incapable of interacting in a healthy way with a child who moves into adulthood because of their own sadness at losing control over the child or losing the closeness that once existed with the child. Crisis workers must be just as empathic to these parents as to the young adult.

Creating a Parental Subsystem

The next potential for crisis in the evolving family occurs when a child is born. Now the parents have to adjust to a third individual, who will have a profound effect on the family unit they have been creating. Parental nurturance of the baby needs to be learned. This nurturance is different than the affection and intimacy between spouses. Each parent needs to develop skills and behaviors to help raise the child. Also, in-law involvement must be determined. Grandparents have rights, and children benefit greatly from healthy grandparental involvement. If parents have not come to terms with their own parents, however, the birth of a child can create tension and conflict.

It is vital to have a strong marital subsystem before creating a parental subsystem. The crisis worker needs to help the couple strengthen their marriage before any real change in parenting function can be made.

Creating Sibling Subsystems

As children grow and new children are added to the family, new tasks of evolution are faced. Parents need to acknowledge that siblings share certain ideas and behaviors that belong to them and not to the parents. Good, strong, even conflictual sibling relationships should be encouraged (though abuse should not be tolerated). These experiences are important to healthy interpersonal functioning later in life. If parents interfere too much, siblings do not learn how to cope interpersonally outside the family.

Also, parents must have different expectations for children of different ages, must assign different responsibilities, and must grant different privileges. A 5-year-old obviously must be treated differently than a 15-year-old in regard to bedtime, curfews, eating habits, social activities, and household chores.

> **Example:** A 15-year-old girl was brought in to counseling because she had been acting out against her parents, frequently opposing them, yelling at them, and demonstrating much unhappiness in general. Evidently, she had been required to come home from school every day and baby-sit her four younger siblings while her parents were at work. Not only did she have to do this, but she was not allowed to be with her peers on weekends. She seemed to have all the responsibilities of an adult but the privileges of her 4-year-old brother.

Crisis intervention involved establishing a new role for her. Her parents were strongly encouraged to allow their daughter to join the volleyball team at school and to find someone else to watch their other children one night a week. The 15-year-old would also be allowed to be with her friends on weekends as long as she spent time with the family on Sundays. Though the parents were inconvenienced, in the long run the family functioned in a more stable fashion.

Creating Grandparental Subsystems

As children grow up and involve themselves in intimate relationships with peers outside the family, parents must relinquish control and move into a more collaborative relationship with their children. This means that the parents must strengthen their marital unit and accept the boundaries that the adult children set. Also, when they become grandparents (i.e., a grandparental subsystem), they need to set boundaries so they are not taken advantage of by their children, either as baby-sitters or as financial contributors.

Grandparents must often sit by quietly as they watch a child or child-in-law make mistakes with grandchildren. Interference is usually not appreciated and can cause problems in the family. The crisis worker needs to explain to well-meaning grandparents that their child and his or her spouse need to make their own mistakes, just as the grandparents themselves did. The counselor can also point out ways in which the grandparents can be supportive of their children without being intrusive.

SITUATIONAL CRISES RELATED TO ADOLESCENCE

A number of situations that can become crises are unique to specific periods of life. Though these situations do not affect all adolescents, they are prevalent enough to warrant a closer look.

Adolescence can be a stormy period, in which teenagers are struggling for independence yet still in need of guidance and emotional support. When a family system does not allow both autonomy and nurturance, teenagers may engage in self-destructive behaviors in order to meet one or both of these needs. Although individual or group therapy is effective with this population and is used widely in teen shelters and group homes, a look at the family structure and intervention with the family are vital for permanent resolution of the problems. For this reason, most adolescent treatment programs require family involvement.

Teen Pregnancy

In 2002, 433,000 teenagers gave birth in the United States. This number does not include pregnancies that were terminated by abortion or miscarriage. The United States has the highest teen pregnancy rate in the industrialized world, and California has the highest rate in the country (U.S. Census Bureau, Statistical Abstract of the United States: 2004–2005).

When pregnant teens are compared with girls who did not become pregnant as teenagers, a number of social factors emerge. Teen pregnancy is linked to other social problems, such as dropping out of high school, dependence on welfare, drug and alcohol abuse, domestic violence, child abuse, and unemployment. Simpson and colleagues (1997) have identified several common risk factors for adolescent pregnancy: being the daughter of a teen parent, poverty, poor academic achievement, low self-esteem, dating at an early age, dating boys or men 5 or 6 years older than oneself, and minority status. Others have suggested that certain family characteristics may also contribute to teen pregnancy. Jacobs (1994) proposes that teenagers' developmental needs of autonomy and attachment seem to be a factor in their desire to be sexually active. This behavior may be perceived by teens as a defiant act of differentiation.

In many families in which a daughter acts out sexually, the parents have not communicated with her about sexual matters and have put excessive restrictions on her. In these families, adolescents do not feel that they can talk to their parents, which increases their secrecy about their social activities. In addition to seeking autonomy, most of the girls seek a closeness that they do not have with their parents. Some choose to keep their babies instead of offering them for adoption because of their misguided belief that the baby will provide them with the nurturing they lacked at home.

Many clinics and shelters have been set up to address the problems peculiar to this group of teenagers. For example, pregnant teen girls can often be cared for in facilities in which they can go to school and learn how to parent the baby. The crisis worker should be aware of the availability of such options in the area. Parents are often willing to help out, and the crisis worker must help the entire family adjust to the pregnancy and the baby. This often means that the girl must drop out of school. More importantly, her social life will change. If the girl does not wish to keep the baby, the crisis counselor must have knowledge of adoption agencies and abortion facilities and present these options to the girl and her parents. When conducting crisis counseling with someone who is considering abortion or adoption, it is imperative to maintain a nonjudgmental attitude. It is not ethical for counselors to persuade a teen to either continue with the pregnancy or terminate it. Instead, counselors should listen, help the girl clarify what she wants to do according to her value system, and provide education and referrals.

Gangs

The issue of teenagers being involved in gangs is extremely difficult for a crisis worker. Local police usually have gang units that can help in counseling these youths and their families. Other options include helping the family move out of the area or helping the youth develop new friends and an improved social attitude. Such complete shifts are difficult to bring about, and cultural sensitivity is of utmost importance.

In trying to understand why some teens join gangs, a worker should look at both the family structure and societal and cultural conditions. Much informative demographic data related to gangs have been produced by research studies. The reader may be familiar with some of the myths commonly believed about gangs:

- Gangs consist only of males in urban areas.
- Only minorities are in gangs.
- Gang activity is limited to low-income youths.
- Gangs are concerned about the safety of a gang member's family.
- Gang leaders care about each member.
- Gangs are made up of a group of loyal friends.
- Gangs do not put members' lives in danger.
- Gangs are only a problem in the United States.

Most research findings do not support these myths. Kenner (1996) reports that gangs exist in most cities and towns in the United States. In addition, surveys show that in 175 cities with populations between 50,000 and 250,000, 84% had gang problems. There has been a 640% increase in U.S cities reporting gang problems from 1970 to 1995. That is extreme. Another finding is that gang activity is not limited to low-income youth, but that middle- and upper-class youth are also involved in it. The acts of vandalism, robbery, and drug

dealing attributed to these groups are often thought of as the result of boredom or alienation from families and peers, not poverty (Kenner, 1996).

The factors associated with gang involvement can generally be grouped as
(1) family dynamics, (2) self-concept, and (3) societal stresses. Drass (1993)
further categorized them as parental neglect, abandonment, and family dysfunction; lack of a sense of self-esteem, absence of personal safety and adult
guidance, social alienation, and boredom; and the lack of job opportunities
and the presence of socioeconomic stresses.

Children who join gangs have sometimes grown up in a family that has little verbal communication. Often, there is only one parent, and that parent has
minimal interaction with the children. Lack of family structure and no sense
of belonging are also associated with gang involvement. The child seems to be
seeking a place to belong—a place with some type of structure, albeit a dangerous and illegal one.

It is not uncommon for gang involvement to be transferred down from one
generation to another; parents who have been in gangs sometimes encourage
gang membership in their children, either overtly or through role-modeling. This
process occurs in Asian, African American, Caucasian, and Hispanic cultures.
When the gang member is the first in the family to be involved in gang activity,
the family of origin may be disengaged, with the children receiving very little
nurturance and guidance. Because of this disengagement, it is easy for the child
to become enmeshed in a gang.

It is much easier to prevent a child from joining a gang than to intervene
after the child has joined a gang. Once the child is a member, getting him or
her out of the gang is extremely difficult. People are often hesitant to talk
about gang activity. It may be easier to ignore gang behavior than report it.
The old cliché "Don't get involved" applies to this problem because of the
reality of retribution by gangs against anyone who testifies against a gang
member. As a society, however, we cannot extinguish gang activity if we do not
talk about it. Gathering accurate information about gangs is a first step.
Learning how to manage tension and conflict in interpersonal relations is the
next step. Be assured that when gang activity is reported or a parent confronts
a child about gang involvement, conflict will follow.

Many parents ignore the way their children dress or the people with
whom they associate because they want to avoid conflict. If parents can set
limits before the child is a full-fledged gang member, they have a greater
chance of preventing gang involvement. Parents need to know what gang
members wear and how they behave to be able to watch for early signs of gang
involvement in their children—just as they need to be aware of early signs of
alcohol or drug use. Then, parents need the courage to speak up and assert
their authority and support.

Intervention tactics include involving the community (as in neighborhood
watch programs) and increasing the gang member's exposure to positive social
activities. These may include counseling, sports programs, mentoring programs, and educational or occupational programs. The most effective interventions address issues of racism, poverty, and family dysfunction and attempt
to create opportunities for the gang member, with the aim of showing him or

her other avenues that will appear more attractive than gang membership. When possible, family involvement should be encouraged.

Runaways

Like teenagers experiencing other crises of adolescence, teens who run away from home are trying to meet their needs for both differentiation and nurturance. If a family prohibits individuation, the teen is unable to establish a mature identity and develop the capacity for intimacy that is needed to assume adult roles and responsibilities. Without the love and acceptance of their families, teens face much anxiety during this most stressful stage of development.

Running away from home is one way to achieve autonomy and independence, but it can be very dangerous. Runaway teens may be drawn into prostitution, pornography, and drug use. They are susceptible to the influence of others because of the sense of aloneness they feel. Often, they feel abandoned by their parents and seek the acceptance of anyone.

In 1999, an estimated 1,682,900 youths had run away or been "thrown away" (i.e., kicked out of the house by parents). Of these youths, 37% were missing from their caretakers and 21% were reported to authorities for purposes of locating them. Youths ages 15–17 years made up two-thirds of the youths with runaway or thrown-away episodes (National Incidence Studies of Missing, Abducted, Runaway or Thrown Away Children Bulletin, 2002).

More and more nonprofit agencies have been created to house teen runaways to prevent them from being preyed on while trying to live on the streets. These teen shelters usually provide brief crisis intervention and family counseling, either to find a permanent residence away from the family or to reunite the family. If the teen is abused, this will be reported, and attempts will be made to help the teen find a safe place to live with the assistance of the state social services department.

In intervention, families are taught more effective communication skills and the counselor attempts to address the needs of the teen for autonomy and support. Cultural differences must be recognized and the counselor must be sensitive to parents' rights and values. This is not an easy task. A good idea is to seek consultation from others who have worked with adolescents and clients from other cultures. Once the crisis intervention is completed, most agencies offer ongoing support groups, continuing family therapy, and follow-up services. The stress in these families must be changed in order for the teen to return home and not act out again.

The past decade has seen an increase in the need for runaway youth shelters. Casa Youth Shelter in Los Alamitos, California, is an example. Gary Zager (1998), the director of the program, describes the purpose of this shelter as a place to help calm down the crisis that began at home and get the minor back into his or her own home. He states that the counselors at the shelter attempt to define the client as "the entire family" rather than pin the label of "bad child" onto the teen in crisis. Extreme physical abuse is a major reason why teenagers run away from home. Zager says that about 20% of girls that run away are pregnant, and many others run away because they have been "kicked out." Unfortunately, the trend is for younger and younger children to be "thrown away" by their parents. Sexual abuse is certainly another reason why teens run away from home. The teen may believe that leaving is the only way to make the sexual abuse stop, especially if he or she has attempted to get support from the nonperpetrating parent and has been ignored or scolded. Others are referred to the shelter by school counselors, juvenile probation workers, and social workers. Shelters such as the one in Los Alamitos are excellent resources for any crisis worker. Once the child is at the shelter, crisis intervention is provided for the child and the parents. In keeping with the theory of crises, a 45-day stay is typical. It is hoped that the crisis can be resolved in this period and reunification accomplished.

The goals of family therapy include creating more appropriate boundaries, "deparentifying" the child, and allowing the individuality of the child. In other words, an attempt is made to create an appropriate structure in the family, where parents are in charge, children get their needs met, and open communication is allowed. Often, the family is a single-parent one, and the mother needs support in developing an emotionally satisfying life for herself. The runaway often leaves so as not to be burdened with tasks normally ascribed to a second parent. Progress is made when the family can demonstrate appropriate communication processes in front of the crisis worker.

Eating Disorders

Although adults suffer from eating disorders such as **anorexia nervosa** and **bulimia nervosa,** teenage girls make up the majority of patients with these disorders. In fact, 90–95% of persons with these disorders are female. Research indicates that substantial proportions of males suffering from eating disorders are homosexual, bisexual, or asexual. There is an increasingly high prevalence of eating disorders among male athletes, however (Carson, Butcher, & Mineka, 2000, found in Association for Advanced Training in the Behavioral Sciences, AATBS, 2005). Approximately 7 million females and 1 million males are afflicted with an eating disorder. Of the females, 86% developed it before the age of 20 years; 10% before the age of 10 years, and 33% between the ages of 11 and 15 years (Radcliffe, 1999, found in AATBS, 2005).

Girls at highest risk for developing an eating disorder are white and middle or upper class. Unfortunately, these disorders are now becoming more prevalent among less privileged girls of minority status as they assimilate into Anglo American culture, in which typical models weigh 25% less than the average woman. Sadly, the media usually present unrealistic body images to the public, not by using ultrathin models in advertising but by using extremely thin actresses in movies and television shows.

Anorexia Nervosa   The central features of this syndrome include an intense fear of gaining weight, refusal to maintain adequate nutrition, erroneous complaints of being fat, loss of original body weight at least to a level 85% of that expected on the basis of height/weight norms, disturbance of body image, and absence of at least three menstrual periods (American Psychiatric Association, 1994).

Bulimia Nervosa   This syndrome differs from anorexia nervosa in several ways. Sufferers binge on high-calorie foods and then, to compensate for overeating, engage in purging behaviors (e.g., self-induced vomiting, taking laxatives) and overexercising. These individuals are usually preoccupied with shame, guilt, self-deprecation, and efforts at concealment, whereas anorexics are usually in denial regarding the seriousness of their disorder (Carson et al., 2000, found in AATBS, 2005).

Personal Characteristics   The following characteristics are common in individuals who develop eating disorders: (1) are highly emotionally reserved and cognitively inhibited; (2) prefer routine, orderly, predictable environments and adapt poorly to change; (3) show heightened conformity and deference to others; (4) avoid risk and react to appetitive or affectively stressful events with strong feelings of distress; and (5) focus on perfectionism, negative self-evaluation, and fears of becoming an adult.

Although it is easy to blame eating disorders on societal reinforcement of slimness in women, this is not the only cause of them. Evidence suggests that hereditary factors may play a role in the development of eating disorders and that biochemical or structural abnormalities in the brain mechanism that controls metabolism or eating may be a cause (Russell & Treasure, 1989; Walters & Kendler, 1995; Fava et al. 1989, and Kaye et al., 1990, found in AATBS, 2005). Another way to understand eating disorders is to see them as a form of addiction. The person is addicted to the act of dieting or binging on food. A depressed or psychologically traumatized individual may use the eating disorder to soothe the self. Eventually, however, the disorder takes over and the person cannot stop it, similar to the process in drug addiction (Castillo, 1997, found in AATBS, 2005).

Treatment Considerations   Because eating disorders may have life-threatening implications, especially for anorexics who weigh less then 70 pounds and for bulimics who vomit daily, physician involvement must be considered by crisis counselors. The client may need medical care in a hospital if physical injuries are present, such as malnutrition, dehydration, or seizures caused by electrolyte imbalances. These patients may also be at risk for heart failure; the singer Karen Carpenter, who had an eating disorder for years, died of heart failure. A physician may prescribe various medications such as antidepressants or other mood stabilizers. Once the target weight has been achieved, psychological treatment can begin. In addition to medical care for eating disorder–related physical conditions, clients are at risk for self-mutilation and suicide. Crisis workers must assess for self-destructive ideation or behaviors. Some perceive the eating disorder behaviors as a form of self-destruction. These clients are often very depressed and suffer from low self-esteem. They often feel worthless, helpless, and hopeless—the perfect equation for suicidal ideation and behaviors.

The family must be involved in treatment because eating disorders affect the entire family unit. The parents often seek crisis intervention in the first place because of their fears about their daughter's health. A challenge encountered with anorexics is helping them face the seriousness of their condition and getting them to cooperate with treatment. They may tell counselors that it is their parents who have the problem and be thoroughly convinced that everyone is making a big deal out of nothing, even though they may only weigh 85 pounds and think that being a size 1 is too big! As with substance abusers, crisis workers must begin by listening with nonjudgmental empathy to the client's side of the story and assess her frame of reference and cognitions about her body and eating habits. She will "hang herself" soon enough because her thoughts are usually illogical and are not supported by evidence. The key is to proceed slowly and kindly, but confrontations must eventually be given to help her see that she does need help.

Instead of focusing solely on her eating, it is wise to explore her role in the family, her identity as a growing woman, and her emotional needs for individuation and nurturance. It is easier to prove that these issues are a problem for her because by the time her eating disorder has become such a problem that her parents seek professional help, she has usually isolated herself socially and is depressed. Remembering that she is a teenager who needs to accept the process of growing up is helpful. Her behavior should be assessed to see how much is rebellion and an attempt to have control over her parents and how much is due to low self-esteem and lack of identity. Sometimes, the eating disorder can be reframed as a form of adolescent oppositional defiant disorder. She may believe that she cannot openly disagree with her parents, so the eating disorder can be a way to have power without openly defying her parents.

As with all crisis interventions, the role of crisis workers is to understand the problem, reframe it, provide education and validation, and get the client to accept referrals for ongoing help. She may need several years of individual therapy, family therapy, and group therapy to overcome her disorder. Some must attend 12-step groups indefinitely. Others need to take medication indefinitely. Family members must participate in treatment; therefore, it is vital to gain their trust and cooperation. If the individual suffering from the eating disorder is seen alone, as if she exists in a vacuum, family members may inadvertently sabotage intervention efforts. It is necessary to remain nonjudgmental toward parents who may seem overcontrolling and rigid. The crisis worker must help them work through the crisis of their teenage daughter growing up.

CRISES OF OLD AGE

Certain issues arising during old age are a direct result of normal development. This is not to say that the following issues affect all elderly people and their families, but they are common enough to be a cause of crises in families. Knowledge about them, as explained in the following sections, is essential for the crisis counselor. The number of people in the United States over the age of 65 years is growing rapidly, and so it is prudent to be knowledgeable about their needs. In 2003, there were nearly 36 million elderly people in the United States, accounting for over 12% of the total population. This age group has grown from 3 million to 36 million since 1900. The population of people age 85 years and older has grown from 100,000 in 1900 to 4.2 million in 2000. It is projected that by 2030, the older population will increase to over 70 million (Federal Interagency Forum on Aging, 2004).

Elder abuse issues will be dealt with in Chapter 12, along with other forms of intimate partner violence. One thing that may differentiate elder abuse from other forms of victimization is that the perpetrators are often employees of homes for the elderly. Many elderly people are treated poorly by service providers because they may be perceived as vulnerable, weak, and unable to speak up for themselves. The following section focuses on Alzheimer's disease, but many of the issues described are relevant to less severe medical problems, such as frailty, heart conditions, diabetes, strokes, and other partially or fully debilitating disorders.

Alzheimer's Disease

An estimated 4 million Americans are afflicted with Alzheimer's disease (Harvard Mental Health Letter, 1998, p. 1). A national survey conducted in 1993 indicated that about 19 million Americans say they have a family member with the disease, and 37 million know someone with it. It is the fourth leading cause of death among American adults. Because the population is aging, an estimated 14 million will have the disease by the year 2050. Ten percent of those over age 65 years and almost half of those over age 85 years have the disease (Alzheimer's Association of Orange County, 1998). These statistics tell us that we need to be aware of the problem and its effects on the significant others of the patient.

What Is Alzheimer's Disease?   Alzheimer's disease is a progressive degenerative disease that attacks the brain, causing impaired memory, thinking, and behavior. Symptoms include a gradual loss of memory, declining ability to perform routine tasks, disorientation, impaired judgment, and personality change. There are also difficulties in learning and loss of language skills. The disease eventually renders its victims totally incapable of caring for themselves.

The course of the disease is 2–10 years, although it has lasted for as long as 20 years in some people. The financial burden is tremendous for families as a result of the many needs and services required for the care of patients. The cost of care from diagnosis through treatment to home care, whether informal or institutional, is estimated to be more than $100 billion each year nationwide. Twenty-four hour care is required during the later stages of the disease for daily activities such as eating, grooming, and hygiene.

Effects on the Caretaker   It is caretakers who often use crisis intervention services because of the emotional drain Alzheimer's patients put on them. Although there is no cure for the disease, caretakers can be supported and referred to groups to vent their frustrations and ambivalent feelings. The crisis worker should be knowledgeable about available services for these families. Alzheimer's disease is particularly difficult because of the pervasive impairments it brings in cognitive, emotional, and physical functioning. Patients are often depressed, paranoid, incontinent, and psychotic. It is very sad for people to see a spouse or parent deteriorate to the point where he or she does not recognize his or her own children. Caretakers need empathy along with education about the disorder.

The following 10 signs of stress in a caregiver may require some form of intervention:

1. *Denial* about the disease and its effect on the person who's been diagnosed
2. *Anger* at the person with Alzheimer's disease or others; that there is no effective treatment or cure; and that people don't understand what's going on
3. *Social withdrawal* from friends and activities that once brought pleasure
4. *Anxiety* about facing another day and what the future holds
5. *Depression* beginning to break the caregiver's spirit and affecting the ability to cope
6. *Exhaustion* making it nearly impossible to complete necessary daily tasks
7. *Sleeplessness* resulting from a never-ending list of concerns
8. *Irritability* leading to moodiness and triggering negative responses and reactions
9. *Lack of concentration* making it difficult to perform familiar tasks
10. *Health problems* beginning to take their toll, both mentally and physically (Alzheimer's Association of Orange County, 1998).

When a crisis worker comes into contact with the caretaker of an Alzheimer's patient, the Alzheimer's Association suggests the following 10 ways to help reduce the caretaker's stress:

1. *Get a diagnosis as early as possible:* Once caretakers know what they are dealing with, they are better able to manage the present and plan for the future.
2. *Know what resources are available:* Adult day care, in-home assistance, and visiting nurses are some of the community services that can help. The local Alzheimer's Association chapter is a good place to start.
3. *Become an educated caregiver:* Care techniques and suggestions can help one to better understand and cope with the many challenging behaviors and personality changes that often accompany Alzheimer's disease.
4. *Educate about getting help:* Trying to manage everything on one's own can be exhausting. Encourage the caretaker to ask for the support of family, friends, and community resources. Support groups and help lines are good sources of comfort and reassurance.
5. *Talk about taking care of oneself:* Caretakers should pay attention to their own needs and attend to their diet, exercise, and sleep. They should use respite services that allow time for shopping, a movie, and other recreational activities.
6. *Suggest ways to manage stress levels:* Stress can cause physical problems and changes in behaviors. Caretakers should use healthy relaxation techniques and perhaps consult a physician.

7. *Help the person to accept changes as they occur:* People with Alzheimer's disease change and so do their needs. An investigation of available care options should make transitions easier.

8. *Talk about legal and financial planning:* Planning now will alleviate stress later. The caregiver can consult an attorney and discuss issues related to durable power of attorney, living wills and trusts, future medical care, housing, and other key considerations.

9. *Be realistic:* Neither the caretaker nor the Alzheimer's patient can control many of the circumstances and behaviors that occur. Caretakers should give themselves permission to grieve for the losses experienced but should also focus on the positive moments as they occur and enjoy good memories.

10. *Talk about giving oneself credit, not guilt:* Occasionally, one may lose patience with oneself. Caretakers should remember that they are doing the best possible. Patients need the caretakers and would thank them if possible. Be proud. (Alzheimer's Disease and Related Disorders Association, Inc., 1995)

CASE VIGNETTES

In the following sample cases, the reader can apply the ABC model of crisis intervention, using knowledge about the type of crisis presented in this chapter. Some hints are provided to assist the reader in providing educational statements, reframes, empowerment statements, and validation and support comments.

Case 1   A husband and wife seek help because they have been fighting all the time. They had their first baby one month ago and were so happy just after the birth, but now they are tense, angry with each other, and have no desire for sex or affection with each other.

    Hint: Assess for child neglect or abuse.

    Hint: Validate how stressful it is to have a newborn and to be deprived of sleep.

    Hint: Educate about how sexual drive is reduced for the mother after birth due to hormonal changes and maternal preoccupation.

    Hint: Reframe the fact that they came to counseling together as evidence that they still love each other and want to regain the affectionate feelings they had. The fact that they take their stress out on each other instead of the baby is a positive thing because they can communicate with each other and modify their behaviors, whereas the infant is not capable of making changes yet.

    Hint: Help them focus on what they can do to make changes that will lower stress, such as having the father help out more and having date night for the husband and wife.

Case 2   A mother comes to you complaining that her 2-year-old must be hyperactive. He makes noises all day, can't sit still, won't listen, bites his older sister when he's angry, says "no" all the time, and refuses to be "potty trained." His sister was potty trained by this age.

Hint: Educate about the normalcy of boys taking longer to be "potty trained than girls." Educate about how one can't diagnose a 2-year-old as hyperactive because much of the behavior is normal.

Hint: Reframe the biting as his only way of communicating because he can't yet talk.

Hint: Reframe his saying no as simply mimicking what is probably being said to him all day.

Hint: Teach the parent how to talk to the child, how to set boundaries appropriately, and how to help the child be structured yet also have some autonomy.

Hint: Some behavioral tips such as the use of positive reinforcement for good behaviors should be offered.

Case 3   A 20-year-old female becomes completely stressed out as she plans her wedding. Both sets of parents are trying to control the whole thing, and she is ready to elope tomorrow. Her soon-to-be husband seems to always take his mother's side and won't speak up to her. The bride-to-be is a nervous wreck. The wedding is in 2 weeks.

Hint: Educate about how this is equally stressful for the parents because they have to let go of their children, which completely changes the dynamics of the family.

Hint: Reframe the parents' controlling behaviors as an attempt to maintain the role of parent, not just to be mean and nasty.

Hint: Reframe her fiancée not speaking up to his mother as possibly not so bad, because it could mean that he respects her and will most likely respect his new wife as well.

Hint: Reframe the situation as an opportunity for her and her fiancée to set the needed boundaries between them as a married unit and their families of origin.

Hint: Validate the fact that most weddings have a considerable degree of stress involved.

Hint: Empower her to take charge of the things that mean the most to her and not fight every battle. There is some power in letting go.

Case 4   A couple in their fifties come to you because they are tired, feel guilty, and are very stressed out. They have been taking care of the wife's father, age 78 years, who started showing symptoms of Alzheimer's disease 2 years ago. Just recently, they have been invited by the husband's company to go on a cruise to the Mediterranean, all expenses paid, but do not have anyone to take care of the father while they are gone.

Hint: Validate their feelings of guilt and depression as normal.

Hint: Educate them on the needs of caretakers.

Hint: Reframe their situation to show that if they don't start taking care of themselves, they won't be able to continue taking care of the father.

Hint: Brainstorm with them about who might be able to help out. Maybe someone could watch him for 2 or 3 days at a time. Maybe there is a facility that could take him for a week.

Case 5 A mother takes her 15-year-old daughter to counseling because she refuses to eat. The mother thinks the daughter has lost over 40 pounds this past year but is not sure. Last week, the daughter fainted after she jogged 5 miles without eating anything all day.

> **Hint:** Ask the daughter what she thinks the problem is.
>
> **Hint:** Find out how the daughter is functioning with friends, at school, and so forth.
>
> **Hint:** Address the issue of not eating as a serious medical issue.
>
> **Hint:** Empathize with the mother's concern.
>
> **Hint:** Talk with the daughter alone and find out about individuation issues and control issues. Find out about her level of depression, suicidal feelings, and self-esteem.
>
> **Hint:** Make sure they follow through with an examination by a physician.
>
> **Hint:** Find out if the mother tries to control the daughter's eating; if so, have her change that behavior. Reframe the eating disorder as an adolescent oppositional behavior.
>
> **Hint:** Get mother and daughter to accept that recovery will be long term. Refer them to groups and experienced therapists.

Case 6 A mother and father bring their 16-year-old son to you because he has been threatening to run away. This week they took his driver's license away from him because he is failing four classes. They don't want him on the streets but feel he must earn the privilege of having a car. The son is oppositional, defiant, and refuses to cooperate.

> **Hint:** Help everyone express angry and fearful feelings.
>
> **Hint:** Reframe the running away as a last-ditch effort to feel some sense of control and independence.
>
> **Hint:** Empower everyone by exploring what can be done to make everyone feel safe.
>
> **Hint:** Assess for child abuse issues.
>
> **Hint:** Assess for violence.
>
> **Hint:** Explore the option of having the son stay at a youth shelter for a few weeks until things calm down.

KEY TERMS FOR STUDY

Alzheimer's disease: A disease that impairs the cognitive, physical, and emotional functioning of the patient. The disease usually affects older people, but it can appear in a person as young as 45 years.

autonomy: A state of independence and self-sufficiency needed to function as an adult in society. Adolescents often struggle to achieve this with their parents.

differentiation: A process whereby an adolescent or young adult establishes a mature identity and the capacity for intimacy needed to assume adult roles and responsibilities.

disengagement: Parental behavior in which parents do not relate to their child in a nurturing manner; the child feels little support or sense of belonging.

enmeshed: A state in which an individual lacks a sense of separateness from others with whom he or she has an emotionally intense relationship.

Erikson's eight stages of development: Often called the psychosocial stages of development. The tasks of growing up that everyone experiences and that often lead to crisis states. They include the following:

1. Infancy: Trust versus mistrust
2. Toddler years: Autonomy versus shame and self-doubt
3. Preschool years: Initiative versus guilt
4. Childhood years: Industry versus inferiority
5. Adolescence: Identity versus role confusion
6. Young adult years: Intimacy versus isolation
7. Middle adult years: Generativity versus stagnation
8. Mature adult years: Ego integrity versus despair

evolutional crises: The normal stages a family experiences as it evolves through the life span of its members. The crises result from having to adjust to the formation of the following subsystems:

> **marital:** The system that refers to the new couple. The couple needs to learn how to set boundaries with each family of origin and set rules for the new family.

> **parental:** The system concerned with parenting. The couple now must establish behaviors that deal with raising children and the ways the marital system changes in response to children.

> **sibling:** The system concerned with relations between siblings in the new family. Another boundary and new rules are established with brothers and sisters.

> **grandparental:** The system establishing the relationship of the couple with their parents after the parents become grandparents. The role of a grandparent must be defined, with boundaries and support.

individuation: See *differentiation*.

nurturance: A sense of emotional support and love.

public guardianship programs: Programs often provided through a department of social services that serves as a public caretaker for the elderly. If an elder is being abused or has no one to care for him or her, the county will serve as the caretaker and make decisions for the elder if he or she becomes incompetent.

self-advocacy: An intervention strategy that aims at increasing feelings of power among the elderly. The elderly population is encouraged to speak out about injustices suffered and to assert its needs.

self-neglect: Condition occurring when elders abuse themselves or cannot seek adequate medical care for themselves.

CRISES OF LOSS

If the topic of loss is discussed, Elisabeth Kübler-Ross's name is bound to be mentioned. She has provided an outline for understanding the different stages people go through in dealing with grief over death and dying. Whether a client is grieving the death of a loved one, a divorce, or loss of a body part or function, the issues are similar.

DEATH AND DYING

Kübler-Ross's five stages of death and dying (1969) can serve as an introduction to the topic of loss. This chapter is an appropriate follow-up to the chapter dealing with crises involving suicide because such crises often bring up death and dying issues for suicidal clients and their significant others. If a suicide attempt is successful, grieving will undoubtedly be the focus of a crisis interview. Understanding the stages of loss is vital for counselors who are helping clients through this process. In addition, these stages can be generalized to other forms of loss. A related issue is the triggering of suicidal thinking in a grieving person, especially after denial and anger pass and depression sets in. This is one reason suicide is addressed in this book before crises of loss. Awareness of the possibility of suicide will help the counselor assess for it with any client, no matter what the presenting crisis.

Kübler-Ross's Five Stages of Death and Dying

After extensive work with terminally ill patients and a long study of the process of dying, Elisabeth Kübler-Ross identified five stages that seem to be universally involved in dying.

1. **Denial and isolation:** Denial and isolation make up the first stage in the dying process. Denial is both a healthy and a familiar initial reaction. It cushions patients from the initial shock and allows them to deal with both their hope and their despair.
2. **Anger:** Anger frequently follows denial as patients begin to accept the real possibility of death. There may be rage, envy, resentment, and bitterness. This frequently includes the "why me?" question that so often has no answer.
3. **Bargaining:** The third stage is bargaining. Usually, bargains are secret pacts made with God, regardless of whether patients have been religious earlier in life. When bargaining fails, the next stage develops.
4. **Depression:** When death is recognized as inevitable and feelings of loss become overwhelming, depression sets in. Depression often includes sadness, pessimism, gloominess, and feelings of guilt and worthlessness along with lethargy.
5. **Acceptance:** Eventually the depression lifts as patients work through mourning the impending loss of their life or a loved one's life and come to accept the inevitable. At this stage, the patient is described as being almost void of feelings. Individuals are in the process of disengaging from this life if they are dying or disengaging from a loved one if that person is dying or has died (Kübler-Ross, 1969, pp. 35–77).

The problem with Kübler-Ross's stages became apparent as her popularity increased. People were only too ready to talk about dying, death, grief, and mourning. Consequently, they frequently accepted the stages as truth with a capital T. Counselors tried to force all patients to move through the stages in the same sequence. They did not understand that the stages were no more than generalizations. Not every patient goes through each stage and certainly does not go through the stages in a predictable, sequential order. Patients struggle back and forth, frequently experiencing other emotions or similar emotions in varying degrees. Although Kübler-Ross is often credited as the originator of the study and treatment of death and dying, others have dealt with this topic over the span of modern history. Ideas from other theorists may help you be more empathetic and offer more effective interventions when working with those who are terminally ill. The theories of Charles Darwin, Sigmund Freud, and John Bowlby preceded and contributed to Kübler-Ross's theories on death and dying.

As early as 1872, **Charles Darwin** commented that the separation reactions resulting from the loss of a loved one were innate. He observed similar body movements in grieving individuals, regardless of their cultural background (Darwin, 1965).

Sigmund Freud defined mourning as a period of gradual withdrawal of libido from the now-missed loved object. He described the reactions as dejection, disinterest in the environment, and detachment from others. He saw the process as self-limiting. The effects cease when the libido has completed its withdrawal from the loved object and is reinvested in a new object (Leick & Davidson-Nielsen, 1991, p. 9).

John Bowlby (1980), noted theorist in the area of attachment and separation, proposed four phases of mourning: (1) numbing, (2) yearning and searching for the lost figure, (3) disorganization and despair, and (4) reorganization (p. 85).

The most well-known person associated with death and dying is **Elisabeth Kübler-Ross,** a Swiss-born psychiatrist who began seminars on death and dying in the late 1960s. She had the courage to bring dying patients into the classroom and openly discuss with them their fears, concerns, and desires as part of the training process for psychiatrists. Until then, few doctors or medical schools openly discussed the need to deal honestly and openly with dying patients and their families (Kübler-Ross, 1969, pp. 35–36). From these courses, she extracted the five stages, described earlier, that she believed were experienced by people who knew they were dying; these emotions are also felt by those who are emotionally close to dying individuals.

Since the beginnings of the study of death and dying issues, behavioral scientists have continued to develop their understanding of the various issues and of the intervention skills that are helpful with these clients. Let's take a look at some concepts that serve as adjuncts to Kübler-Ross's stages.

Definitions

As with any topic, understanding is predicated on shared definitions. In this book, the following terms are used.

Bereavement: A state involving loss. To bereave means to take away from, to rob, to dispossess.

Grief: The feelings of sorrow, anger, guilt, and confusion that arise when one experiences a loss. It is the affect that accompanies bereavement. One can be bereaved without grief, although full recovery seems to include some affective experience of the bereavement, usually in terms of grief.

Mourning: The overt expression of grief and the usual response to bereavement. Frequently, it is culturally modified and influenced. Whether one wears white or black, dances or cries, drinks or prays is often the result of cultural tradition.

Tasks of Mourning

Rather than think solely in terms of stages of grieving, the crisis worker can consider tasks of mourning (see Table 8.1). Tasks imply no time sequence. Tasks can be experienced as they arise rather than in any particular order. In addition, tasks imply that some action must be taken by the bereaved person. There is a need to do or experience something, to work toward a concrete

TABLE 8.1 | A COMPARISON OF KÜBLER-ROSS'S STAGES OF DEATH AND DYING AND WORDEN'S TASKS OF MOURNING

Kübler-Ross Stage	Worden Task
Denial	Accepting the reality of the loss
Anger, Bargaining, Depression	Feeling the pain and expressing grief
Acceptance	Adjusting to life without the deceased
	Withdrawal of energy from the deceased and reinvestment of it into something or someone else

goal. Worden (1982) offers four tasks for the person working through the mourning process:

Task I: Accepting the Reality of the Loss   As Kübler-Ross discovered, most people have difficulty accepting death. After a loved one dies (or a body part is amputated), the defense mechanism of denial is typically used to cope until the person can assimilate the knowledge that the loss is real. Denial can take different forms. There can be denial of the facts of the loss, the meaning of the loss, or the irreversibility of the loss. Denial can be a buffer, but it can become pathological if it continues indefinitely. Worden's first task of mourning is for the person grieving to accept that the loss is real. Eventually, denial of permanent loss must be replaced by realization that the loss has happened and that the person can survive the loss. The crisis worker can help by encouraging clients to release their denial slowly, accept the reality of the loss, and move toward the expression of grief. The time it takes for denial to lessen varies from person to person. When people do begin to feel anger and other aspects of grief, it is usually a sign that there is some acceptance that the loss is real. Crisis counselors can educate people about this and reframe the expression of feelings as a sign that the person is actively working toward surviving the loss and that the first step, lessening denial and facing the reality of the loss, has been accomplished.

Task II: Experiencing the Pain of Grief   The next step toward working through loss is for the person to fully experience the feelings associated with it. The broadest possible expression of pain is what needs to be experienced by clients. This experiencing of the pain of grief may manifest itself in the form of crying, yelling, or ruminations. It may be more intense for some than others, but everyone needs to come to the point of experiencing the void that is left in his or her life and the pain associated with that. One way to avoid experiencing the pain is not to feel. Our society has been good at fostering this avoidance in a subtle way. We are not comfortable around people who are in pain; therefore, we give a subtle message to them not to express their grief. More directly, we give the message "It's time to get over this" after the socially acceptable mourning period of 4 weeks has elapsed. However, as was pointed out by Caplan (1964) (see Chapter 1), mastering one's feelings is one of seven characteristics of people who cope effectively and should be encouraged by crisis counselors.

Task III: Adjusting to an Environment from Which the Deceased Is Missing   For many widows and widowers, realizing that they must cope on their own takes several months. Often, about 3 months after the loss they realize that they can in fact manage to live in their new environment. It is helpful for them to look at all the roles the deceased played in their life and to develop ways to cope with new demands and new roles they must take on because of the loved one's absence. They often resist developing new skills at first, but eventually they become proud of their newfound abilities and feel the beginning of a new self-esteem.

Task IV: Withdrawing Emotional Energy from the Deceased and Reinvesting It in Another Relationship   For many, the idea of withdrawing their emotional energy from the dead loved one is seen as betrayal; the guilt that comes with this must be overcome. Working through this task means acknowledging that there are others to love. It does not take away from the earlier relationship; it is simply different. Mourning can be considered finished when the tasks of mourning are over. This certainly does not happen in 4 weeks. Mourning is an individual process; therefore, any attempt to set time limits is artificial and arbitrary. However, most literature supports the need for a year to pass before the loss is fully resolved. At least that much time is usually needed for a person to let go of old memories and begin to build new ones, which will help facilitate the grief process. Holidays, seasons, and family events all must come and go during the mourning period before resolution is complete. That does not mean that the expression of grief will be strong for the entire year, but the process of mourning continues and is experienced during all those events. One indication that mourning may be finished is when the person is able to think and talk about the deceased without pain. The sadness at this point lacks the tearing quality of loss. Studies of widows in particular find that a year is frequently not enough time for them to recover. Often, they need 3–4 years to find stability in life again. One thing is clear: Mourning is a long-term process.

Manifestations of Normal Grief

Regardless of the period required for mourning, people who experience normal grief share common manifestations. The ones seen most often are listed here:

> *Feelings:* Sadness, anger, guilt, and self-reproach; anxiety, including death awareness and phobia; loneliness, fatigue, helplessness; shock—particularly with sudden death; yearning and pining; emancipation, which can be a positive response; relief, particularly from suffering; and numbness

Physical Sensations: Hollowness in the stomach, tightness in the chest and throat, sense of depersonalization, breathlessness, weakness in the muscles

Cognitions: Disbelief, confusion, preoccupation, sense of presence, hallucinations (usually transient)

Behaviors: Sleep disturbances, such as early morning awakenings; appetite disturbances; absent-minded behaviors; social withdrawal (usually short lived); dreams of the deceased; restless overactivity; sighing or crying; fear of losing memories; treasuring objects

Determinants of Grief

A person's response to loss will largely be influenced by several factors of the nature of the loss:

- Who the person was in relation to the survivor is important.
- The nature of the attachment—whether the deceased provided strength, security, or ambivalence in the relationship—will be influential.
- The mode of death will determine reactions. Natural death is easier to cope with than accidental death, suicide, or murder. At least one is somewhat prepared for the death of an 86-year-old grandfather who has been hospitalized on and off for several years. When a loved one is murdered or commits suicide, however, issues of blame and anger become very difficult to overcome.
- Prior grief experiences and mental health in general influence one's grief reactions.
- One's religious beliefs will affect the grieving process.

An individual may seek crisis intervention for grief issues at various points in the grieving process. As the counselor assesses the client's subjective distress, the counselor will determine the stage of grief and decide which interventions will be helpful. Many crisis workers are emotionally taxed when dealing with death and dying. Counselors must come to terms with their own fears of death and beliefs about death and grieving. If the crisis worker is in denial about death and mortality, she or he may inadvertently send messages to clients that grieving and connecting fully with one's pain are not necessary. The crisis worker must be able to handle the pain involved in mourning for clients to grieve as needed. To do this, the worker must be able to be both truly empathetic and objective and rational. The counselor then becomes a sort of emotional tranquilizer for clients in a bereaved state.

Intervention

As with any crisis state, workers must be alert for symptoms that may require the attention of a physician. If the emotions are so strong and out of control that they prevent clients from sleeping, working, eating, or taking care of themselves, medication may be necessary for a brief time. Remember that the counselor does not recommend medication; the counselor's responsibility is to refer the client to a physician if symptoms cause moderate to severe dysfunction. If the client's symptoms seem to be typical grieving reactions, then counseling can assist the mourning process and help the client work through the normal expression of grief.

Before clients begin the process of grieving, they must be informed of the loss, whether it is a death or a serious, or terminal, illness. The person breaking this news might be a doctor, lawyer, police officer, or friend or family member. How the loss is presented may affect the person's ability to accept it. It may even determine the person's emotional reactions.

In general, most people do not like to be lied to or patronized. Such behavior is disrespectful and may lead to feelings of resentment beyond the normal anger involved in grieving. A direct, honest approach is best. Empathy skills are most helpful at this time. Following are some specific ways that professionals or family members might break the news of a death or loss:

> PHYSICIAN: He didn't make it. I am very sorry for your loss. May I contact someone for you? Do you need some space to be alone?

> LAWYER: I have been given the legal responsibility of informing you of some tragic news. Please accept my sympathy for the loss of your father, who has asked me to read you his will.

> POLICE OFFICER: Mrs. Jones, I have come to you in person to ensure that you hear some tragic news with someone near you. Sadly, your child was fatally wounded in a car accident tonight. Please feel free to talk to me tonight about your grief. The loss of your child is a tragedy that no one else can understand but you, but I'd still like to assist you if I can.

> FRIEND: Kathy, it's Jenny. I need to see you in person immediately. (After they meet.) Kathy, Margaret died today. We need to cry and talk together.

> FAMILY MEMBER: Honey, your father became ill last night and didn't make it through the night. Please call your brother and sister for me. Let's all meet at my house as soon as possible.

If the person hearing the news loses control with grief, it is good to have another person available to help contain her or him. Emergency rooms are open 24 hours a day, and medical personnel there can give medication to someone who is a danger to himself or herself or others because of shock. However, people usually become numb after hearing the news of a death and just need to have someone around for emotional support and to help take care of any legal or business details. Uncontrollable emotions might come during the funeral or weeks later, when the person has had time to accept the loss.

Counseling Principles and Procedures

Counseling someone through a loss is difficult. However, knowing certain procedures and their underlying principles is helpful. The following list should be useful to workers counseling someone who is suffering a loss.

1. Help survivors actualize the loss. Talk about the loss. What happened? Ask.

2. Help them identify and express feelings. If they are dealing with anger, be indirect (what do you miss the most/least?). Four common difficult emotions are anger, guilt, anxiety, and helplessness.

3. Help survivors in living without the deceased. The problem-solving approach works well for this. Discourage major life changes for a while.

4. Facilitate emotional withdrawal from the deceased. Encourage survivors to go on.

5. Provide time to grieve. Crucial times include 3 months and 1 year after the death, anniversaries of the death, and holidays. Help clients prepare in advance for these.

6. Educate clients about customary grieving reactions of other individuals to help normalize the experience.

7. Allow for individual differences. Be sensitive to individual styles.

8. Provide for continuing support. Encourage clients to join support groups.

If a client's symptoms and grief reactions appear to be delayed, chronic (i.e., last longer than 1 year), exaggerated, or masked, longer-term therapy may be required. This individual may have an underlying pathologic disorder. In this type of grief therapy, the person's defenses and coping styles would be assessed; and most likely, issues about loss and abandonment will surface. The counselor can best assist this type of client to get through the most recent loss by helping her or him grieve previous losses first. If the previous losses are great, therapy will probably be a 2- to 5-year process. The two examples given next compare responses to crisis intervention with responses to grief therapy.

> **Example 1:** A 45-year-old woman was referred to me for crisis intervention by the Victim Witness Assistance Program. Her 21-year-old daughter had been murdered horrifically 4 months earlier. The woman hadn't been able to work, continued to have nightmares, cried uncontrollably, and was having communication problems with her husband. Her grieving had continued to be strong and painful.

This client has a strong support system in her parents, who are still married; all of her other family members are still living; her own 25-year marriage is a loving one; and she has two remaining daughters who are 17 and 11 years old. She had a very stable and appropriate childhood and responded well to the ABC crisis intervention model. In the B section, she was helped to discuss what her daughter's death meant to her and how her life perspective had changed. Her functioning level was assessed for symptoms and behaviors at each session. In the C section, she was encouraged to consult with a physician because of a sleep disturbance; she was given medication for about 6 months. She was referred to a support group for parents of murdered children. This woman will do well with continuing crisis intervention that focuses on the current precipitating event—the death of her daughter. Her childhood does not have to be dealt with because she demonstrated excellent premorbid functioning. Her present symptoms can be assumed to be related strictly to the death of her daughter.

> **Example 2:** A 35-year-old woman comes for counseling after the death of her older sister. Before we were able to process her grief over her sister, we had to

discuss her childhood and young adulthood losses. This client's method of coping with trauma can best be described as a defensive style called denial. In her family, she was told not to be aware of her own feelings, that her mother and father knew her better than she knew herself. They beat her and degraded her, and then abandoned her. Her only ally was the older sister who had just died.

Not only did this client need to grieve her sister's death; she also had to deal with abandonment by her parents. Being without her sister caused unbearable feelings of aloneness and emptiness for her. She was completely emotionally dependent on this sister, who had offered the only nurturing the client had experienced in her life. The parents had offered no affection. As you can see, the complexity in this case would require a longer-term approach. The client would need to grieve her past losses and come to terms with her aloneness and her own death in addition to grieving the loss of her sister.

Losing a Child

The interventions discussed thus far can be used with all grieving clients. When parents have lost a child, some special considerations are needed as well. As Nancy Ludt (1993) said in her presentation, "Losing a child has a different meaning than losing a parent. When you lose a parent, you lose your past, but when you lose a child, you lose your future." It is this dream of the future that the crisis worker will need to discuss with the surviving parents.

If the parents are married at the time of the death, their relationship is usually weakened. This is especially true if the child died unexpectedly, as in an accident. After such trauma, most couples have a lot of trouble getting along with each other as well as with their other children. They no longer feel like the same people they were before the tragedy occurred because their life has been so drastically changed. The divorce rate of bereaved parents is 92% if the couple does not receive some form of help. However, receiving help can make a measurable difference in helping a couple survive the loss of a child. Ludt said that of the 1,500 people who had attended her support group over the last 16 years, only two couples had later divorced. This is a great incentive for crisis workers to recommend to bereaved parents that they attend support groups! In these groups, the couple can say things to each other that they normally would not say at home. Also, the father has an opportunity to express his hurt as openly as the mother. This is helpful, considering society's perpetuation of the stereotype of the strong man: He can't cry but instead must be strong and go to work even after the death of a child. It is obvious that if the father has a forum where he can communicate openly and express his feelings, the marital relationship has a greater chance of working.

Societal norms also affect parents regarding working after the loss of a child. Many places of employment allow only 3 days of leave for a death. This is inadequate, considering that the attention span of a grieving parent is about a minute and a half. Because of this, many parents may lose their jobs, further complicating their crisis state. It would be nice if people could grieve within tidy time frames, but this is not reality.

Crisis workers can ease the grieving parents' burden by listening. Because the parents' concentration is greatly affected, counselors should minimize their own talking, offering very brief educational and supportive comments. One reason that self-help groups are more popular than professional counseling groups is that parents feel they can just talk and be listened to, no matter what the topic. Structure will not be helpful, because the parents have changing needs, which may shift from one minute to the other. Guest speakers are usually not welcome, because group members want to talk. If a grieving client comes to you on an individual basis, don't be a guest speaker. Let the client be the speaker.

Other things a counselor can do for grieving parents is help them feel normal and not inhibit them if they want to talk about their children. Eventually, they need to remember the child's life, not the child's death. Probably the best thing a crisis worker can do for parents whose child has died is to connect them to a support group. In the group, they can feel whatever is in their hearts and say whatever is on their minds with no fear of ridicule or invalidation. Many times, parents will laugh when talking about the death. To many people, this behavior would appear insensitive. In a group with other grieving parents, it would be understood and shared.

Ludt (1993) lists 10 reasons why grieving parents prefer a support group. Some parents may stay in a group for as long as 10 years after the loss of a child. According to the members of Ludt's support group, the group serves these functions:

1. It is a place of safety where it is all right to say anything. ("I'd trade my living son for my lost son.")
2. It fulfills the need to be with understanding people; even if members don't attend, they know it's available. ("Feelings change over the years and although we don't need to come now, who knows when we will need to come?")
3. It is our child space. ("We can talk about our child all night without any inhibitions. Often talking about memories hurts family members too much, but in group, our child is alive for 2 hours.")
4. It helps us to understand the death emotionally versus intellectually. ("If we say he's dead enough times, we begin to believe it.")
5. It allows a hope for socialization in the future. ("We often feel guilty when we have fun, but we learn here that we can have fun.")
6. It has no time frame. ("He's dead forever, so it will hurt forever.")
7. It allows parents to laugh or cry and not hurt anyone's feelings.
8. It allows parents to express their thoughts with no need to explain them.
9. It can save a parent's life. ("Suicidal thoughts are strong, and the group gives some hope and help.")
10. It is a place where I know that you know that I know that you know.

If the crisis worker cannot locate a group in the client's area, these ideas need to be implemented during the course of counseling.

DIVORCE AND SEPARATION

Divorce, separation, and relationship breakups are extremely common presenting problems in crisis intervention centers. Reactions to separations, whether the partners are married or not, may create dysfunctional states in an otherwise normally functioning person. The reactions range from severe depression to anxiety attacks. As with any situational crisis, how well the person copes with a breakup will depend on material, personal, and social resources. Why are relationship losses so devastating? Often, a person's entire life and self-concept is based on being part of a couple. After a breakup, major adjustments have to be made, sometimes even more than when a spouse dies. Divorce can be thought of as a failure of one or both spouses to live up to the projected expectations of the other. These expectations were established by the family of origin of each spouse, which created a sense of what a family was supposed to be. When a couple divorces, one or both spouses have realized that his or her emotional needs just haven't gotten met (Bell, 1999).

About 50% of marriages end in divorce, and probably more nonmarital relationships than that end at some point. Separations are usually experienced as a loss, even if they are desired and sought (Gilliland & James, 1988, p. 409). Because the issues surrounding loss and mourning have been covered previously, they are not repeated here. Crisis workers should know that each partner needs to complete the tasks of mourning as he or she passes through each stage. In general, the longer the couple was together, the stronger the feelings of loss. If children are involved, the suffering is increased and complicated. Parents often feel guilt and embarrassment when explaining divorce to the children. Rage and frustration are typical emotions that surface when parents are setting up custody arrangements. Crisis workers often step in to mediate these procedures.

There is also loss of financial status and social networks. Losing friends and in-laws often increases the partners' feelings of depression and loneliness. Financial problems create anxieties and often lead to a lowered standard of living. Adjusting to these losses is another focus of crisis intervention in these cases. The person who was "left" often seeks out crisis intervention and seems to suffer the most. This person may be at high risk for suicide and may have the potential for increased drug and alcohol abuse. These possibilities must be assessed, appropriate contracts developed, and 12-step groups encouraged. This person in particular needs to rebuild a support system. Church, family, athletic organizations, and school ties can be helpful. Also, many excellent books are available that can give solace.

The partner who "left" has different issues to face. This person may alternate between feelings of grief and resentment. At one moment, he or she may still try to take care of the spouse; the next, this person may be reckless and irresponsible as he or she goes out "partying" and living the much-missed single life. Although at first this crazy, wild fun seems great, eventually depression usually sets in. It is hard to be single when one has been used to companionship, even though it was miserable.

Intervention

The overall goal is to help the client grieve. This individual needs encouragement to cry, write, read, pray, and go to divorce support groups. The crisis worker, as usual, needs to be soothing, comforting, and optimistic. Letting the person know that many people survive divorce and breakups is helpful. The counselor should remind the client that although he or she may not believe it now, things will eventually be better. Completing mourning can take up to 5 years for some people. Educating clients about the grief process will help normalize their experience. Other helpful educational statements that a counselor can offer deal with the client's concerns about children and in-laws.

Children and Divorce

Most parents are concerned about the effects of divorce on the children; many believe that divorce will damage the children. About 26% of children under 18 years of age (17 million) live with a divorced parent, separated parent, or stepparent. Careful attention must be given to the direct effects of divorce on children, such as changes in the child's living situations and economic status. In 1991, 39% of divorced women with children lived in poverty. Though divorce is difficult for children, they adjust fairly well to the situation. A small minority of children, however, will need mental health treatment. Findings indicate that the custodial parent's own adjustment is the best predictor of child adjustment (Johnston, 1994, pp. 174–175). Johnston's research also found that a history of physical aggression in the family was strongly associated with emotional, behavioral, and social problems in the children.

A crisis worker is often able to point out that whether children are hurt depends on how the parents deal with them and each other during the divorce. Civility and assurance that both still love the children help them greatly. Unfortunately, as a result of the tremendous pain they are enduring because of the divorce, many parents use the children to vent their anger at the other partner, which places children in the dangerous middle. Often, a worried parent should be told that more damage may be done to the children if parents stay together than if they divorce, especially if the marital relationship has been abusive and love and affection has been lacking. This perspective allows them to reframe their perception that it is best to stay together no matter what. Another piece of information that may comfort a parent is that the average family is no longer a nuclear family, so their children need not feel weird or unusual compared with their friends.

Interventions for children may be child oriented or family oriented. Child-oriented interventions alleviate emotional and behavioral problems associated with adjustment to divorce. These interventions may include group sessions in which children meet on a regular basis to share their experiences, learn about problem-solving strategies, and offer mutual support. Individual therapy may include play therapy that allows free expression of feelings.

In regard to in-laws, it is probably best not to tell them everything. What if the couple decides to get back together? A spouse may be able to forgive, but an in-law may not. Also, after a divorce the children will still be involved with both sets of in-laws; therefore, the less the grandparents know, the better, so they are free to be completely supportive and nurturing to their grandchildren. Often, denial is very strong for the spouse being "left," and this partner must be helped gently to confront reality. The counselor can encourage this person to ask whether he or she truly wants someone who does not want him or her. Confronting such a question can give "discarded" partners some control over retaining their dignity. This is an example of empowerment. In a final note regarding legalities, it is good to be familiar with legal clinics and divorce lawyers in your area. Clients may need referrals to these professionals to avoid being taken advantage of or to obtain a restraining order.

Crises Related to Blended Families

Many families come in with crises stemming from the joining of two families when divorced parents have married. The Brady Bunch system is not as much fun as it was portrayed in the 1970s television show. Many of the conflicts in blended families arise because of the developmental stages of the children, the maturity level of each adult involved, and the stage of grieving over the divorce each adult is working through. It is rare for each biological parent to set aside his or her own personal power struggles and resentments for the sake of the children. When four adults are involved, at least one is bound to react dysfunctionally after the divorce and subsequent remarriage. Of course, in some cases, one of the persons marrying into a family with children has not been married before or has no children from an earlier marriage. This circumstance may disentangle the web slightly, but it certainly does not ensure complete cooperation and facility in adjustment.

> **Example:** A 45-year-old man comes to counseling because his girlfriend moved in with him and his 13-year-old daughter after he had been separated from his wife for 5 months. He was very stressed because his girlfriend complained about the amount of time he devoted to his daughter. The girlfriend felt deprived. Subsequent couples counseling brought out the girlfriend's perception of being disliked by the daughter and her feelings that her boyfriend was too focused on his daughter.

Crisis counseling focused on educating the girlfriend about parental attachment and responsibility. This helped alter her view that the father was "overly devoted." She began to understand that his attention to his daughter was normal. The daughter was brought in as well to explore the girlfriend's perception that the daughter disliked her. The daughter said that she did not dislike the girlfriend but that she felt awkward about liking her, considering that the girlfriend had now taken on her mother's former role. Crisis intervention explored loyalty issues and allowed each to clarify her expectations of the other.

Loyalty issues are common for children in cases where a stepparent becomes part of their home life. Children often feel guilty about bonding with another adult for fear it will make their natural parent angry or hurt. If possible, the crisis worker may bring in the natural parent to tell the child it is acceptable to be nice to the stepparent. This will not be an easy task, however, if the parent is still grieving the divorce or has a serious personality disorder.

Incorporating the stepparent's rules and expectations into an existing system is another area in which a crisis worker may be needed. Here, a very brief problem-solving approach is useful. Everyone is encouraged to speak up and give suggestions and can perceive himself or herself as validated.

In conclusion, as with all people in crisis, clients divorcing and forming blended families will fare worse if they have little ego strength and a low level of maturity. Although most people in this situation will suffer, not all will suffer in the same way.

Exercises

Conduct role-play interviews using some of the following ideas and case vignettes. Use the ABC model of crisis intervention.

First, here are a few things *not* to say. These comments are often made by friends and family, well-wishers who tend to discount the grief and seek to deny the experience:

"Cheer up."

"Don't be so depressed."

"Isn't it about time you got over this?"

"It'll get better."

"At least she's with God."

"Just think of the good things; don't dwell on it."

Now, here are some ideas that may be useful with the case vignettes and with your clients who are mourning. During the B section of the ABC model, crisis interventionists can offer various therapeutic statements as they explore the client's belief system, knowledge, support systems, and self-esteem.

Reframes will help the client think about a disturbing event differently:

"Rather than view yourself as weak and out of control when you cry, you might consider understanding this behavior as a sign of your love and part of the process it takes to learn to accept the loss strongly and boldly."

Educational statements will help normalize the client's experience and clear up confusions and misconceptions:

"The grieving process usually takes a full year. Every holiday, birthday, and anniversary of her death will need to be experienced without the person you have lost."

Supportive comments do not mean that you should take away the person's pain. Rather, they let the client know that you understand her or his feelings:

"I wish I could make the pain go away. But you and I both know that's impossible. I can be here to listen as you process your loss."

Empowerment comments will help show clients they have some control and choice despite not having control over the loss:

"You don't have control over the reality that your wife will die of cancer, but you can make choices about how you will live your life with her until that time comes."

Be creative and look for clients' strengths. Having some knowledge about death and dying will help you work meaningfully with your clients. This is also a good chance for you to become aware of your own issues of loss and feelings about death.

Case 1 A minister referred a 37-year-old woman to the crisis intervention center because she has just lost her husband. The minister is concerned because the woman and her two children have not cried since the death of her husband. She is still confused as to why she needs to come in. She tells the counselor that she does not think about his death. When probed a little more, she begins to cry. She has been left without any money, and has two children to feed. She was married for 10 years, and they were good years. Her husband died in an automobile accident, and the driver of the other car was drunk at the time.

Case 2 A 24-year-old woman comes to you because she is depressed and angry. Her father died a year ago, and she got married 1 month after his death. She has never discussed his death with anyone. She and her father were very close. He was the most supportive person she knew. Her marriage is not doing very well. She feels her husband is not as supportive as her father. Her work is beginning to suffer, and she has often been absent from work lately. When questioned about her father's death, she talks as if he is not dead. Her mother was always jealous of her relationship with her father.

Case 3 A 39-year-old woman was referred to the counselor by her doctor. She lost her son to cancer. She feels she cannot go on living. Life seems worthless and meaningless. Her son died when he was only 6 years old. Her husband does not understand her feelings.
     Hint: Suicide assessment.

Case 4 A 45-year-old man comes to counseling feeling very confused. He cannot pinpoint the reason. He tells the interviewer that he wonders how she can possibly be of help to him. The counselor looks as though she has never experienced a separation. Two months ago, his lover of 3 years left him suddenly and he has been waiting for her to return. Yesterday, he saw her with another man; they were holding hands and acting very much in love.
     Hint: Denial, supportive feedback, self-disclosure, and empathy.

Case 5 A friend has told a 35-year-old woman to come to the clinic. She has been yelling at everyone. She is not aware of how angry she feels. She tells the counselor that he looks like an inexperienced person and far too happy to be in touch with reality. The truth is she is very scared because for the first time in her life she feels alone. Her spouse of 7 years left her 3 months ago, and so far she has been saying "Good riddance." The truth is that this is the first time she has ever been hurt by someone close to her.
     Hint: Check out current functioning in all areas and support systems. Educate about loss.

KEY TERMS FOR STUDY

bereavement: A state involving loss; a period of time when something has been taken away from someone.

blended families: The joining of two previously separate families. This often means that children have stepparents, a situation that leads to many conflicts and requires adjustment to new rules.

effects of divorce on the children: Suffering often experienced by the children of divorcing parents because of the power struggles and immaturity of their parents. This does not have to occur. Often, counseling is necessary to ensure that parents do not direct their feelings of anger and pain toward their children.

grief: The feelings of sorrow and sadness that follow a loss.

Kübler-Ross's five stages of death and dying: Five stages that Kübler-Ross believes all people go through after the death of a loved one or while in the process of dying. They are as follows:

> **denial and isolation:** The person is in shock or in a state of nonacceptance about the death or dying.

> **anger:** The person becomes aware of feelings, especially about the unfairness of death, and feels rage and intense pain.

> **bargaining:** The person may try to make deals with God, the doctors, or a loved one.

> **depression:** The person experiences true mourning and grief, feeling sad, nonenergetic, and despondent.

> **acceptance:** The person finally pulls out of the depression, accepts the death or loss, and is able to move on.

loyalty issues: Issues experienced in a blended family when the children sometimes feel guilty for loving or bonding with a stepparent. Their fear is that the natural parent will be angry or hurt. Unfortunately, it is often true. Crisis workers attempt to help both the children and natural parent come to terms with the reality of the blended family.

support: Help that is considered essential for clients experiencing a loss. Validation of such clients' feelings of pain is an important function of the crisis worker. Support groups have also been found to be helpful.

tasks of mourning: Four proposed tasks a person needs to complete in order to grieve a loss fully. They are as follows:

> Accepting the reality of the loss

> Experiencing the pain of grief

> Adjusting to an environment in which the deceased is missing

> Withdrawing emotional energy from the deceased person and reinvesting it in another relationship or activity

CRISES RELATED TO AIDS AND HIV

Many of the issues and dynamics found in the previous chapter on death and dying will be useful in dealing with crises related to HIV (human immunodeficiency virus) infection and AIDS (acquired immunodeficiency syndrome). However, there are also many issues and facts relating specifically to HIV/AIDS with which crisis workers should be familiar. If a counselor is working with an AIDS patient who is terminally ill, death and dying interventions are applicable. However, if one is working with a symptom-free client, the interventions will be different.

First, check your current knowledge about HIV/AIDS by taking the quiz in Box 9.1. Mark each statement T (true) or F (false). The answers are at the end of the quiz.

Box 9.1 *HIV/AIDS Quiz*

T 1. The AIDS antibody test will tell you if the HIV virus is present in your body.

F 2. Oral sex is the most common way of transmitting HIV/AIDS.

T 3. There is a difference between being "exposed" to HIV and being "infected" by HIV.

F 4. There has not been a verified case of a man being infected with the AIDS virus through vaginal intercourse with a woman.

T 5. Current estimates are that 25–50% of those exposed to HIV will go on to develop AIDS.

BOX 9.1 *Continued*

F̶ 6. The AIDS antibody test tells whether a person will develop AIDS.

T 7. It is possible to be infected with HIV without having a sexual encounter.

F 8. In spite of publicity about it, the incidence of diagnosed AIDS among heterosexuals has not changed in the past year.

F 9. Condoms have been proven to protect against sexual transmission of HIV.

F 10. You can tell by looking at a person if he or she has been infected by the AIDS virus.

F 11. It is safe to have sexual contact with a person who has shown you his or her negative AIDS antibody test results.

F 12. If you are in a relationship, you do not need to take any precautions against AIDS.

F 13. Everyone who develops some symptoms of AIDS goes on to develop one or more of the opportunistic diseases that are usually fatal.

F 14. White splotches on the tongue or throat are the first signs of AIDS.

T 15. The most common opportunistic disease is a particular type of pneumonia.

F 16. Any swelling of lymph nodes is an early sign of HIV infection.

F 17. Health care workers are taking a considerable risk when they treat AIDS patients.

T 18. The average life expectancy of a person formally diagnosed with AIDS varies.

F 19. A positive AIDS antibody test indicates the severity and extent of HIV infection.

F 20. If both partners in a relationship test positive for the AIDS antibody, there is no value in practicing safe sex.

F 21. Dispensing disposable needles to intravenous drug users would completely solve the problem of HIV transmission among that group.

F 22. An oily (petroleum-based) lubricant is not recommended for sexual intercourse.

F 23. Sexual intercourse (vaginal or anal) is safe if a proper spermicide is used before and after.

T 24. A woman who is infected with HIV can pass it on to her unborn baby.

F 25. Self-masturbation is safe only if a condom is used.

T 26. Research indicates that some people have a natural immunity to HIV.

T 27. When a vaccine is developed for HIV, it will not be effective in those who have already been exposed to and tested positive for the virus.

F 28. HIV can be absorbed through the outer layer of the skin into the bloodstream.

F 29. The incubation period for HIV infection is the 2- to 8-week period during which antibodies develop after a person is exposed to HIV.

Answers: 1: T; 2: F; 3: T; 4: F; 5: T; 6: F; 7: T; 8: F; 9: F; 10: F; 11: F; 12: F; 13: F; 14: F; 15: T; 16: F; 17: F; 18: T; 19: F; 20: F; 21: F; 22: T; 23: F; 24: T; 25: F; 26: T; 27: T; 28: F; 29: F. (Brown, 1990)

BASIC STATISTICS ABOUT AIDS

This section provides some statistics about HIV infection and AIDS. The outline and list format should make the information easier to grasp, and they emphasize the starkness of the information. The section begins with explanations of a few essential acronyms. Crisis workers should share some of this information with clients if it is relevant.

Acronyms and Terms

Table 9.1 lists acronyms and terms with which counselors should be familiar.

A Brief Outline of the History of AIDS

Table 9.2 shows a historical outline of the discovery and spread of HIV/AIDS.

The cumulative estimated number of diagnoses of AIDS through 2003 in the United States is 929,985. The cumulative estimated number of deaths of persons with AIDS through 2003 is 524,060. The largest percentage of these cumulative AIDS cases in the United States is in persons 35–44 years of age, and the second largest percentage is in persons 25–34 years of age. Surprisingly, there are more cases of AIDS in children under 13 years of age than in adolescents 13–14 years old. This may be due to lack of knowledge in the 1980s and 1990s about infected breast milk, which can transmit the disease to infants. The number of cases in persons between 15 and 24 years of age is 37,599. In the year 2003, 1,991 persons between the ages of 15 and 24 years had AIDS; only 59 persons under 13 years of age and only 59 persons 13–14 years of age had the disease.

During 2003 in the United States, the highest number of cases occurred in blacks (21,304). The number of cases in whites was 12,222; in Hispanics, 8,757; in Asian/Pacific Islanders, 497; and in American Indian/Alaska Natives, 196. Male-to-male sexual contact continued to be the main method of transmission in 2003. Heterosexual contact was the next most common method and injection drug use the third most common (U. S. Centers for Disease Control, 2005).

What Is AIDS?

AIDS is the disease that develops when the HIV virus invades the body and disrupts the immune system so that it cannot ward off deadly infections such as cancer or pneumonia. AIDS is a life-threatening disease that sooner or later kills almost everyone who has it. Once a person has AIDS, he or she may die

TABLE 9.1 | HIV/AIDS ACRONYMS AND TERMS

AIDS virus: HIV (human immunodeficiency virus)

Asymptomatic infection: Infection is present but no symptoms are evident

ARC: AIDS-related complex

AIDS: Acquired immunodeficiency syndrome

TABLE 9.2 | HISTORY OF HIV/AIDS

1977–1978   First cases of AIDS probably occur in the United States, Haiti, and Africa.

1979   Aggressive Kaposi's sarcoma and rare infections first seen in Europe and Africa.

1981   Kaposi's sarcoma and rare infections first reported in homosexual men in the United States; link with sexual transmission suspected.

1982   U.S. Centers for Disease Control (CDC) establishes AIDS case definition; formal surveillance starts in United States and Europe.
First educational efforts started in United States by local homosexual groups.
AIDS linked to blood transfusions, intravenous (IV) drug use, congenital infection

1983   2,500 AIDS cases reported in United States.
HIV identified in France and United States.

1984   First studies indicate AIDS is common among heterosexuals in Africa.

1985   Enzyme-linked immunosorbent assay (ELISA) blood test developed to detect HIV antibodies. United States begins screening donated blood.
HIV is isolated in brain cells and cerebrospinal fluid.
First controlled clinical trials of anti-HIV drugs begin in United States.

1986   Estimated 5–10 million people infected with HIV worldwide.
World Health Assembly recommends global strategy for AIDS control.
Some estimates indicate 1–3 million people infected in the United States. Estimate is reduced by Reagan administration.
Several governments start national communication programs.

1987   National Education Association (NEA) publishes "The Facts about AIDS" and joins Health Information Network.
Education programs begin to expand; so does the number of AIDS cases.

1988   The Names Project creates the AIDS quilt, which helps publicize the epidemic.

1989   Over 100,000 AIDS cases in United States.

1990   International AIDS conference held in San Francisco. Many new treatments and potential vaccines discussed.
Federal Drug Administration (FDA) loosens regulations to allow AIDS patients to have access to experimental medication.

1996   Discovery of "triple whammy" doses of (1) the original antiretroviral drugs, such as AZT; (2) the nonnucleoside reverse transcriptase inhibitors, such as nevirapine; and (3) the newest class of drugs, protease inhibitors, such as invirase. The combination is expected to increase life expectancy of HIV-positive patients by suppressing the development of resistance to a drug type and producing a rapid and sustained drop in viral load. (Association for Continuing Education, 1997, p. 115)

TABLE 9.2 | CONTINUED

1996	U.S. AIDS deaths = 39,200
1997	U.S. AIDS cases (reported) = 58,493 cases
1999	U.S. AIDS cases = 41,900 (42% gay men, 33% heterosexuals, and 25% IV drug users). (Centers for Disease Control and Prevention, 2000)
2003	U.S. AIDS cases = 43,171 (31,614 in males, 11,498 in females, 59 in children under age 13). Estimated number of deaths of persons with AIDS = 18,017.

within a few days or a few years from infections that attack the immune system. In the past, most people died within 6 months to 2 years after being diagnosed with AIDS. Today, medications that fight opportunistic infections prolong life for people with AIDS. Because of advancements in antiviral medications, many people infected with HIV live for 10–20 years without developing AIDS.

SIGNS AND SYMPTOMS OF AIDS

Patients with AIDS have different signs and symptoms as the infection progresses. According to the Centers for Disease Control and Prevention (2002), some of the symptoms that indicate that infection has begun to destroy the immune system include:

Fever

Fatigue

Diarrhea

Skin rashes

Night sweats

Loss of appetite

Swollen lymph glands

Significant weight loss

White spots in the mouth or vaginal discharge

Memory or movement problems

As the virus continues to destroy the immune system, infections not normally seen in people with healthy immune systems may occur. These infections, which are referred to as opportunistic infections, include invasive cervical cancer, Kaposi's sarcoma, lymphoma, pneumonia, and tuberculosis.

Misconceptions about AIDS

Misconceptions about AIDS are numerous and widespread. The following information should help to dispel the most common of these.

Misconception 1: AIDS can be spread by kissing. New research suggests that saliva from healthy individuals actually inactivates the AIDS virus. Although HIV can be isolated from saliva, the concentration of the virus is so low that the likelihood of someone becoming infected from kissing is very remote.

Misconception 2: AIDS can be spread by touching. HIV is present in sweat and tears; however, its concentration in these fluids is extremely low. Studies of health care workers who are in close contact with AIDS patients have shown that the risk of infection through patient contact is remote (less than 1%). For persons coming into casual contact (e.g., hugging and shaking hands), the risk of HIV transmission is nonexistent.

Misconception 3: AIDS can be spread by sharing eating utensils. The HIV concentration in saliva is too low to cause infection and, also, saliva inactivates the virus.

Misconception 4: A person can contract AIDS by being near someone with it. This is more a psychological response than a physical threat. People are generally repulsed by disease, especially a disease that is known to be infectious and is poorly understood. It is important to remember that HIV is not transmitted through the air, as influenza or cold viruses are. HIV is spread solely through the exchange of bodily fluids, primarily semen and blood.

Modes of Transmission

As important as it is to dispel misconceptions about the ways HIV can be spread, it is equally important to know how the disease is transmitted. The five common modes of transmission are these:

1. Person-to-person transmission through sexual behavior that involves the exchange of body fluids such as vaginal fluid and sperm
2. Use of HIV-contaminated injection equipment by more than one person (e.g., needles for injecting heroin, tattoo needles) involving the exchange of blood
3. Mother-to-infant transmission during pregnancy, labor, and delivery or breast-feeding
4. Transfusion of infected blood or blood products (Association for Continuing Education, 1977, pp. 21–22)
5. Contact with infected feces that enter the bloodstream

HIV may also be spread in other ways, but such instances are much less common. One may contract HIV infection by kissing an infected person if both people have open sores in the mouth. Also, health care workers and police officers may become infected by inadvertent punctures from HIV-contaminated needles.

Progression of HIV Infection to AIDS

The development of AIDS can be thought of as a five-stage process:

1. *Acute infection:* The virus enters the body and replicates itself.

2. The second stage may take one of two forms:
    2a. *Acute symptomatic illness (primary HIV infection):* Within the first 2–4 weeks, some people experience fever, weakness, sore throat, skin rashes, and lethargy. This stage can last 1–2 weeks.
    2b. *Immune reaction against HIV:* The body begins to produce antibodies to fight infection. Within 2 months after infection, typical HIV testing procedures can detect the virus. For 95% of those infected, antibodies can be detected within 6 months.
3. *Asymptomatic HIV infection:* The HIV-infected person shows no symptoms for 6 months to 15 years or longer, depending on medical treatment.
4. *Chronic or symptomatic infection:* This stage was previously called AIDS-related complex (ARC) because it was believed that full-blown AIDS would be seen after these symptoms occurred. Medical interventions have delayed the onset of AIDS in the last 10 years. Symptoms include fever, fatigue, diarrhea, skin conditions, thrush, and bacterial, fungal, and parasitic infections.
5. *AIDS:* The person develops one or more of the 26 AIDS-defining opportunistic infections or has a T-helper cell count below 200 cells in conjunction with HIV infection or T-helper cells that register less than 14% of total lymphocytes. (Association for Continuing Education, 1997, pp. 10–14)

AIDS Testing

An AIDS antibody test is available. A positive test result does not mean that a person will develop AIDS. The test cannot predict whether the individual will eventually develop signs of illness related to the viral infection or, if the person does, how serious the illness will be. A positive test result does indicate that the person has been infected by HIV and can transmit it to others. When a person tests positive on the first test, another test is used that is more sophisticated and provides a more accurate diagnosis of exposure to HIV. The second test also helps to rule out a false-positive result on the first test. The first test is used because it is less expensive than the second one and can rule out infection in people who think they may be infected but are not.

Treatment

To date, there is no curative treatment for AIDS. There is no vaccine available, despite many years of research for one. Many AIDS patients and HIV-positive patients take a variety of medications, the most popular being zidovudine (AZT), the original medication for AIDS patients. The triple whammy regimen can affect the virus so significantly that it does not show up on a blood test in some people. The purpose of these medications is to block the deterioration of the immune system.

The outline below tells how HIV infection develops and how the triple whammy medications attempt to block it:

Stage 1: *Binding.* On entering the bloodstream, HIV binds to a receptor on the surface of an appropriate host cell. The only cells it targets are those that display a surface molecule called CD4 (T4). T-helper cells carry the CD4 surface marker. When HIV randomly encounters a T-helper cell, the proteins on its envelope bind to CD4 receptors on the cell.

Stage 2: *Uncoating.* HIV is then internalized by the host cell. The virus enters the cell by means of the same CD4 surface molecule to which it was originally bound. Once inside the cell, HIV sheds its protective coating, or envelope. Shedding, or uncoating, exposes the genetic material (RNA) at the core of the HIV virus.

Stage 3: *Reverse transcription.* HIV transcribes its RNA into DNA, a process accomplished by means of a viral enzyme called reverse transcriptase. (At this stage, the reverse transcriptase inhibitor drugs, such as AZT and 3TC, can be effective.)

Stage 4: *Integration.* The retroviral DNA (the virus's DNA) is incorporated into the genetic material (DNA) of the host cell. Incorporation is achieved by means of a viral enzyme called integrase. The integrated retroviral DNA can remain as a latent infection in the host cell's genetic material for a variable period of time. (The drugs known as integrase inhibitors can stop this process.)

Stage 5: *Transcription.* Either immediately or when activated, the integrated retroviral DNA (provirus) works inside the host cell, using the cell's metabolic machinery to transcribe viral messenger RNA. Once transcribed, viral RNA can serve to produce more copies of HIV.

Stage 6: *Protein synthesis.* Viral RNA makes structural proteins in the production of new viral RNA and envelope proteins.

Stage 7: *Assembly.* New viruses are assembled. The new viral RNA is incorporated as the core of newly produced envelope proteins. A viral enzyme called protease is necessary for the assembly of new viruses. (Drugs called protease inhibitors block this stage.)

Stage 8: *Budding.* Assembled viruses (viral copies) eventually "bud," are released from the host cell, and infect other appropriate cells.

Social Aspects

Despite increased knowledge and education about the AIDS virus, a stigma continues to be attached to people with AIDS. The stigma comes not only from the public but from professional health care workers as well. Much of the negative reaction toward AIDS patients stems from negative attitudes toward homosexuality and IV drug users. The generally accepted view is that the spread of AIDS started with gay men and heroin addicts. Many consider the lifestyles of these two groups to be wrong, and extremists believe those afflicted are getting what they deserve because they are being punished by God. As a result of these views, many AIDS patients have been isolated from family and friends, who stay away because of fear and self-righteousness. Being a social outcast only worsens the trauma of AIDS.

Just as the general population discriminates against gays and IV drug users because of their perceived immorality, many professionals also discriminate against these patients, patients who frequently don't comply with traditional medical model treatment plans. Some HIV-positive IV drug users suffer from personality problems that do not respond to education and counseling. Because many people are disdainful of heroin addicts, it is not uncommon for addicts to be deprived of needed treatment. According to Slader (1992), the HIV-infected IV drug user often feels entitled to use drugs and manipulates people relentlessly to get a fix. He asserts that many continue to share needles despite treatment and education. They behave as if they do not care about their health because the "high" they get from the drug is all-important to them. Treatment of IV drug users infected with HIV must be different from the treatment of others. The next section explores various approaches to crisis intervention in working with populations infected with HIV.

INTERVENTIONS

According to Bulnes (1989), crisis workers providing counseling for those suffering from AIDS should keep in mind various issues about the individual. Identification of these issues furthers the workers' understanding of the subjective distress and helps the worker to choose coping alternatives.

1. Diagnosis: Whether the client has tested positive for HIV, has developed ARC, or has full-blown AIDS
2. Inception: How the person became infected: by at-risk sexual contact; sharing of needles; or blood transfusion
3. Lifestyle: Do the person's significant others know about his or her sexual behaviors, drug use, or other risky behaviors?
4. Marital status: Involvement of significant others?
5. Developmental stage
6. Personality style: Dependency issues, losses, narcissism
7. Cultural background
8. Social support network

Some issues have to do with a person's sense of loneliness and inability to relate to others; how to help clients relate to the disease and their body; clients' feelings of self-worth, guilt, sex, love and hate, anger, depression, anxiety, and control; and issues of survival and death.

Individuals diagnosed with AIDS as well as the precursor symptoms often suffer as much psychologically from the diagnosis as they do physically; therefore, psychological counseling is very appropriate for this population. With proper counseling, patients may be able to reduce their feelings of stress and depression, enabling them to enjoy a better quality of life. Counseling can also help clients address issues of death and dying and the denial, anger, and frustration associated with these events. Isolation often compounds these emotions and is reinforced by the withdrawal of family and friends once the AIDS diagnosis becomes known. Counseling must also focus on the psychosocial issues brought on by the stigma associated with the disease, homophobia, and loss of friends, work, housing, insurance, and other essentials of life (Baker, 1991, p. 66).

Treatment Issues

In 1991, the Ackerman Institute AIDS Project developed a training video dealing with crisis intervention for HIV/AIDS patients and their families. This film is addressed to the types of clients who may seek crisis intervention. It offers valuable insights into the psychological and interpersonal issues involved in the various stages of distress in which clients are first seen by the crisis worker.

The first group the intervention worker should consider is also the largest: the worried well. Many of these individuals experience sexual guilt caused by fear of AIDS. They are often anxious about their own mortality and their children's future. They are ambivalent about being tested for HIV. While waiting for their test results, they often experience fear arising from their past sexual behaviors.

For example, if a man is gay but has been living as a heterosexual—even a married heterosexual—issues of disclosure about his homosexuality often need to be discussed. As a reframe, the crisis worker might say, "This can be an opportunity to bring out past lies, which may help open up relationships and enhance communication."

Issues of suicide must be taken seriously. For example, a bisexual man may believe suicide would be preferable to telling his wife and children that he has engaged in risky behaviors such as oral or anal sex with a gay man. He may believe suicide would spare his family embarrassment. The crisis worker can reframe this issue by pointing out the burden his family would feel if they lost him suddenly to suicide. After all, his wife can choose to leave him or stay with him. Is it really his right to make that choice for her?

A second type of client is one who is pondering whether to be tested for the virus. Issues of denial may be present, a sense that "it could never happen to me." Some people may suspect they are infected but may have irrational thoughts such as, "If I find out, I may really die." Also, moral issues may cause the person to think, "If I don't get tested, I don't have any responsibility to tell any sexual partners."

Other people cope by using a form of denial in which they just assume they are positive and restrict their sexual behaviors. If they don't get medical help, however, they put themselves at risk. Therefore, denial can be dangerous for others as well as for the possibly infected person.

A crisis worker can explain how the test detects the virus and how knowing whether one is infected can prevent exposing others to the virus. Several reframes will also be useful. The worker can point out that even if the client tests positive, at least the client can use the knowledge to prolong life through nutrition, medications, and physical wellness. This is a common experience for people who have had near-death experiences.

Another reframe could ask, "Wouldn't it help you to know you aren't positive? At least then you can carry on with life rather than be paralyzed with fear from day to day." Encourage the client to talk to others who have been tested to gain support and encouragement for completing this step.

A third group who come to the crisis interventionist's attention is made up of clients who are dealing with an HIV-positive test result. Many issues must be explored during the time following the news of the result. A crisis worker can use Kübler-Ross's stages as a starting ground and help clients work through each stage. However, denial can be honored for a while because an HIV-positive test result is not a death sentence. The client's energies will be best spent in attending optimistic support groups, complying with medications, and learning to engage in healthy behaviors that lead to good health and low risk for infecting others. Kübler-Ross's stages may be more helpful when a client becomes terminally ill, which may not happen for many years.

Once persons are infected, they may believe that they have lost a world of free and unencumbered sexual activity and any opportunity for childbearing. They may experience feelings of ostracism from family and friends. In the beginning, there may be a ceaseless vigil for symptoms; this is a waste of the person's valuable time and energy. Listening while the client expresses his or her pain and despair is helpful to the client.

Two struggles to be aware of are disclosing the condition to partners and changing sexual practices. Denying the impact of a positive result—that it can lead to AIDS—can be useful in the beginning as the client works on these struggles and the impact of the infection on her or his relationships.

Some clients may struggle with losing their partner if they disclose the positive test result. The counselor will need to support both partners as they express fear, pain, anger, and sadness. When clients choose not to tell a partner, counselors must struggle with their own responsibility to let the partner know. Workers should encourage clients to explore both positive and negative reactions to disclosure.

Changing one's sexual practices is a completely private issue for most people. Sensitivity to cultural and family traditions is vital because resistance to safer sex can often be understood better in these contexts. Some uninfected partners may feel guilty, so they will have unprotected sex to risk becoming infected as a form of punishment. Others may become suicidal at the thought of losing their infected partner to AIDS. In some marital situations, the woman may feel a need to protect her husband's masculinity by not requiring him to wear a condom.

Support groups that focus on optimism and education are an excellent resource for HIV-positive clients. Here, clients can share common concerns and offer one another practical problem-solving advice that may not be well received from a well-meaning counselor who is not HIV positive.

All of the struggles of the HIV-positive client are delicate and difficult to talk about openly. These issues need to be addressed by crisis workers in a nonjudgmental manner. This is not easy for workers. Workers must stop and ask themselves how they are feeling at various points.

A fourth group that will need the help of a crisis worker is made up of those who start to develop symptoms (usually of precursor illnesses). These clients commonly feel dirty and contaminated. Fears of physical deterioration often lead to thoughts such as, "I just want to die because I know sooner or later ARC will turn into AIDS." Such clients may not allow themselves to get close to others because of their extreme fear of an imminent and painful death.

The counselor can help by working to restore a sense of hope. Typical clients have the attitude that AIDS equals death. The counselor can begin to reframe the condition as a catalyst for a more meaningful life, in which clients can learn to appreciate more fully what they have. Rather than creating distance from others, disclosure can rekindle relationships and create closeness.

Educational comments pointing out that family members are probably curious but afraid to ask about the diagnosis may encourage clients to open up to those who live with them. Once disclosures are made and the client has adjusted to changed sexual behavior, the person's crisis state will stabilize. Medical issues, of course, will continue to appear, as will death and dying issues once opportunistic diseases begin.

Since the scientific community began to do research on AIDS and HIV, the professional literature has been addressing the counseling of those afflicted. Education and support seem to be the prevalent modes of counseling for all levels of infected persons, from asymptomatic persons to patients with chronic pneumonia (Price, Omizo, & Hammett, 1986; Slader, 1992). In his residential treatment house for HIV-positive IV drug users, Slader focuses on teaching clients the skills to help them live a healthy life. The focus for this particular population is mainly on preventing spread of the virus. Eliminating needle sharing is the most effective prevention. Some would say that treatment should focus on complete sobriety; but stopping heroin use quickly is extremely difficult, so treatment may have to be more realistic. Many infected IV drug users need to be told that they will die more quickly if they continue to use drugs because drug use damages an already deficient immune system. Pointing out that sharing needles could cause infections with other diseases, which deplete the immune system further, is an example of a useful educational comment. Support groups that deal with feelings and groups such as Narcotics Anonymous can also be helpful with this population.

A counselor may want to reassure clients that their status is guarded by confidentiality ethics, though disclosure to partners will most likely be recommended by the physician. Counselors can also point out that HIV infection does not equal having AIDS. The HIV-infected person is encouraged to avoid infecting others and to stay in good physical condition rather than focus on preparing for full-blown AIDS.

Crisis workers often give the information in Box 9.2 to HIV-positive clients:

BOX 9.2 *How to Reduce the Risk of Infecting Others*

- Reduce the number of sexual partners, preferably to one.
- Practice safe sex, and have all sexual partners tested.
- Use condoms.
- Do use fondling, mutual masturbation, and other safe sexual practices for gratification.

- Clean up accidental spillage of body fluids, especially blood and semen but also feces and vomitus. Fortunately, the AIDS virus is destroyed easily by alcohol, hydrogen peroxide, and bleach.
- Do not pass or receive body fluids, especially blood and semen.
- Do not engage in any form of sex that can cause injury to body tissues (such as rectal sex).
- Avoid poppers and other drugs that can cloud thinking and reduce self-control.
- Avoid intravenous or other injectable drugs.
- Follow the rules of ordinary good personal hygiene. Give special attention to bathing before and after sex and keeping the mouth, teeth, and tongue clean.
- Avoid sharing personal items, especially those that may be contaminated by a small amount of blood, such as razors and toothbrushes.

For those already ill with AIDS, support groups are recommended. Participation will create a sense of family and reduce feelings of isolation. For the counselor, this is a time to model efforts to initiate and maintain contact with AIDS clients. These contacts will help reduce clients' feelings of dirtiness. Because brokering appropriate services is a vital part of any crisis intervention, knowledge of AIDS service centers in the area is helpful for crisis workers and their clients.

Table 9.3 provides a concise summary of the major issues related to AIDS.

Before concluding this chapter, it is vital to point out that there are many other sexually transmitted diseases (STDs) that are more common than HIV infection. Counselors have the obligation and privilege to educate people about risky behaviors that may increase the likelihood of other infections. According to the 2003 surveillance report by the Centers for Disease Control and Prevention, chlamydial infection is the most commonly reported infectious disease in the United States. In 2003, 877,478 chlamydial infections were reported to the Centers for Disease Control. Because this disease is probably underreported, the actual number is probably 2.8 million new cases each year. Cases of gonorrhea are at an all-time low number, but it is still the second most commonly reported infectious disease in the United States, with 335,104 cases reported in 2003. Syphilis has increased among men who have sex with men and has decreased in other populations; about 7,177 cases were reported in the United States between 2002 and 2003.

Other STDs such as herpes, genital warts, trichomoniasis, and bacterial vaginosis also compel people to use precautions when engaging in sexual activity. Crisis workers may come across clients who are in crisis because they are suffering from one or more of these infections. Many of the issues discussed in the section on HIV and AIDS apply, such as disclosure, safe sex, medication management, and prevention of further infection.

Exercises

Practice role-playing the following vignettes using the ABC model. Try to use some of the suggested reframes and educational knowledge presented to you

TABLE 9.3 | HIV AND AIDS-RELATED ISSUES AND INTERVENTIONS

HIV *Human immunodeficiency virus*	AIDS *Acquired immune deficiency syndrome*
Contracted through: 1. sperm 2. blood 3. mother's milk 4. feces 5. vaginal fluid	**When diagnosed?** 1. opportunistic infection 2. T-cell count below 200
Progression: 1. 1 to 2 weeks after infected may have coldlike symptoms, feel run down 2. 6 months to 1 year may be dormant with no symptoms 3. Within 6 months to 1 year may test sero-positive; antigens show up in a blood test	**Progression:** 1. Without medication, new opportunistic infections occur 2. Needs antiviral and antibacterial medications
Crisis issues: 1. Death sentence 2. Fear of disclosure 3. Fear of lifestyle changes 4. Medication cooperation (denial) 5. Suicide as only way out	**Crisis issues:** 1. Death and dying issues 2. Medical care 3. Financial issues 4. Disability issues 5. Caretaker issues 6. Suicide issues
Intervention strategies: 1. Education 2. Suicide prevention 3. Optimistic groups 4. Medication 5. Honor the denial 6. Family therapy 7. Practice safer sex 8. Increase healthy lifestyle	**Intervention strategies:** 1. Grief therapy 2. Case management 3. Suicide watch 4. Medical intervention issues 5. Support groups 6. Hospice

in this section. Keep Table 9.1 handy when you are making assessments for possible issues. Students role-playing the part of client should also use this table to better play their parts.

Case 1   A 32-year-old male comes to you just after he has gotten the results of his HIV test. He tested seropositive. He has been living a closet gay life; his family and employer do not know he is gay. He does not have a current partner but has several buddies with whom he parties. He's depressed but feels good physically, so he's not very worried.

Case 2 A 50-year-old man comes to you on referral of the medical social worker at the hospital. His longtime companion of 20 years has contracted AIDS and is currently suffering from the opportunistic infection pneumonia. He is drained and misses his friend's youthfulness and lively character.

Case 3 A 30-year-old man comes to you after finding out that he is infected with the HIV virus. He found out at the public health department. He is married but does not have children yet. He thinks he contracted the disease from a prostitute. His wife does not know.

Case 4 A female heroin addict comes to you worried that she will get AIDS. She shares needles on a regular basis but feels uncomfortable asking whether the other users have been tested for HIV.

KEY TERMS FOR STUDY

AIDS (acquired immunodeficiency syndrome): Disease caused by HIV infection either when an opportunistic infection has invaded the body or when the T-cell count is very low.

ARC (AIDS-related complex): A term seldom used today. It originally referred to patients who had symptoms such as night sweats, thrush, and lesions but had not yet caught an opportunistic infection. It is a state between dormant HIV infection and full-blown AIDS.

HIV (human immunodeficiency virus): The virus that usually leads to AIDS. It depletes the body of T-cells, which fight off bacteria and viral infections.

how to reduce the risk of infecting others: Ways to reduce the spread of the disease. Crisis workers must be familiar with these. Safe sex includes the use of latex condoms, dry sex, mutual masturbation, and fantasy. Blood should not be exchanged in any way, including via needles, razors, or feces.

intravenous (IV) drug use: Use of syringes by people to inject themselves with an illicit drug such as heroin. Such people who share needles have a high risk of spreading HIV because the virus is directly transmitted into the bloodstream.

misconceptions about AIDS: Mistaken ideas about how the virus is transmitted. AIDS cannot be spread through casual contact, but people often feel worried about hugging and touching an HIV-infected person. HIV is spread through the bloodstream. Even kissing has not been shown to be a likely way to spread HIV. Also, many people think only gay people or drug addicts get AIDS. Actually, the virus is well established in the heterosexual population and is appearing in more and more teenagers in the United States.

types of clients who may seek crisis intervention: People may seek help related to AIDS for a variety of reasons. Four typical types of clients are the following:

> *Worried well persons:* People who feel guilty about past risky behaviors and are almost paranoid about being infected. They may overtest themselves, even if test after test shows negative results.

Clients pondering whether to be tested: Persons who may have had unsafe sex or shared a needle and who may be in denial or just plain scared. Crisis workers can be a great support to these persons by offering education and reframes.

HIV-positive clients: Once a person tests positive for HIV, the person may be in a crisis and is often suicidal. Education, support, and empowerment are needed to help this person through a very difficult time.

Patients who are starting to have symptoms of HIV infection: The patient is moving into the world of terminal illness. This person will be dealing with issues similar to Kübler-Ross's stages of dying. As with all persons dealing with HIV or AIDS crises, disclosure becomes necessary and is often very traumatic.

CRISES RELATED TO SUBSTANCE ABUSE

The media, celebrities, and politicians have been campaigning against drug abuse since the "Just Say No" campaign of Nancy Reagan began in the 1980s. In the 1960s and 1970s, by contrast, the slogans were "tune in," "trip out," "experience," "turn on," and "try it, you'll like it." Drug use was "in"; now, drug abuse is no longer a respectable recreation. Why, then, will so many families and individuals be severely affected by alcohol and drug abuse?

Any crisis interventionist will, in time, see a considerable number of substance abusers and their significant others. In 2003, an estimated 21.6 million persons age 12 years or older were classified as having substance dependence or abuse (9.1% of the total population). Of these people, 3.1 million were dependent on or abused both alcohol and illicit drugs; 3.8 million were dependent on or abused illicit drugs only; and 14.8 million were dependent on or abused only alcohol (National Survey on Drug Use and Health, 2003). The term *substance abuse* as used in this chapter means the use of alcohol and drugs that affects a person's occupational, academic, family, social, emotional, or behavioral functioning.

Although some would include overeating, cigarette addiction, or caffeine use as substance abuse, these behaviors are not examined here. Before reading the information presented in this chapter, take a moment to complete the following quiz about drug use. The answers appear at the end of the quiz.

1. The most commonly abused drug in the United States is
   a. marijuana b. alcohol c. cocaine d. heroin
2. People who are dependent on heroin keep taking it mostly to
   a. experience pleasure b. avoid withdrawal c. escape reality
   d. be accepted by peers
3. Which of these is not a narcotic?
   a. heroin b. marijuana c. morphine d. methadone
4. Which age group has the highest percentage of drug abusers?
   a. 10–17 b. 18–25 c. 26–35 d. 36–60 e. 61 and over
5. Which drug does not cause physical dependence?
   a. alcohol b. morphine c. peyote d. secobarbital e. codeine
6. Most drug users make their first contact with illicit drugs
   a. through pushers b. through their friends c. accidentally
   d. through the media
7. What is the most popular drug at underground "rave" parties?
   a. ecstacy b. heroin c. LSD d. alcohol
8. Which of the following is not a stimulant?
   a. amphetamine b. caffeine c. methaqualone   d. methamphetamine
9. The majority of inhalant abusers are
   a. men b. children c. women d. the elderly
10. Which of the following poses the greatest health hazard to the most people
    in the United States?
    a. cigarettes b. heroin c. codeine d. LSD e. caffeine
11. Which of the following poses the greatest immediate risk to users?
    a. marijuana b. nicotine c. LSD d. inhalants
12. Which drug was believed to be nonaddictive when it was developed in the
    1800s as a substitute for morphine and codeine?
    a. LSD b. heroin c. horseradish d. PCP
13. When does a person become hooked on heroin?
    a. first time b. after 45 times c. 20 times or more
    d. different for each person
14. What causes a drunk person to sober up?
    a. cold shower b. black coffee c. traffic ticket d. time e. walking
15. Which of the following should never be mixed with alcohol?
    a. amphetamines b. sedatives c. cocaine d. cigarettes
16. Medical help for drug problems is available without legal penalties
    a. if the patient is under 21 b. under the protection of federal law
    c. in certain states
17. Stopping drug abuse before it starts is called
    a. prevention b. withdrawal c. tolerance d. education
18. How long does marijuana stay in the body after smoking?
    a. 1 day b. 12 hours c. up to 1 month d. 1 hour
19. The use of drugs during pregnancy
    a. should be limited to tobacco and alcohol
    b. may be harmful to the unborn child c. should cease at 25 weeks
20. What makes marijuana especially harmful today?
    a. It is much stronger than it used to be b. It could affect physical and
    mental development c. Younger kids are using it d. all of these

How did you do? Here are the answers:
1. b; 2, b; 3. b; 4. b; 5. c; 6. b; 7. a; 8. c; 9. b; 10. a; 11. d; 12. b; 13. d; 14. d; 15. b; 16. b; 17. a; 18. c; 19. b; 20. d

RECOGNIZING SUBSTANCE DEPENDENCE AND SUBSTANCE ABUSE

If you scored high on the quiz, you have a good general knowledge about drugs and their use and abuse. As a crisis worker, however, you need to combine this information with other, more specific data to be able to identify a person who is dependent on or abusing drugs. The following two sections set out criteria for helping you make these determinations.

Criteria for Substance Dependence

In using the criteria for substance dependence given below, the mental health worker needs to specify which substance is being used. Essentially, however, the criteria fit most street drugs, prescribed medications, and alcohol. (Note that the terms *alcoholic* and *drug addict* are not used in the formal nomenclature.)

A maladaptive pattern of substance use, leading to clinically significant impairment or distress, as manifested by three (or more) of the following, occurring at any time in the same 12-month period:

1. tolerance, as defined by either of the following:
   a. a need for markedly increased amounts of the substance to achieve intoxication or desired effect
   b. markedly diminished effect with continued use of the same amount of the substance
2. withdrawal, as manifested by either of the following:
   a. the characteristic withdrawal syndrome for the substance
   b. the same (or closely related) substance taken to relieve or avoid withdrawal symptoms
3. the substance often taken in larger amounts or over a longer period than intended
4. a persistent desire or unsuccessful efforts to cut down or control substance use
5. a great deal of time spent in activities necessary to obtain the substance (e.g., visiting multiple doctors or driving long distances), use the substance (e.g., chain-smoking), or recover from its effects
6. important social, occupational, or recreational activities given up or reduced because of substance use
7. substance use continued despite knowledge of having a persistent or recurrent physical or psychological problem that is likely to have been caused or exacerbated by the substance (e.g., current cocaine use despite recognition of cocaine-induced depression, or continued drinking despite recognition that an ulcer was made worse by alcohol consumption)

Specify if:

With physiological dependence: evidence of tolerance or withdrawal (i.e., either item 1 or 2 is present)

Without physiological dependence: no evidence of **tolerance** or withdrawal (i.e., neither item 1 nor 2 is present).

(*Source:* Reprinted with permission from the *Diagnostic and Statistical Manual of Mental Disorders, Fourth Edition, Text Revision.* Copyright 2000 American Psychiatric Association.)

If item 1 or 2 is present, the crisis worker needs to make sure that appropriate medical personnel are involved in the case. Withdrawal from certain substances such as alcohol, Valium, and barbiturates can have life-threatening consequences.

Criteria for Substance Abuse

The criteria for substance dependence and substance abuse are similar. All are generally applicable to the most commonly abused substances.

A. A maladaptive pattern of substance use leading to clinically significant impairment or distress, as manifested by one (or more) of the following, occurring within a 12-month period:
    1. recurrent substance use resulting in a failure to fulfill major role obligations at work, school, or home (e.g., repeated absences or poor work performance related to substance use; substance-related absences, suspensions, or expulsions from school; neglect of children or household)
    2. recurrent substance use in situations in which it is physically hazardous (e.g., driving an automobile or operating a machine when impaired by substance use)
    3. recurrent substance-related legal problems (e.g., arrests for substance-related disorderly conduct)
    4. continued substance use despite having persistent or recurrent social or interpersonal problems caused or exacerbated by the effects of the substance (e.g., arguments with spouse about consequences of intoxication; physical fights)

B. The symptoms have never met the criteria for substance dependence for this class of substance.

(*Source:* Reprinted with permission from the *Diagnostic and Statistical Manual of Mental Disorders, Fourth Edition, Text Revision.* Copyright 2000 American Psychiatric Association.)

TYPES OF DRUG ABUSE CRISES

When dealing with substance abuse problems, the crisis worker can be most effective when the person is truly in crisis. A crisis condition is needed to confront clients successfully about the negative impact the drug is having on their functioning. Over time, crisis workers generally see four types of crises in relation to drug abuse. These will differ, depending on the substance being abused.

Medical Crises

Medical problems are most severe when alcohol or barbiturates are the substance of abuse. Seizures, heart attacks, strokes, and liver failure are some of the common reasons for hospitalization. For someone who is physiologically dependent on either of these two categories of drugs, medical detoxification is necessary because life-threatening complications can occur when a person tries to withdraw from the drug.

Despite the many stereotypes about heroin withdrawal, the medical risk is actually not serious. To the heroin addict, however, coming off the drug feels like a crisis of enormous proportions. For several days, the addict experiences flulike symptoms that often prompt a visit to an emergency room. Although heroin addicts in withdrawal may feel as though they are dying, they are seldom in danger. Most medical facilities encourage abrupt and complete (cold turkey) withdrawal. Some outpatient clinics provide an alternative to heroin called methadone. These clinics allow the addict to withdraw from heroin slowly under the supervision of medical professionals while taking the substitute, methadone.

Medical crises also occur with abuse of stimulants, such as cocaine, crack, or crystal meth (methamphetamine). Some users have seizures or heart attacks and require emergency medical treatment. These events can be life threatening, but they can also pave the way for clients to confront the addiction and do something about it.

At times, drug users take more than one drug, such as ecstasy, alcohol, and marijuana, and have negative reactions. They may pass out or get ill and need to be taken to a hospital. Adolescents are particularly at risk for this type of medical emergency because they do not often think before they take drugs, especially at "rave" parties and other social gatherings.

Legal Crises

Another reason that substance abusers and their families may seek crisis intervention is because of an arrest or some type of court-ordered mandatory counseling. A common arrest for alcohol abusers is drunk driving or public drunkenness. Most states require not only a fine but also counseling and participation in Alcoholics Anonymous as part of the sentence for these crimes.

In addition to being arrested for being under the influence of alcohol or drugs, a person may be arrested for drug possession or sale of drugs. Because of overcrowding in jails and prisons, many diversion programs have been established to provide rehabilitation in lieu of incarceration in traditional correctional facilities. These programs almost always include counseling and education. Diversion programs are especially common for juveniles who are caught with drugs at school. They often lead to increased family involvement as well as cessation of abuse by the teenager.

At times, a state's child protective agency may discover that parents are substance abusers, and the workers will remove the children from the home. The agency may require the parents to enter counseling as a condition of having their children returned to them. The premise for this condition is that having one's children taken away should be a motivator for parents to stop the substance abuse; unfortunately, the desired result is not always obtained.

Substance abuse is often related to domestic violence against a spouse, so similarly, a person convicted of domestic violence may be required to enter substance abuse treatment as part of his or her sentence.

Psychological Crises

Many people seek crisis counseling because of intense anxiety and depression associated with both the use of certain drugs and the sensation of "coming down" after the drug effects wear off. Most of the drugs in the "speed" category create feelings of paranoia when too much is ingested or during the phase following a major binge. People who snort cocaine, smoke crack cocaine, snort or inject crystal meth, or take Ritalin experience a sense of unreality and often have delusions that they are being followed or are in danger. In addition, a profound depression often follows several days of using and can precipitate suicide attempts or ideation.

Lysergic acid diethylamide (LSD) has long been associated with "bad trips," or adverse reactions to its ingestion. The affected person may be pseudopsychotic and delusional to the point of not being in control of his or her mind. People in this state need to have someone with them constantly to talk them through these derealized and depersonalized feelings. They need to be told continually that all the bizarre sensations they are experiencing are a result of the LSD and that in 8–12 hours, the trip will end.

Spiritual Crises

A spiritual crisis involves a parting from the normal sense of self. People in these crises realize that they are no longer who they once were. Such an individual may have a revelation after staying up all night smoking crack in a motel room with a prostitute. Perhaps the person looks in the mirror and sees a skeleton who hasn't slept or had a decent meal in months because of using speed. Maybe the person runs into an old buddy who is not a drug user and remembers a life before drugs. Whatever the spiritual awakening, the emotional result is often anxiety and depression; the person's self-esteem needs bolstering and his or her suicide liability needs to be assessed. One man had a spiritual crisis when he realized that his 5-year-old son had caught him with a straw up his bloody nose while he was in the midst of a cocaine binge.

Whatever the crisis that brings substance abusers into counseling, crisis workers will be most helpful if they can show clients how their current state of functioning is directly related to substance use. Clients must understand the consequences of substance use in clear and practical terms that are presented in a nonjudgmental manner.

ALCOHOL: THE MOST COMMON DRUG OF ABUSE

Although much media attention lately has focused on the use of speed and heroin, alcohol remains the number one most abused substance. Alcoholism affects the alcoholic's entire family, job performance, and health. It is extremely costly to the nation. Groups such as MADD (Mothers Against Drunk Driving) have lobbied for stricter drunk-driving laws in an effort to reduce alcohol consumption and the resulting deaths caused by drunk drivers. Other efforts to minimize alcohol use include an increase in sales taxes on alcohol products and the reduction of alcohol consumption by characters on television programs. In addition, many television movies and soap operas have been portraying realistic alcoholic dynamics in both teens and adults.

Unfortunately, alcohol, like drugs, is big business; corporations and underworld drug lords are not likely to encourage consumers to stop using. However, certain television commercials have been promoting responsible drinking.

Facts about Alcoholism and Alcohol-Related Problems

Most of the facts and statistics in this section were compiled by the National Council on Alcoholism, based on several research studies. They offer a disturbing view of the pervasiveness of alcohol abuse and the destruction it causes.

- It has been estimated that 13,760,000 people ages 18 years and over in the United States were either dependent on alcohol or abused alcohol in 1992. Approximately 3,953,000 were women and 9,806,000 were men (Grant et al., 1994).
- It has been projected that by the year 2000, there would be 10,940,000 alcohol abusers, suggesting less dependence on alcohol (Williams et al., 1989).
- Alcohol is known to cause or contribute to fatal illnesses, including cardiac myopathy, hypertensive diseases, pneumonia, several types of cancer, diabetes mellitus, tuberculosis, and cirrhosis of the liver.
- In 1997, 11,945 Americans died from alcohol-related liver cirrhosis.
- Alcohol is also related to accidents and injuries to a person using pedal cycles, water transport vehicles, air transport vehicles, and motor vehicles. It is related to accidental drowning, falls, fires, and homicides as well (Saadatmand et al., 2000).
- In 1998, there were 12,663 alcohol-related traffic fatalities. The largest percentage of persons involved were ages 25–44 years (45.3%) (Yi et al., 2000).
- 472,066,000 gallons of alcohol were consumed in the United States in 1998 (Nephew et al., 2000).
- Alcohol-related highway deaths are the number one killer of 15- to 24-year-olds. The 1995 Public Health Services Sourcebook reports that 18 million people, 16 years old and older, had driven under the influence of alcohol or drugs (Rouse, 1995, p. 19).
- Alcohol is associated with attendance problems in the workplace (Rouse, 1995, p. 26).

The Alcoholic

The person with an alcohol problem may be called an *alcoholic, problem drinker,* or *alcohol abuser.* Many people working in the field of chemical dependency see alcoholism as a disease in which alcohol abuse covers up other underlying problems. Feelings such as shame, guilt, disgust, remorse, anger, and fear are denied by the alcoholic and anesthetized by alcohol consumption.

When alcoholics stop drinking they may exhibit symptoms of the *dry alcoholic* as they struggle with the emotions that used to be covered up by the effects of alcohol. Family members often complain about newly sober alcoholics because they often behave worse than when they were drinking. This phenomenon underscores the necessity of intervention on the part of the entire family while the alcoholic is recovering.

Family involvement is one aspect of alcoholism that makes it different from other types of diseases. Another aspect is that alcoholics can control their own disease and accept full responsibility for the consequences of their actions. This assumption is one of the basic tenets of Alcoholics Anonymous (AA). However, AA's 12-step program suggests that alcoholics participate in the program and accept the support of a sponsor as part of assuming responsibility and controlling the disease.

Although **alcohol dependence** probably has some genetic and biological components, it is largely a psychological disorder in the beginning stages. In other words, a person experiences emotions and problems, or was socialized in an alcoholic home, and turns to a substance (alcohol) to deal with life stresses. Once used, alcohol helps the person cope with stress by denying and minimizing his or her feelings.

The criteria for determining substance dependence and abuse appeared earlier in this chapter and contain the formal terminology used in most mental health agencies, both profit and nonprofit. There are, however, other practical ways for a crisis intervention worker to understand the patterns and psychological processes of the substance abuser and his or her significant others.

Gilliland and James (1988) offer some useful definitions of defense mechanisms often observed in alcoholics. Detecting and understanding them can aid the crisis worker in capturing the essence of the person's emotional concerns and needs.

1. *Denial:* Emotional refusal to acknowledge a person's situation, condition, or event the way it actually is. This is believed to be the favorite defense of alcoholics and all substance abusers and their families.
2. *Displacement:* The ventilation of hostility on a person or object, neither of whom deserves it. This allows the addict to shirk responsibility for her or his problems.
3. *Fantasy:* A state related to the euphoria brought on by alcohol intoxication. It allows the person to live in a world different from reality (which the person perceives as intolerable otherwise).
4. *Projection:* The attribution of one's own motives and wishes to significant others. Because of alcoholics' low self-esteem and shame issues, they cannot cope with any flaws in themselves. This defense creates poor

communication patterns because the alcoholic appears hostile, suspicious, and oversensitive.

5. *Rationalization:* Making excuses to support one's behaviors and drinking.
6. *Minimizing:* Playing down the seriousness of one's addiction. Many alcoholics will say, "I only drink on weekends."
7. *Repression:* The practice of alcoholics in burying hurtful, threatening, and shameful events in the unconscious; when sober, often remembering nothing of their behavior while intoxicated (pp. 285–287).

Addicts seem to have strong dependency needs and anger issues. Crisis workers need to be aware of these shame issues and build an environment of safety in which the client may express these emotions and still feel accepted by the counselor. Denial is strong in these types of clients because most of them who come in for counseling are still capable of functioning on the job; therefore, they do not see themselves as addicts.

Intervention

Treatment of the alcoholic ranges from education about the disease of alcoholism to psychodynamic characterological analysis, family therapy, behavior modification, and detoxification. The most popular approach is involvement in AA (Alcoholics Anonymous). Because AA (like all **12-step programs**) is not costly for the client, it is by far the most practical treatment approach on a long-term basis that most would agree is necessary for an addict.

Before the long-term approaches in treating alcohol abuse are explored, some general techniques and suggestions need to be examined for dealing with the crisis state. Once the crisis is identified and the ABC model is applied, the client can be referred to the most appropriate setting. Following is a list of actions for the worker in a crisis situation:

- If the client is under the influence, ask questions that will let you know what he or she took and when it was ingested. Do not try to conduct any type of therapy if the person is intoxicated.
- Safety comes first—your safety, that is. Also, do not let an intoxicated client leave your office in a car. You may be held responsible should the client be involved in a car accident.
- Try not to be alone in a building or office with an addict or alcoholic, especially one who is under the influence of the drug.
- If the client is not currently intoxicated, find out when the client last used drugs and what types of substances were used. Remember, polysubstance abuse is very common.
- Check for lethal combinations.
- Find out pertinent medical information, including prescribed medications and illnesses.
- Inquire about possible genetic predispositions by asking whether any family members are drug or alcohol abusers.
- Get a picture of what the person's abuse is like: When does the client typically use? With whom? Under stress?

- Get as much information as possible about the client's functioning level and relationships.
- Find out what in the person's life might be falling apart now.
- Find out why he or she keeps using.
- Begin to confront the client on how the alcohol or drug use is tied into his or her overall problems once enough information has been gathered.
- Deal with the crisis presented.
- Never minimize the crisis or the abuse level.
- Deal with the family when possible.
- Encourage a crisis in the family when possible in order to disrupt the status quo.
- Keep the focus on behavior that is a result of the abuse rather than focusing on the drinking or drug use itself.

Alcoholics Anonymous (AA)   Alcoholics Anonymous was created in 1935 by Bill Wilson, an alcoholic New York stockbroker, with the help of Robert Holbrook Smith. It has about 2 million members worldwide. AA is a mutual self-help group that follows a holistic philosophy. During a meeting, members focus on a person's physical, psychological, emotional, and spiritual aspects. Members are able to explore such issues as how they feel about themselves, their jobs, their families, and other interpersonal relationships and issues dealing with self-image and self-esteem.

There are also purely educational meetings that attempt to break through denial and other defense mechanisms as well as provide information. Many people convicted of drunk driving are ordered by the court to attend these types of meetings, evidence of the respect society holds for the AA program.

The basis of Alcoholics Anonymous is a 12-step program. Following is a list of the 12 steps:

1. We admitted we were powerless against alcohol, that our lives had become unmanageable.
2. Came to believe that a Power greater than ourselves could restore us to sanity.
3. Made a decision to turn our will and our lives over to the care of God, as we understood Him.
4. Made a searching and fearless moral inventory of ourselves.
5. Admitted to God, to ourselves, and to another human being the exact nature of our wrongs.
6. Were entirely ready to have God remove all these defects of character.
7. Humbly asked Him to remove our shortcomings.
8. Made a list of all persons we had harmed and became willing to make amends to them all.
9. Made direct amends to such people wherever possible, except when to do so would injure them or others.
10. Continued to take personal inventory, and when we were wrong, promptly admitted it.

11. Sought, through prayer and meditation, to improve our conscious contact with God, as we understood Him, praying only for knowledge of His will for us and the power to carry that out.
12. Having had a spiritual awakening as the result of these steps, we tried to carry this message to alcoholics and to practice these principles in all our affairs.

Lancer (2004) shares her view of the 12-step process from a Jungian perspective. She says that recovering from an alcohol or drug abuse problem is a process. The addict or abuser uses the 12 steps to work through the process. The steps are not necessarily linear, however. The process may be circular, that is, working through one step may affect the work a client has done in a previous step, work that the client thought was sufficient. In general, addicts deal with each of the following situations during their recovery process:

1. Facing the problem
2. Surrender
3. Self-awareness
4. Inventory: building self-esteem
5. Self-acceptance and transformation
6. Compassion for others
7. Tools for daily growth

Twelve-Step Facilitation (TSF)   Although 12-step groups are not facilitated by mental health clinicians, counselors and crisis workers may play a large part in facilitating the involvement of addicts with appropriate 12-step groups. This model of crisis intervention consists of a brief, structured, manual-driven approach to facilitating early recovery from alcohol and drug abuse and addiction. It is intended to be implemented on an individual basis in 12–15 sessions and is based on the principles of AA. The goal of TSF is to help clients accept the fact that they need to abstain from alcohol and drug use and surrender to the fact that they are helpless to control their behavior and therefore need to participate in a 12-step fellowship in order to remain sober (Nowinski, 2000).

Family Therapy   Another treatment model for alcoholism is to bring the family together and give the alcoholic a choice: Either go into treatment or move out of the family home. The idea is that if the family system changes, the alcoholic can no longer live comfortably in it. To change requires much effort from co-dependent family members, who are used to and comfortable with enabling behaviors (discussed later in the chapter).

Once the alcoholic is in treatment, family sessions can be conducted to explore new patterns of living for all family members. Sometimes, when the alcoholic sobers up, marriages end because the alcoholic decides he or she no longer wants the partner. Being intoxicated was often the only way the alcoholic could tolerate the spouse.

> **Example:** An attractive, verbal, successful 44-year-old woman came to therapy very much in crisis because her husband, whom she described as an alcoholic, had become verbally abusive to her children (his stepchildren) and she couldn't cope

with this behavior. She believed that if only he would stop drinking, everything would be all right.

The husband had been drinking since they met, however, so there had never been any relationship based on sobriety. After a few individual sessions, she and the children confronted him and told him to stop drinking or they were moving.

The husband stopped drinking for about 1 month. During this time, marital sessions were conducted in which the husband decided that he didn't want to be a part of this family emotionally. The wife found this unacceptable, so they decided to divorce.

Medical Approaches   One of the most important aspects to consider in assessing the needs of a substance abuser is whether he or she needs medical intervention. Providing medical care is particularly vital when the abuser is physically addicted to alcohol, barbiturates, tranquilizers, or heroin. There are many types of withdrawal symptoms with each of these drugs, some of which are life threatening.

Detoxification usually takes 2 to 30 days, during which the person is in a hospital and provided with medical attention. People undergoing withdrawal are given various alternative drugs, such as minor tranquilizers, to ease them through this very difficult time. These drugs must be given in some cases to prevent seizures and convulsions.

Heroin addicts can more readily be detoxified abruptly (cold turkey) than other abusers, though this is not popular among this population of addicts. At times, they might receive a mild tranquilizer or begin a methadone program as a substitute for the heroin addiction.

Once the drug is out of the person's system safely, other psychological and social methods of intervention can be instituted. During the hospital stay, clients participate in many groups and activities, such as occupational therapy, recreational therapy, assertion training, educational classes, and groups for building self-esteem. Often, an individual therapist will be assigned to provide psychological counseling as well. A psychiatrist may also be part of the team approach and may prescribe such medications as antidepressants or lithium.

Some hospitals that have alcohol or drug rehabilitation programs have designed partial hospitalization programs or day treatment programs. These offer the same groups and activities as inpatient facilities, but the client lives at home and goes to work during the day, attending the groups daily. This type of program has been widely accepted as more cost effective than residential treatment and is probably the way of the future. These hospitals offer a variety of therapies ranging from behavioral methods to social methods.

Behavior Modification Approaches   A number of behavior modification approaches are used with drug abusers. Two of them are discussed below.

Aversion Therapy   **Aversive conditioning** is based on Pavlov's classical conditioning model, which pairs noxious stimuli with the alcohol (or drugs). Schick Shadel started this treatment in 1935. Its popularity has lessened in recent years because its effects are not long lasting. After patients have been detoxified physiologically with the aid of antidepressants or mild tranquilizers, they are ready for this "throw-up" therapy. On an empty stomach, they drink two large glasses of salt water and take Emetine, a drug that makes them nauseated. A bottle of their favorite liquor is then placed in front of them. First they sniff it, then gargle and swallow it. They immediately vomit. This is repeated several times.

The next day, patients are given the "butterfly," a combination drink that smells like beer and continues the nausea. The third day, they are given a truth serum, sodium pentothal, and are asked if they want their favorite drink. If they say no, they are asked if they would like another kind of drink. If they say yes, the aversion process is repeated with that type of alcohol.

This same process is used for cocaine addicts with a substance that looks, tastes, and smells like cocaine. Treatment usually takes 10 days and costs about $11,000. After 30 days and 60 days, the patient returns for 2-day follow-ups.

Synanon Charles E. Dederich, a former alcoholic, developed a confrontational style of group therapy in 1958. He started **Synanon,** a self-help therapeutic community based in a Venice, California, storefront and run by recovering addicts.

The basic goal of Synanon is to have drug abusers undergo a complete change in lifestyle; this includes abstaining from the drug, breaking patterns of criminal activity and learning job skills, developing self-reliance, and cultivating personal honesty. Counselors help residents confront their behavioral problems, mainly in group therapy sessions. A resident usually singles out another resident and confronts that person with an issue. The discussion goes from there.

Although Synanon emphasizes rejection of life outside the community during the program, reentry into society is a major goal (Orange County Register, 1990, p. M3).

Most communities have a few of these recovery, residential, or halfway houses, though the need far outweighs the availability. The Synanon approach is not practiced in its pure form in most homes, but the idea of change in social life is still a prominent component. Phoenix House is a popular example of one of these residential treatment facilities.

Biopsychosocial Model Probably a more common type of residential program is a community in which the medical, psychological, and social aspects are treated. Gerry House West in Santa Ana, California, is an example of a successful home. Francis (1998) explains the philosophy of this one-year residential facility, where drug addicts live while they undergo structured treatment. One of the beliefs of the staff is that drug use starts in adolescence as experimentation and rebellion. As the user continues into adulthood, the reason for the rebellion gets lost but the user still acts like an adolescent with many narcissistic thought patterns. The narcissism necessitates providing a lot of attention to these addicts, who need to feel special. Much of the therapy is cognitive based; the addict is forced to examine the many unrealistic thought patterns that lead to negative feelings and behaviors. Some typical irrational thoughts include:

- Catastrophizing: The "Chicken Little" complex (i.e., everything is going to turn out badly).
- Personalizing: The tendency not to look for facts but instead think that everything is about me.
- Mind reading: Making other people's choices for them about me.
- Fallacy of fairness: "I've done what I'm supposed to do. Why aren't good things happening to me?"
- Always or never: Approaching life in absolutes.

The treatment model progresses from complete containment and restriction to integration into the community. Much of the focus is on skill building and relapse prevention. A "trigger chart" has been developed to help clients look at their cognitive distortions and the ways in which those distortions lead to inappropriate behaviors.

Crisis intervention is a large part of the treatment. Effective crisis intervention begins with a containment and time-out so that clients may focus on their thoughts. The counselor then provides active listening so clients can feel heard and empowered. This approach, by the way, is exactly the way in which parents are often encouraged to communicate with an "acting-out" adolescent.

Brief Intervention for Alcohol Problems   Some clients may not need to be hospitalized or live in a residential facility. They may be able to control their drinking and function adequately by participating in a few sessions with a health professional who does not specialize in addiction treatment. This brief intervention therapy is most often used with clients who are not alcohol dependent; the goal may be moderate drinking rather than total abstinence. These clients may be abusing alcohol and may be at risk for developing alcohol-related problems. Miller and Sanchez (1993) proposed six elements summarized by the acronym FRAMES for this type of intervention. The crisis worker may offer feedback of personal risk, focus on the responsibility of the patient to change, give advice to change, offer a menu of ways to reduce drinking, create an empathetic counseling style, and encourage patients to believe in their own self-efficacy to make changes. Research has shown that brief intervention for alcohol problems is more effective than no intervention and often as effective as more extensive intervention (Bien, Miller, & Tonigan, 1993; Fleming et al., 1997), so if clients refuse to go to a 12-step group or other forms of treatment, this type of approach may be effective.

The Co-Dependent

In the past two decades, many books have been written dealing with the psychological and behavioral dynamics of the spouses and children of alcoholics and drug abusers. A **co-dependent** is an individual who is closely involved with the person who is dependent on alcohol or drugs and engages in behaviors that enable the alcohol or substance abuse or feels the need to control it, or both.

The co-dependent experiences many of the same emotions as the substance abuser—guilt, resentment, fear, shame, and low self-esteem. The hallmark of co-dependents, or **enablers,** is the need to be in control, whereby they do not allow users the dignity of living their own life as they choose. Instead, co-dependents' lives center around the activities of the users. They usually try to get users to stop using or worry about whether users are getting into trouble because of their addiction.

Davis (1982) has designed an outline that describes various enabling behaviors of the co-dependent (Table 10.1). These are defense mechanisms that maintain the alcoholic family system in its disease form.

Adult Children of Alcoholics   Adult children of alcoholics are often co-dependents and enablers, who have been socialized in an alcoholic home. In this environment they learned about finances, relationships, jobs, isolation, and self-esteem. Adult children often develop problems in these areas because they did not learn realistic coping mechanisms for dealing with life's stresses. Instead, they learned to use denial in dealing with their feelings.

Treatment for the Co-Dependent   Whereas about 40% of substance abusers seek mental health treatment because of outside pressure, a much larger

TABLE 10.1 │ ENABLING BEHAVIORS

1. Denying: "He's not an alcoholic or other drug addict." As a result:
   a. expecting him to be rational
   b. expecting him to control his drinking
   c. accepting blame

2. Drinking with the alcoholic or using with the addict

3. Justifying the use by agreeing with the rationalization of the alcoholic or addict (e.g., "Her job puts her under so much pressure.")

4. Keeping feelings inside

5. Avoiding problems: keeping the peace, believing lack of conflict makes a good marriage

6. Minimizing: "It's not so bad. Things will get better when . . ."

7. Protecting the image of the alcoholic or user; protecting the alcoholic or user from pain or the co-dependent from pain

8. Avoiding by numbing feelings with tranquilizers, food, or work

9. Blaming: criticizing, lecturing

10. Taking over responsibilities

11. Feeling superior: treating the alcoholic or addict like a child

12. Controlling: "Let's skip the office party this year."

13. Enduring: "This too shall pass."

14. Waiting: "God will take care of it."

percentage of the significant others of abusers seek counseling voluntarily. These people are often in a crisis state, feeling nervous and depressed because they cannot control the drinking or substance abuse of their spouse, parent, or child.

As with all people involved in alcoholism, the crisis worker must provide an atmosphere of warmth and safety, for these people have little trust in the world. Many have had to grow up early because of parental irresponsibility. They feel as though they should be able to handle everything on their own because they have always had to do so.

Education works well with this population. Most are willing to read books that describe their personality patterns and needs. Also, educating them about substance abuse is helpful.

Reframing can be useful as well. Co-dependents often perceive themselves as being helpful to the user. It is easy to reframe this thinking by suggesting that their help is actually perpetuating the abuse. Rather than treating the user like a mature responsible adult, the co-dependent has taken away the user's dignity and respect.

Co-dependent people may present as though they are in full control. However, it is easy to show them how controlled they are by their significant other. The crisis worker can empower these people by releasing them from the responsibility of "fixing" the abuser. They must be shown that they need to develop their own life in a way that doesn't revolve around the addict if they are to regain self-control.

Davis (1982) offers empowering advice to those whose loved one is an alcoholic:

> Don't regard this as a family disgrace. Recovery from alcoholism can come about as in any illness.

> Don't nag, preach to, or lecture the alcoholic. Chances are he has already told himself everything you can tell him. He will take just so much and shut out the rest. You may only increase his need to lie or force him to make promises he cannot possibly keep.

> Guard against the "holier than thou" or martyrlike attitude. It is possible to create this impression without saying a word. An alcoholic's sensitivity is such that he judges other people's attitudes toward him more by small things than spoken words.

> Don't use the "if you loved me" appeal. Because the alcoholic's drinking is compulsive and cannot be controlled by willpower, this approach only increases guilt.

> Avoid any threat unless you think it through carefully and definitely intend to carry it out. There may be times, of course, when a specific action is necessary to protect the children. Idle threats only make the alcoholic feel you don't mean what you say.

> Don't hide the liquor or dispose of it. Usually this only pushes the alcoholic into a state of depression. In the end, he will simply find new ways of getting more liquor.

Don't let the alcoholic persuade you to drink with him on the grounds that it will make him drink less. It rarely does. Besides, when you condone his drinking, he puts off doing something to get help.

Don't be jealous of the method of recovery the alcoholic chooses. The tendency is to think that love of home and family is enough incentive for seeking recovery. Frequently the motivation of regaining self-respect is more compelling for the alcoholic when he turns to other people for help in staying sober. You wouldn't be jealous of the doctor if someone needed medical care, would you?

Don't expect an immediate 100% recovery. In any illness there is a period of convalescence. There may be relapses and times of tension and resentment.

Don't try to protect the recovering alcoholic from drinking situations. It is one of the quickest ways to push him into a relapse. He must learn on his own to say "no" gracefully. If you warn people against serving him a drink, you stir up old feelings of resentment and inadequacy. (pp. 1–2)

As a crisis worker, you may want to offer these suggestions to your co-dependent clients.

12-Step Groups   You may also recommend groups to co-dependent clients. Several have been created on the model of Alcoholics Anonymous and use the 12-step, peer, mutual self-help pattern. Al-Anon, Co-Dependents Anonymous (Co-Da), and Adult Children of Alcoholics Anonymous (ACA) have been created for the spouses, relatives, and children of alcohol abusers. Their purpose is to help these individuals cope with their feelings and unproductive behaviors associated with trying to control and change the alcoholic. At these mutual support, self-help meetings, the members receive support for nonenabling behaviors, and their feelings of isolation are reduced. Because these 12-step groups are free, widely available, and effective, crisis workers should have knowledge about the ones in their community.

The Role of Hospitalization   Just as some alcoholics and drug addicts undergo treatment in a hospital, some co-dependents will also benefit from hospitalization. If the person is extremely depressed and suicidal, hospital treatment may be indicated. There are even hospital wards specifically designed for this population.

In summation, alcohol abuse affects all family members, and crisis workers need to be sensitive to the needs of all. It is particularly important for them to be informed about community resources dealing with alcoholism because treatment is usually long term.

The next sections briefly examine other substance abuse issues. Most of the information about alcoholism applies to these issues also. The following sections should provide enough information about specific issues, however, that you will not be totally naïve when you come into contact with drug abusers. Most people realize that substance abuse is a serious national problem.

COCAINE, CRACK, AND CRYSTAL METH

Every crisis worker should at least know the facts about **cocaine,** one of the most pervasive illegal drugs in today's society. Health Communications, Inc., has developed pamphlets that describe cocaine and other drugs. They are updated regularly and can be ordered from the organization at this address: Health Communications, Inc., 2119-A Hollywood Boulevard, Hollywood, FL 33020.

Cocaine is a central nervous system stimulant possessing both anesthetic and vasoconstricting properties. It produces a combination of amphetamine-like energy with the numbing (anesthetic) effect of some narcotics. It has been misclassified by the Drug Enforcement Administration for years as a narcotic. In recent years, cocaine use has increased rapidly, most notably in the educated middle-class population. There were an estimated 1.2 million cocaine users and 265,000 crack users in the United States during 2000 (U.S. Department of Health and Human Services, 2001).

Cocaine is derived from the coca bush. The leaves are 1–4 inches in length and are harvested three times a year. The leaves are reduced to coca paste by the use of petroleum solvents, and the result of this manufacturing process is a white powder.

Cocaine is rarely available in its pure form. Common additives are lactose, procaine, lidocaine, benzocaine, tetracaine, and amphetamines. The amphetamine enhances the high-energy effect and the other additives produce the anesthetic effect.

The most common way of using cocaine is by sniffing, or **snorting,** it. One popular technique is to form lines of cocaine on a mirror and sniff it through a straw or rolled-up dollar bill. The drug takes effect within 3 minutes after snorting. A riskier technique—shooting—is to dissolve the cocaine in water and inject it by needle; the drug takes effect in about 20 seconds. Shooting puts impurities into the blood, and shared needles can spread infectious diseases, including hepatitis and AIDS. The fastest way to get cocaine to the brain is by smoking it in a freebase form such as crack or rock. This creates a very intense high in less than 10 seconds. Smoking cocaine can cause addiction in weeks (StayWell Company, 1998, p. 5).

After ingesting low doses of cocaine, users usually experience a short-lived (20- to 30-minute) sense of exhilaration and euphoria. They tend to talk a lot and feel energetic and self-confident, but the exhilaration is very short lived. After the initial euphoria, psychological depression, nervousness, irritability, loss of temperature sensations, and muscle tightening or spasms may occur. To prevent these coming-down effects, users must use the drug every 20 minutes or so.

Another form of cocaine is **crack** cocaine, that is, cocaine in smokeable (freebase) form. People have been smoking freebase for some time. Before crack was developed, however, they had to convert cocaine into freebase with highly flammable chemicals that only users were foolish enough to risk handling. You may remember the comedian Richard Pryor, who nearly died from burns caused by converting cocaine to freebase.

Now there is a safer way to convert cocaine into freebase. Ammonia or baking soda and water are used. The result is crack, so-called because of the crackling sound it makes when smoked. The crack looks like shavings or chips scraped from a bar of soap and is packaged in small plastic vials that sell for 10–20 dollars each. Crack may be smoked through the stem of a specially designed glass pipe or sprinkled on tobacco or marijuana and smoked.

When smoked, crack triggers an explosive release of neurotransmitters in the brain and depletes the brain's supply of these natural substances, producing an intense craving for more stimulation. The user takes more and more crack to appease a craving that can never be satisfied.

Initially, the user will experience euphoria and excitement, but soon avoidance of coming down becomes the reason for using. Crack is almost instantly addicting. As the addiction takes hold, the user experiences memory problems, insomnia, fatigue, depression, paranoia, irritability, loss of sexual drive, suicide attempts, and violent behavior.

Soon, crack becomes the most important thing in the user's life and overpowers such other needs as eating, sex, family life, personal health, and career. In addition to these effects, physical dangers are associated with crack use. About 64% of users report chest congestion, 40% have a chronic cough, and 7% say they have suffered brain seizures with loss of consciousness. Many others report chronic hoarseness; they produce black phlegm when they cough or suffer persistent bronchitis (National Council on Alcoholism of Orange County, 1986).

Another illegal drug is **crystal methamphetamine,** or "meth," which is a form of speed. Its popularity reflects its low cost and its strong potency in contrast to cocaine. An estimated 4.7% of Americans have used some form of stimulant and an estimated 0.4% currently use stimulants (U.S. Bureau of the Census, 1998, p. 151). "The Feds call meth the nation's most serious drug problem, surpassing even cocaine. Once prevalent in the biker world, speed, with recipes available on the Internet, has gone upscale, used by professionals in search of endless energy or endless sex." (Fischer, 2000, p. 141). Speed is a stimulant that is snorted, injected, or smoked as "ice." It can cause paranoia, weight loss, and disturbed sleep.

Crystal meth is highly addicting; the heavy addict often needs hospitalization to detoxify as well as participation in a 12-step program. The psychodynamics and treatment are similar to those for cocaine addicts and abusers. The major difference between speed and cocaine is that speed lasts longer; therefore, the user doesn't spend all night trying to track down more of the drug, as does the cocaine user. Unfortunately, long-term use often leads to paranoia, violence, and serial arrests or psychological crises.

Methamphetamine is dangerous and can cause physical harm to the brain, heart, and general health. Users often binge for several days before taking a break from using it, a practice that takes a heavy toll on the body.

Another stimulant became popular in the mid-1990s: Ritalin. Historically, this drug has been used in the treatment of hyperactive children, as it has a paradoxical effect on them. Although it is a stimulant, Ritalin acts to calm these children. Many of their older brothers and sisters, however, have been using the drug as an upper, or stimulant, and this use has spread across high school campuses. Even pharmacists have been caught snorting Ritalin at work. This is a drug the crisis worker must know about and inquire about when substance abuse is suspected.

Effects of Cocaine and Speed on the Family

When cocaine or speed controls someone in the family, life for that family can't be normal. Dependence on these drugs makes the user behave in hurtful ways to family members. The drug occupies most of the user's time, money, and attention. The family often suffers from the following emotions:

- *Suspicion and insecurity:* This leads to frequent conflicts over drug use. Money and time become a focus of the family member's insecurities.
- *Resentment and disappointment:* Family members must often make unreasonable compromises. As a result of the user's focus on drugs, the family feels deprived because the joys of normal family living are sacrificed to the chemical dependency.
- *Isolation and hurt:* The user often withdraws from participation in the family. Often children and spouses feel they cause this isolation.
- *Fear and guilt:* The family often fears the consequences for the addict as well as for the family, often blaming itself for the addict's behaviors. (Staywell Company, 1998, pp. 10–11)

In order to help family members cope with the user's behaviors, the crisis worker can teach members how to stop enabling the user and how to properly intervene and help the addict get professional treatment. Once the family understands that it cannot fix the addict, it is freed up to return to healthy living.

MARIJUANA

People rarely seek crisis intervention for **marijuana** abuse; nonetheless, crisis workers should be familiar with it. Marijuana, or "pot," is widely used and may impair a person's functioning and coping while the person is in a crisis. Also, rather than use sober coping strategies, many people use marijuana to deal with stress. The average new user is 16–17 years old. It is estimated that 32% of Americans have tried marijuana (U.S. Bureau of the Census, 1998, p. 151). Of the 6.8 million persons classified with dependence on or abuse of illicit drugs, 4.2 million were dependent on or abused marijuana. This represents 1.8% of the total population age 12 years or older and 61.4% of those classified with illicit drug dependence or abuse (National Survey on Drug Use and Health, 2003). Of the 6.3% of the population using illicit drugs, 59% reported using marijuana only, and another 17% reported using it with other drugs (U.S. Department of Health and Human Services, retrieved 11/4/01).

Take a moment to see how well informed you are about marijuana by comparing facts with myths:

1. *Myth:* Only a few hippies, radicals, and artists smoke pot.
   Fact: One in three Americans has tried pot.
2. *Myth:* Marijuana is a safe drug.
   Fact: Pot has been linked to lung cancer, loss of short-term memory, and slowed reaction times when driving.
3. *Myth:* Marijuana isn't addictive.
   Fact: People can become psychologically dependent on pot and have physical withdrawal symptoms after stopping heavy use.
4. *Myth:* Marijuana makes people more creative and social.
   Fact: Frequent use blunts emotions and may lead to paranoia.
5. *Myth:* If parents don't smoke pot, their kids won't either.
   Fact: If parents misuse any drug, including alcohol, their kids are more prone to drug dependency.
6. *Myth:* Marijuana dependency is an individual problem.
   Fact: Family members get trapped, too, in enabling roles that help drug abuse continue.
7. *Myth:* Teachers would know if a student were dependent on marijuana.
   Fact: The signs of dependence are often too subtle to spot.
8. *Myth:* Pot is not a problem at work; cocaine and alcohol are.
   Fact: Marijuana use is more common than cocaine use and harder to spot. (Krames Communications, 1995, p. 3)

Marijuana is the unprocessed dried leaves, flowers, stems, and seeds of the *Cannabis sativa* plant. Delta-9-tetrahydrocannabinol (THC) is thought to be the primary psychoactive, or mind-altering, compound in this plant. The drug is usually rolled with cigarette papers into a joint or reefer and smoked like a cigarette or in a pipe or "bong." Hashish is the solidified resin of the *Cannabis sativa* plant (Zimbardo, 1992, p. 129). It is usually smoked in a pipe as a brownish chunk and is many times stronger than marijuana. Marijuana and hashish may also be baked and eaten in brownies.

The common street names of marijuana are pot, weed, reefer, smoke, hooch, and dope. Its effects depend on the potency of the particular plant, experience of the user, and user's expectations. Some marijuana users describe a subjective state of increased sensory awareness to music, touch, light, and social interaction. Other users experience anxiety, fear, and withdrawal from social interaction because of drug-induced paranoia.

Research by Health Communications, Inc., indicates that the following may be chronic effects of marijuana over long periods of time:

- *Respiratory system:* Bronchial problems, sore throats, coughing, susceptibility to bronchitis and pneumonia. Tar and cancer-causing agents in marijuana smoke are 5–10 times the amount in a typical tobacco cigarette.
- *Immune system:* Reduced ability to fight infection from bacteria and viruses.

- *Endocrine system (maturational):* Possibly impeded physical, emotional, and mental development for 11- to 15-year-olds using marijuana.
- *Reproductive/hormonal system:* Possible reduction in both male and female hormones. When this occurs, it can affect fertility, sperm reproduction, menstrual cycles, and ovulation. Sperm that are damaged and diminished in size have been reported. These hormone reductions are also related to the maturational processes, particularly in regard to secondary sex characteristics.
- *Intelligence and behavior:* Decreased ability to store information, concentrate, make decisions, handle complex tasks, and communicate. (Health Communications, Inc.)

Marijuana use is often regarded as "soft" drug abuse. However, counselors should remember that marijuana is illegal. Clients may find themselves in legal difficulties because of pot use, and this may be the reason for their seeking intervention. Also, many companies are requiring drug screenings prior to employment or as grounds for continuing employment. A person may need help in staying off pot for this reason.

Marijuana use may be a special problem on the job or at school as well. It interferes with performance and safety. Signs of marijuana dependence are hard to spot, but the following are some of the signs that may indicate chronic pot use:

- Absenteeism
- Erratic performance
- Errors in judgment
- Lack of fitness for duty
- Risk to co-workers
- Frequent accidents

Other psychological and social risks often associated with marijuana use include missed milestones such as graduation (the stoned person is in a "cloud" emotionally), emotional immaturity (feeling most comfortable in superficial relationships), and amotivational syndrome (lacking initiative) (Krames Communications, 1995, p. 6).

Signs that a student is using marijuana in school may include:

- Giving in to peer pressure
- Impaired short-term memory
- Low energy
- Low achievement. (Krames Communications, 1995, pp. 10–13)

Pot Smokers Anonymous or Narcotics Anonymous may be helpful for marijuana users. Users typically need to develop a social network of nonusing people with whom they can have fun and interact socially.

Denial is a large part of the marijuana smoker's perception of her or his problem. This person minimizes the extent of use or the idea that it is a problem. The crisis interventionist may want to help the smoker explore what life is like when he or she is sober. Also, remember that the marijuana grown today is unusually potent compared with that grown even 10 years ago.

LSD (LYSERGIC ACID DIETHYLAMIDE)

LSD is also known as acid. It is taken orally in tablet form or licked off paper. A crisis worker may treat someone on a "bad trip" that has extreme panic associated with it. Many emergency room doctors and nurses as well as mental health workers have had to talk someone through a crisis state set off by LSD. An estimated 9.7% of Americans have used some form of hallucinogen (U.S. Bureau of the Census, 1998, p. 151), and one million stated having used a hallucinogen in 2000 (U.S. Department of Health and Human Services).

LSD distorts the person's sensory perception and sense of self. He or she may resemble a psychotic person because of having hallucinations and delusions. The effect usually lasts 10–12 hours, and the person needs comfort and reassurance that the feelings are due to the acid.

LSD has made a major comeback in the 1990s, perhaps because teenagers are trying to imitate the perceived excitement of teenagers in the 1960s. The drug is frequently associated with underground "rave parties," the location of which is unknown to parents and authorities. The music is loud and teens and young adults engage in wild dancing. If a young client is brought in from a party, the crisis worker should probe to discover the nature of the party.

Many teens use LSD daily or for an entire weekend. This drug can precipitate a psychotic reaction in otherwise normal teens, but it is less prevalent than other drugs.

Ecstasy (3,4-methylenedioxymethamphetamine, or MDMA) is another hallucinogen that has grown in popularity since the 1990s for adolescents and young adults. An estimated 6.4 million people reported having tried ecstasy in a 2000 National Household Survey (U. S. Department of Health and Human Services). It was first synthesized by German chemists in 1912. It was considered for use as an appetite suppressant but was rejected because of its side effects (Harvard Mental Health Letter, 2001). Its effects are unpredictable and include extreme states of altered consciousness. It is often combined with other drugs and alcohol, leaving the young user in a vulnerable state.

Ecstasy affects the body like a stimulant. Other effects have been reported, also, such as strong feelings of intimacy, which often lead to intimate revelations or personal decisions that are later regretted.

> **Example:** A 16-year-old girl went to a rave party. She had lied to her parents about her whereabouts. After consuming alcohol and ecstasy, she passed out. Her pants were undone when she awoke, and she needed to be rushed to a hospital because she couldn't function. Her family was in a crisis because of their fear of what might have happened if the police hadn't "busted" the party.

HEROIN

Approximately 130,000 Americans used **heroin** in 2000 (U.S. Department of Health and Human Services). This drug is usually injected and is highly addictive. A person withdrawing from heroin will experience flulike symptoms and may do anything to get a **"fix"** of the drug. Methadone is often prescribed in oral-liquid form to help addicts withdraw from heroin; and sometimes an addict may be talked through an abrupt (cold turkey) **withdrawal.**

Unfortunately, quitting permanently is very difficult because heroin covers up all pain and stress. When sober addicts must deal with normal life stresses, they are not prepared to cope; starting to use again is a strong temptation. Residential halfway house programs are somewhat effective for heroin addicts, but as with all substance abusers, heroin users must make a complete lifestyle change to be cured.

Users usually start by snorting, then move into mainlining (injecting the drug directly into a vein). After 3 or 4 days, the physical craving is so strong that they feel they have no choice but to use. At this point, they are using the drug to keep from getting sick. The term "kicking the habit" is derived from the miniconvulsions users often go through when withdrawing; they want to avoid this trauma at all costs (Turning Point, 1994).

Because of the high rate of return to heroin use and because the user's life is completely wrapped up in how to get the next drug fix, this addiction needs a great deal of attention. Knowledge of how to work with this population is beneficial for crisis workers. Many mental health and medical health practitioners avoid working with heroin addicts because the addicts are so difficult, but the impact on the community (e.g., crime, AIDS, welfare) is significant and needs to be addressed.

A crisis worker can only point the way and offer information about resources. The addict must do the rest. Give yourself a break and don't accept responsibility for substance abuse clients. Burnout can be high when dealing with this population if the counselor doesn't relinquish responsibility. Table 10.2 summarizes the various drugs of abuse and their effects.

As you practice the case vignettes related to drug and alcohol issues, use the outline in Table 10.3 to assist you in proceeding through the ABC model. It encompasses the multitude of assessment needs, therapeutic interactions, and referral options.

TABLE 10.2 | DRUGS OF ABUSE AND THEIR EFFECTS

Drug	Method of Use	Effects
Alcohol	Drink	Depressant; euphoria, blackouts, slowed reaction time
Marijuana	Smoke	Euphoria, slowed reaction time, munchies, amotivation syndrome
Cocaine	Snort	Upper; high, speeded up thoughts
Crack	Smoke	increased activity, heart racing
Crystal meth	Snort	paranoia, agitation
Heroin	Snort, inject	Depressant; euphoria, nodding out; highly addictive
Ecstasy	Take pill	Euphoria, opening of the mind, increased focus on feelings
LSD	Swallow	Hallucinations, increased sensory stimulation

TABLE 10.3 | DRUG AND ALCOHOL ISSUES

1. Assess the crisis
   a. What brought the person in?
   b. What triggered the crisis?
   c. Was it a medical issue?
   d. Was there a legal issue?
   e. Is there a significant other involved?
   f. Is the person suicidal?

2. Assess the impact of drug or alcohol use
   a. Assess typical use
      (1) How long using?
      (2) How much?
      (3) When and where?
      (4) What is being used?
      (5) Remember, abusers tend to be in denial. Stay nonjudgmental!

   b. Identify how the abuse is related to the crisis
      (1) Help client experience how his or her distress is related to use
      (2) Help client to see past problems related to abuse

   c. Educate about abuse
      (1) Abusers and addicts are powerless over drugs and alcohol
      (2) Although the substance used to be a friend, it is now working against the user
      (3) Stay objective and supportive
      (4) Don't confront denial. Educate about denial and relapse.

   d. Empowerment
      (1) Point out choices
      (2) Help client see how new decisions can be made
      (3) Show client how each experience can be a learning opportunity
      (4) Relapse can even be a learning opportunity

   e. Reframe when possible
      (1) Help client think differently about behaviors
      (2) Perhaps abuse of drugs and alcohol is a form of self-medication
      (3) If so, then what is being medicated away?
      (4) Insecurity, depression, fear of rejection?
      (5) This crisis may be the opportunity to get counseling for other issues.

3. Treatment options
   a. Goal of crisis management is to get client to continue with further treatment
   b. Treatment ranges from 12-step programs to inpatient detoxification and rehabilitation programs

Exercises

Role-play the following vignettes using the ABC model and the outline above. If you are the client, try to use some of the defense mechanisms that alcoholics, addicts, and co-dependents use.

Case 1   A 54-year-old woman comes to you. She is chronically depressed but is still able to work and is not suicidal. Her husband has been drinking beer for as long as they have been married, and she tries to control his drinking.

Hints: Try one or more of the following statements with this client.

Educational statements: People who live with alcoholics often try to control their drinking; this has been termed co-dependency.

Reframe: Although you think you are helping him by focusing on his behavior, you are really showing disrespect for him and taking away his dignity, which probably makes him feel the need to drink more.

Supportive statement: I can understand how hard it must be to have to be the only responsible person in the family.

Empowering statement: Although you cannot control his drinking, you can control whether you focus on him or on your own needs in life.

Case 2   A 17-year-old boy is sent to you because his parents found a vial of cocaine in his bathroom. He tells you this was the only time he's used cocaine.

Case 3   A 30-year-old man comes to you because he has been missing work a lot lately. He drinks and smokes pot daily.

Case 4   A 28-year-old woman and her husband come to you because of financial difficulty. The wife has spent more than $30,000 over the past year on her cocaine habit.

KEY TERMS FOR STUDY

alcohol abuse: A formal term used in the DSM-IV that refers to the person who drinks when the drinking leads to impairment in functioning in one or more areas. This person may also be drinking for psychological comfort.

alcohol dependence: A term from the DSM-IV referring to the person who is physically addicted to alcohol and would suffer withdrawal symptoms if he or she were to quit drinking.

alcoholic: A term often used by laypeople to mean anyone with a drinking problem.

amotivational syndrome: A term used to describe a chronic marijuana smoker's lack of initiative and drive.

aversive conditioning: A behavioral approach to help drug addicts and alcoholics quit by pairing the substance with a noxious stimulus such as emetine, electric shock, or dirty water. Formerly used frequently at Schick centers.

cocaine: A white powder that is usually snorted, giving the user a sense of being high and euphoric, an effect that lasts 20–30 minutes. The drug is highly addictive.

co-dependent: Significant other involved with a substance abuser and the controlling and helping behaviors associated with this family member or friend.

crack: A form of cocaine that is smoked. Crack is highly addictive and can have serious side effects such as heart failure, stroke, and brain cell destruction. A very popular drug in the 1980s.

crystal methamphetamine (crystal meth): A form of speed that is growing in popularity and can be made in home laboratories. It is cheap and highly addictive.

denial: Considered to be the number one defense mechanism associated with substance abuse. The addict or family members simply refuse to see that a problem exists.

detoxification: Cleaning a person's system of a drug. When a person is physically dependent on a substance, it usually takes 3–5 days for the substance to be flushed out of the body. Detoxification often needs to occur in a hospital setting under the care of a physician.

ecstasy: A hallucinogen that creates euphoria and an altered state of consciousness. Its effects can be unpredictable. It is associated with rave parties.

enabler: The nonusing member in a family who encourages or helps the substance abuser continue to use.

fix: A slang term for the dose or unit of consumption of a drug addict. Most commonly associated with heroin addicts.

freebase: The procedure for changing cocaine to crack. To make crack, cocaine and certain chemicals have to be combined. The rock form of cocaine is smoked. Often, a large flame is needed for the best results.

heroin: A narcotic that is highly addicting. It is often first snorted, but soon the user injects it. The sensations are reported to be strongly euphoric.

LSD: Often called acid. LSD is a hallucinogen. The user experiences distortions in sensory perception and feels either euphoric or paranoid if he or she experiences a bad trip. LSD is not considered addictive.

marijuana: A plant that contains THC, which creates a sense of euphoria in the user. It is smoked in pipes, bongs, or joints.

snorting: A way to use drugs by sniffing powder up the nose through a straw.

synanon: A type of treatment for addicts that relies on confrontation and a strong social support network to change the user's lifestyle.

tolerance: Resistance to a drug. After prolonged use of drugs or alcohol, the body builds up resistance to them. More and more of the substance must be used for its effects to be felt.

12-step programs: Considered the most effective model in treating substance abusers. These programs are based on the Alcoholics Anonymous model, which acknowledges that users need to seek out and trust a higher power in order to overcome their lifelong problem with a substance.

withdrawal: Symptoms experienced when a user stops taking a drug. The user experiences various physical and psychological symptoms such as nausea, depression, paranoia, convulsions, and anxiety.

II | CHAPTER | PTSD, COMMUNITY DISASTERS, AND TRAUMA RESPONSE

POSTTRAUMATIC STRESS DISORDER (PTSD)

Posttraumatic stress disorder (PTSD) is a broad category that applies to people who have been severely traumatized at one or more times in their lives; at present, they are not functioning effectively because they have not integrated the trauma and laid it to rest. The cause is exposure to a situation perceived to be threatening to oneself or one's loved ones.

The American Psychiatric Association's *Diagnostic and Statistical Manual of Mental Disorders, Fourth Edition, Text Revision* (DSM-IV-TR) (1994) defines PTSD this way:

A. The person has been exposed to a traumatic event in which both of the following were present:

    1. The person experienced, witnessed, or was confronted with an event or events that involved actual or threatened death or serious injury, or a threat to the physical integrity of self or others.

    2. The person's response involved intense fear, helplessness, or horror. **Note:** In children, this may be expressed instead by disorganized or agitated behavior.

B. The traumatic event is persistently reexperienced in one (or more) of the following ways:

    1. Recurrent and intrusive distressing recollections of the event, including images, thoughts, or perceptions. **Note:** In young

children, repetitive play may occur in which themes or aspects of the trauma are expressed.

2. Recurrent distressing dreams of the event. **Note:** In children, there may be frightening dreams without recognizable content.

3. Acting or feeling as if the traumatic event were recurring (includes a sense of reliving the experience, illusions, hallucinations, and **dissociative** flashback episodes, including those that occur on awakening or when intoxicated). Note: In young children, trauma-specific reenactment may occur.

4. Intense psychological distress at exposure to internal or external cues that symbolize or resemble an aspect of the traumatic event.

5. Physiological reactivity on exposure to internal or external cues that symbolize or resemble an aspect of the traumatic event.

C. Persistent avoidance of stimuli associated with the trauma and numbing of general responsiveness (not present before the trauma), as indicated by three (or more) of the following:

1. efforts to avoid thoughts, feelings, or conversations associated with the trauma

2. efforts to avoid activities, places, or people that arouse recollections of the trauma

3. inability to recall an important aspect of the trauma

4. markedly diminished interest or participation in significant activities

5. feeling of detachment or estrangement from others

6. restricted range of affect (e.g., unable to have loving feelings)

7. sense of foreshortened future (e.g., does not expect to have a career, marriage, children, or a normal life span)

D. Persistent symptoms of increased arousal (not present before the trauma), as indicated by two (or more) of the following:

1. difficulty falling or staying asleep

2. irritability or outbursts of anger

3. difficulty concentrating

4. hypervigilance

5. exaggerated startle response

E. Duration of the disturbance (symptoms in Criteria B, C, D) is more than 1 month.

F. The disturbance causes clinically significant distress or impairment in social, occupational, or other important areas of functioning.

(*Source:* Reprinted with permission from the *Diagnostic and Statistical Manual of Mental Disorders, Fourth Edition, Text Revision.* Copyright 2000 American Psychiatric Association.)

If the clinical symptoms do not meet these criteria exactly (e.g., the symptoms happen within 1 month of the stressor), the person may be suffering from **acute stress disorder.** The crisis worker should be particularly alert to this possibility. If intervention can be done within the first month, future problems can be prevented, as discussed in Chapter 1.

Diagnostic Criteria for Acute Stress Disorder

The DSM-IV-TR also sets out criteria for acute stress disorder.

A. The person has been exposed to a traumatic event in which both of the following were present:

1. The person experienced, witnessed, or was confronted with an event or events that involved actual or threatened death or serious injury, or a threat to the physical integrity of self or others.
2. The person's response involved intense fear, helplessness, or horror.

B. Either while experiencing or after experiencing the distressing event, the individual has three (or more) of the following dissociative symptoms:

1. a subjective sense of numbing, detachment, or absence of emotional responsiveness
2. a reduction in awareness of his or her surroundings (e.g., being in a daze)
3. **derealization**
4. **depersonalization**
5. dissociative amnesia (i.e., inability to recall an important aspect of the trauma)

C. The traumatic event is persistently re-experienced in at least one of the following ways: recurrent images, thoughts, dreams, illusions, flashback episodes, or a sense of reliving the experience; or distress on exposure to reminders of the traumatic event.

D. Marked avoidance of stimuli that arouse recollections of the trauma (e.g., thoughts, feelings, conversations, activities, places, people).

E. Marked symptoms of anxiety or increased arousal (e.g., difficulty sleeping, irritability, poor concentration, hypervigilance, exaggerated startle response, motor restlessness).

F. The disturbance causes clinically significant distress or impairment in social, occupational, or other important areas of functioning or impairs the individual's ability to pursue some necessary task, such as obtaining necessary assistance or mobilizing personal resources by telling family members about the traumatic experience.

G. The disturbance lasts for a minimum of 2 days and a maximum of 4 weeks and occurs within 4 weeks of the traumatic event.

H. The disturbance is not due to the direct physiological effects of a substance (e.g., a drug of abuse, a medication) or a general medical condition, is not better accounted for by Brief Psychotic Disorder, and is not merely an exacerbation of a preexisting Axis I or Axis II disorder.

Source: Reprinted with permission from the *Diagnostic and Statistical Manual of Mental Disorders, Fourth Edition, Text Revision.* Copyright 2000 American Psychiatric Association.

There are several different categories of experiences that typically cause PTSD or acute stress disorder. They include being in combat or in a war zone, suffering personal or family victimization, living through a natural disaster, or experiencing a manmade disaster. Each situation creates different emotional experiences for the survivors and different cognitions associated with the trauma. However, survivors of all these experiences tend to have the symptoms of PTSD. A crisis worker is bound to come into contact with clients who did not deal with traumas immediately after they occurred, and so they have most likely been living in some state of PTSD for some time. An event in the present often triggers a memory of the trauma, or the person's functioning may diminish to the point that he or she can't deal with society any longer, so the person seeks the help of a mental health worker.

Some victims exist in a chronic crisis state, never really functioning at all. They often go from one therapist to another or from hospital to jail to clinic looking for coping skills to deal with their current problems. Unfortunately, many cannot be effective in the present until they deal with their past traumas.

Serving in Combat or Living in a War Zone

Counselors first became aware of PTSD when they were dealing with war veterans, especially those of the Vietnam War. Often, they were 19-year-old boys who were sent across the world lacking the coping skills to deal with seeing their buddies blown up and small children killed. Vietnam veterans' symptoms have included re-experiencing the sounds of war, suffering from nightmares, and being unable to manage interpersonal relationships effectively. Support groups were set up to allow these veterans an opportunity to discuss their traumas and find ways to integrate their war experiences into present-day functioning.

The veterans of World War II had similar responses to their combat experiences. Anyone who exhibited signs of trauma was said to have **shell shock.** Unfortunately, World War II veterans did not seek or receive mental health treatment when they returned home. They were encouraged to "buck up" and "be a man." Recent films such as *Saving Private Ryan* have put a realistic perspective on the extent of the trauma experienced by these men. It is easy to forget that they suffered because, unlike their Vietnam veteran counterparts, World War II veterans received a hero's welcome when they returned home. World War II was a popular war, and most Americans were supportive of the efforts of the military.

When soldiers are engaged in combat and see the trauma of war, some do experience acute stress disorder. They are often treated by doctors and given time to recuperate. However, the military does such a good job of training soldiers to numb themselves to war trauma that the majority are able to deal with combat as it is happening. It is when they return home that they show signs of PTSD. The disorder has been delayed, almost by training. Once soldiers return home, many have difficulty adjusting to civilian life. They report being preoccupied with the troops that are still fighting. They often feel guilty for leaving the other soldiers and think they should return to help fight.

The recent wars fought in Iraq and the Persian Gulf have also left emotional scars on combat veterans. Some refer to the PTSD experienced by soldiers who fought to free Kuwait in the 1990s as Persian Gulf syndrome. It is still a bit early to properly identify the effects of combat in the current war against the rebels in Iraq, but since these soldiers are observing killings and other gruesome acts of war, there is little doubt that they will also experience PTSD.

Suffering Personal or Family Victimization

Sadly, we live in a society where people are frequently victimized by others who intend to kill, harm, or intimidate, or all three. The prevalence of child abuse, spousal abuse, and sexual assault is so high that all of Chapter 12 is devoted to these topics. In fact, sexual abuse survivors constitute the largest number of PTSD victims (Shapiro & Forrest, 1997, p. 132).

Many perpetrators of this type of victimization know their victims personally. This adds to the emotional trauma for the victims in ways that "impersonal" traumas such as an earthquake might not. Trust becomes a big issue for people who are attacked by someone they know.

In addition to physical and sexual assault, the following types of trauma may lead to PTSD:

- witnessing a loved one being murdered
- witnessing or being part of a gruesome car accident
- being kidnapped or being the parent of a child who is abducted
- having personal property vandalized (e.g., tires slashed)
- having one's home burglarized
- being robbed at gunpoint

PTSD for survivors of these types of trauma may be severe or mild, depending on the perceived level of threat. They often suffer from feelings of paranoia, **hypervigilance,** and powerlessness. They are usually angry and fearful.

Living Through a Natural Disaster

Natural disasters include landslides, floods, fires, earthquakes, hurricanes, and other storm conditions that wreak havoc on humans. The most recent example was the devastating Hurricane Katrina of 2005, which nearly destroyed the city of New Orleans and caused billions of dollars worth of damage in several states bordering the Gulf of Mexico. As of the writing of this book, the exact death toll is unknown, but this disaster is considered the worst in American history. The flooding of a large area of New Orleans left thousands of people homeless and without food, water, and electricity for several days, until rescue workers arrived to help evacuate those stranded. Several concepts from previous chapters can be observed in the aftermath of this devastating natural disaster.

Material Resources   As was discussed in Chapter 1, individuals with access to material resources such as personal transportation, saving accounts, and home-owner's insurance will undoubtedly manage this crisis more easily than those without them. To start, people who owned cars were able to evacuate New Orleans prior to the hurricane and subsequent flood. Additionally, those who had homeowner's insurance and money in savings accounts will be better able to start over once the acute crisis phase is over and rebuilding begins.

Perception of the Precipitating Event Leads to Subjective Distress   Because of the delay in rescuing many of those stranded in the flood, who had to cling to rooftops for several days, and also the delay in providing food and water for survivors, many survivors and other concerned citizens formed ideas about the reasons for the delays. Many people blamed government officials at all levels for failure to act quickly. This blame led to feelings of rage. When one explores the cognitive tree further, one sees that the blame was fueled by beliefs that racism and classism were reasons for the delays. Because most of the people who needed immediate assistance were poor African Americans, many believed that the failure to rescue and provide was due to the lack of importance given to this subgroup in American culture. This cognition, of course, led to much subjective distress, primarily anger.

Crisis as Danger and Opportunity   As in many other community disasters, people in the United States and around the world responded to Hurricane Katrina with charity and activism. Of course, this disaster has strong elements of danger. People died, homes and businesses were lost, and the historic city of New Orleans was all but destroyed. However, opportunity also arose during this crisis. Americans and people from other countries were enlightened about the disparity that exists between the poor and the upper classes. The disaster provided an opportunity for people to show their humanity, pitch in and help, and engage in dialogue about how to ensure that a similar situation does not occur again.

The catastrophic tsunami that occurred on the coasts of Indochina and other countries in 2004 is another example of the devastation caused by natural disasters. Throughout time, many people have been traumatized by the powerful destruction of earthquakes, blizzards, storms, and floods. These types of disasters make people feel helpless. They may even become angry with God.

When a disaster hits, communities tend to go through certain **phases** to overcome the psychological and physical consequences of the disaster. The Mental Health Center of North Iowa, Inc. (retrieved 6/8/2005) provides information about these phases. The first stage is the heroic phase. This usually occurs during and immediately after the disaster. Emotions are strong and direct. People find themselves being called upon for and responding to demands for heroic action to save their own and others' lives and property. Altruism is prominent, and people expend much energy in helping others to survive and recover. People have a lot of energy and motivation to help. Everyone pitches in to help people that they might not ordinarily have assisted. The second stage is the honeymoon phase, which lasts from 1 week to 6 months after the disaster. There is a strong sense of having shared with others a dangerous, catastrophic experience and having lived through it. Survivors clean out mud and debris from their homes and yards, anticipating that a considerable amount of help will soon be given them to solve their problems. Community groups that are set up to meet specific needs caused by the disaster are important resources during this period. The third stage is the disillusionment phase. When the "honeymoon high" wears off, people realize that life isn't a "bowl of cherries." They realize that people have returned to their normal states of greed, jealousy, and selfishness. The "utopia" they had envisioned doesn't materialize. Strong feelings of disappointment, anger, resentment, and bitterness may arise if promised aid is delayed or never arrives. Outside agencies may leave the affected region, and some community groups may weaken or may not adapt to the changing situation. There is a gradual loss of the feelings of "shared community" as survivors concentrate on rebuilding their lives and solving their own individual problems. The final stage is the reconstruction phase, in which survivors realize that they will need to rebuild their homes, businesses, and lives largely by themselves, and gradually assume the responsibility for doing so. This phase might last for several years following the disaster. Community support groups are essential during this phase as well.

The National Center for Post-Traumatic Stress Disorder (retrieved 6/8/2005) refers to these phases as the impact phase, immediate postdisaster phase, recoil and rescue phase, and recovery phase. The phases are observed when people face natural disasters, personal trauma such as rape (rape trauma syndrome will be discussed in Chapter 12), and manmade disasters.

Surviving a Manmade Disaster

Recall from Chapter 2 that crisis work began when a manmade disaster, the Coconut Grove fire, occurred. Many disasters of this magnitude or worse have occurred since the fire. Sometimes they are accidental, as when a plane crashes; others are perpetrated on purpose and with malicious intent.

World Trade Center and Pentagon Attacks   One such manmade disaster was the terrorist-hijacked airplane crashes into the New York World Trade Center and the U.S. Pentagon on September 11, 2001. These traumas lead to the death of over 5,000 people, the highest disaster-related death toll in U.S. history. Most of us can still remember how the entire country proceeded through the different phases discussed above. The pictures are etched in our minds of men and women working day and night to remove debris from the areas affected by the attacks. This behavior helped to increase feelings of power in all of us. At least something could be done. Unfortunately, this tragedy did not end with the plane crashes but continued with the introduction by terrorists of the anthrax virus into the U.S. Postal System. In 2005, terrorists left bombs in backpacks in the London transit system, reminding us that the threat continues.

A True Story   A powerful story related to the World Trade Center attacks was told to the author by a former student. He had become a sheriff at a local law enforcement agency. After he completed his masters degree in psychology, he was asked to fly to New York and help out. He didn't know exactly what he would be doing, but he was ready to do anything. When he arrived, he went right up to the emergency workers, firefighters, and police, who were heaving heavy cement pieces from Ground Zero, searching for bodies. They were sweating, breathing heavily, and crying. He started helping them, until one of the workers told him to stop. The student said, "But I'm here to help." The worker looked at him and with tears in his eyes said, "This is our job. Your job is to take care of us. There are over 600 people in that building over there who need someone to talk to, share their feelings with, and we hope you can do this." The student walked over to the building and was met by hundreds of people that had been working day and night, survivors of the attacks, and people who had lost loved ones in the attacks. At this point, he certainly felt needed. He was able to use the ABC model that he had just learned to help these people begin to put their lives back together.

Oklahoma City Federal Building Bombing   The bombing of the Oklahoma City federal building in April 1995 is yet another example of a monumental disaster, in which more than 200 people, including preschool children, were killed and many others injured. Complete crisis intervention and critical incident debriefing services were needed to help the survivors of this bombing and of the New York City attack, as well as people in the community, deal with these traumas.

INTERVENTIONS

When disasters happen, they affect not only those directly involved but others who suddenly feel that their security is threatened. Communities throughout the United States responded to the recent traumatic events by providing much-needed support.

Examples of community support included relief funds for families of the victims, generous donations to the **Red Cross,** and crisis response units established in a variety of locales such as elementary schools and even public parks. The crisis intervention was aimed at helping children and adults deal with beliefs that the community is no longer a safe place. Shock that something like this could happen to "me and my family" was a common response by many. Crisis workers needed to help people think differently about the situation, showing the secondary victims through education and empowerment statements that they could cope with this situation.

To function during an emergency situation, people must put their feelings and normal human reactions aside. This state of denial allows individuals to act in order to survive. If this initial shock did not exist, people would be so overwhelmed with feelings that they could not function at all. After the emergency is stabilized, those involved can come to terms at an appropriate pace with what has happened. This process is referred to as a delayed reaction and is the basis for PTSD.

The tendency is for individuals who have been traumatized to seek resolution at some point in some way. This resolution takes a variety of forms and may occur at conscious as well as unconscious levels. For example, nightmares that replay the event are common in PTSD. It is as if the unconscious mind is trying to help the person bring closure to the trauma by creating stress at night so the person will be motivated to deal with the trauma in a wakeful, conscious state.

Once individuals have allowed the trauma to surface, floods of feelings are aroused. Professional help is then needed to channel those feelings into productive avenues for growth. As with all crisis situations, people need to see that some new meaning can be ascribed to even the most devastating trauma. Victor Frankl's work on logotherapy (meaning therapy) is a good example; it shows how he used his trauma as a Nazi concentration camp survivor to create growth in himself as a person. Despite the catastrophic nature of his experience, he found a way to see meaning in it. This ability no doubt helped him survive psychologically.

If people do not receive help after a trauma, the posttraumatic symptoms get worse over time, and the individuals learn to adjust to life in a less functional way. Such people will have less psychic energy available for dealing with daily stresses, because they are using their energy to continue to deny the feelings associated with the trauma. These people will most likely have difficulty in interpersonal relationships, which require feelings if they are to be at all satisfying.

Critical Incident and Debriefing

Because of the extent of manmade and natural disasters, mental health professionals have developed special programs and training that focus on helping people and communities overcome the effects of traumas, or critical incidents. All of the traumas discussed so far in this chapter are examples of critical incidents. Some mental health professionals refer to this process as trauma response or disaster mental health (Ladrech, 2004). Special training programs are available for workers wanting to help victims of disasters through the Red Cross and other responding organizations such as the International Medical Corps. Disaster mental health is a crisis intervention method that "stabilizes, supports and normalizes people in an effort to strengthen their coping abilities, and hopefully, prevent long-term damage such as PTSD, substance abuse, depression, and family and relationship problems. It is not meant to be treatment" (Ladrech, 2004, p. 21).

There are a few special considerations to keep in mind when dealing with people who have experienced a critical incident. The Los Angeles County Department of Mental Health (2001) has listed common signs and signals of a stress reaction to a traumatic event. Most of these symptoms correspond to those listed in the above definition of PTSD. This information is useful for crisis workers so that they may educate victims of trauma about the normalcy of such symptoms. Knowing that these symptoms are typical may relieve victims who thought they were going "crazy."

Physical signs include fatigue, nausea, muscle tremors, twitches, chest pain, difficulty breathing, elevated blood pressure, rapid heart rate, thirst, visual difficulties, vomiting, grinding of teeth, weakness, dizziness, profuse sweating, chills, shock symptoms, and fainting. Typical emotional and behavioral signs of critical incident stress include anxiety, guilt, grief, panic, fear, uncertainty, loss of emotional control, depression, irritability, apprehension, change in activity, change in speech patterns, withdrawal, outbursts, suspiciousness, loss or increase of appetite, alcohol consumption, antisocial acts, pacing, hyper-alertness, and startle reflex.

There may also be cognitive symptoms such as blaming, confusion, poor attention, poor decisions, poor concentration, memory problems, increased or decreased awareness of surroundings, poor abstract thinking, loss of time, place, or person, nightmares, and intrusive images. Counselors should assess whether these symptoms are due to a serious mental disorder such as schizophrenia or part of the PTSD.

Red Cross workers (2001) suggest that these initial symptoms may change over time and have observed certain responses occurring in the weeks and months following a critical incident. Sometimes, a person may not connect these symptoms to the trauma because of the time that has elapsed between the symptoms and the incident. Crying for no apparent reason; apathy and depression; frustration and feelings of powerlessness; increased effects of allergies, colds, and flu; moodiness; disappointment with, and rejection of, outside help; isolation; guilt about not being able to prevent the disaster; and domestic violence are common delayed responses. Table 11.1 provides a summary of the causes and symptoms of PTSD.

Effects on Young Children

Children may be prone to exhibit certain behaviors after exposure to a trauma. These symptoms are similar to those seen in abused children. The following behaviors are common in young children after a critical incident:

- returning to earlier behavior, such as thumb sucking or bed wetting
- clinging to parents
- being reluctant to go to bed
- having nightmares
- having fantasies that the disaster never happened
- crying and screaming
- withdrawing and becoming immobile
- refusing to attend school
- having problems at school and being unable to concentrate (American Red Cross, 2001)

Debriefing Process

The debriefing process after a critical incident follows the same process as the ABC model of crisis intervention and uses Caplan's model regarding characteristics of people coping effectively (see Chapter 1). According to both the American Red Cross (2001) and the Los Angeles County Department of Mental Health (2001), coping with stressful situations begins with listening

TABLE 11.1 | SUMMARY OF PTSD CAUSES
AND SYMPTOMS

Posttraumatic stress disorder (PTSD)

Causes	Real or perceived threat or harm to oneself or close loved ones
Symptoms	Recurring nightmares, re-experiencing the event, hypervigilance, anxiety, sleeplessness, numbness, dissociation
Precipitating events	Loved one is murdered or dies in accident suddenly; assault; rape; war; bombings

Types of PTSD

Acute stress disorder	Symptoms of PTSD lasting only 1 month
Delayed PTSD	When situation is not dealt with, person uses defenses to cope, so symptoms subside until something triggers an acute reaction

and empathizing. Both groups further suggest that traumatized persons need someone to spend time with them. Support and reassurance about safety is critical, as is respecting the need to grieve losses. Support statements that tell the person you're sorry the event occurred are better than statements such as, "You're lucky it wasn't worse." It is also helpful to encourage the traumatized person to talk to others about the trauma and accept help from others. Providing information about special assistance for victims of the traumatic event is vital. Crisis interventionists should also help people to be tolerant of irritability in others and redefine priorities and focus energy on those priorities. This is similar to Caplan's suggestions about pacing oneself and breaking tasks down into manageable bits.

Traumatized people should be encouraged to function where possible and maintain healthy eating habits and sleep patterns. Actively seeking information about the trauma should be encouraged as well.

The crisis worker should be well informed about community support groups. Talking with others who have experienced the same trauma is helpful. Any educational statements, empowerment statements, support statements, or reframes are useful and helpful with the person and the family.

Other Therapeutic Approaches Commonly Used to Treat PTSD

According to the National Center for Post-Traumatic Stress Disorder (2005), the first phase of treatment with PTSD survivors and their families includes educating them about how people get PTSD and how it affects survivors and their loved ones, and other problems that are commonly associated with PTSD symptoms. It is helpful to inform people that PTSD is a medically recognized anxiety disorder that occurs in normal individuals under extremely stressful conditions. Another aspect of this first phase of treatment is exposure to the event via imagery, as this allows survivors to re-experience the event in a safe, controlled environment as they examine their reactions and beliefs about it. It is also necessary to have clients examine and resolve strong feelings such as anger, shame, or guilt, which are common in survivors of trauma.

Cognitive-behavioral techniques such as teaching clients how to engage in deep breathing and relaxation exercises, manage anger, prepare for future stress reactions, handle future trauma, and communicate and relate effectively with people are useful.

A relatively new treatment approach for traumatic memories, **eye movement desensitization and reprocessing (EMDR)**, involves elements of exposure therapy and cognitive-behavioral therapy. The theory and research are still evolving for this form of treatment, but there is some evidence that it may facilitate the accessing and processing of traumatic material (Shapiro, 2002). For clients who do not respond to brief crisis intervention, trained EMDR therapists are an invaluable resource in overcoming PTSD.

Group therapy is also a good resource. Trauma survivors can share traumatic material within an atmosphere of safety, cohesion, and empathy provided by other survivors. By sharing their feelings of shame, fear, anger, and self-condemnation, survivors are enabled to resolve many issues related to their trauma.

Medication may be necessary for some trauma survivors. It can reduce the anxiety, depression, and insomnia often experienced. It is useful for relieving symptoms so that the survivor is able to participate in psychological treatment.

Case Vignettes

Practice the ABC model with the following cases. Try to incorporate the information from this chapter about critical incident debriefing and community response and trauma response models.

Case 1   An 11-year-old boy saw his grandfather killed in a car accident while they were vacationing in Mexico. He cannot concentrate in school and refuses to go anywhere in a car.

    Hint: Assess for other PTSD symptoms.

    Hint: Give support and validation statements about how traumatic this experience was.

    Hint: Assess cognitions about the accident. Does he feel guilty for surviving?

    Hint: Reframe that his grandfather wouldn't want him to do poorly in school because of this event.

    Hint: Let him talk.

    Hint: Educate about car accidents and how to be safe.

Case 2   A 40-year-old college professor went to the parking lot after work and found that three tires on her car were flat. They had been slashed by a knife. She is paranoid, thinks someone is out to get her, and constantly worries about her car being vandalized again. She is hypervigilant and notices every minute change in her environment. She is not able to have fun any more.

>   **Hint:** Educate about PTSD.

>   **Hint:** Give support statements about how scary this situation would be.

>   **Hint:** Empower by pointing out that by not enjoying life, she lets the **perpetrator** continue to victimize her.

>   **Hint:** Reframe the paranoia as having been appropriate for a brief time, but now her fears are working against her, not for her.

Case 3   A 33-year-old city worker was squatting on one knee, fixing a fire hydrant, when a man held a knife to his throat and told him to hand over his wallet. Since then, he has not been able to work, cannot sleep, and will not let his children go out at night.

>   **Hint:** Support his fears.

>   **Hint:** Let him talk.

>   **Hint:** Educate about PTSD.

>   **Hint:** Empower him.

Case 4   An 8-year-old boy was brought in by his parents after a magnitude 6.6 earthquake occurred in his town. He is anxious all the time and won't play. He perseverates about the earthquake and says he has nightmares all the time.

>   **Hint:** Educate the parents and the child about PTSD.

>   **Hint:** Let the child talk.

>   **Hint:** Educate about earthquakes.

KEY TERMS FOR STUDY

acute stress disorder: A condition that occurs within 1 month of a severe trauma. The symptoms are the same as for PTSD.

critical incident: A serious trauma that often causes PTSD.

debriefing: Intervention after a person has been assessed to be affected by a critical incident. It includes listening, empathizing, educating, and supporting.

depersonalization: PTSD sufferer no longer feels like his or her normal self. Person has trouble connecting personally with others.

derealization: People suffering from PTSD often feel that life is not the same and things don't seem real. They feel as though they are walking around in a fog.

disaster mental health: A specialty field of mental health treatment in which counselors are trained how to respond with people after they have experienced some form of community disaster. Often referred to as *trauma response*.

dissociation: A defense mechanism that assists people who have experienced trauma to continue to function. They split off from the terror and fear of the event and push their feelings into their subconscious.

EMDR (eye movement desensitization and reprocessing): A type of treatment for PTSD that combines cognitive, behavioral, and exposure therapies.

hypervigilance: A state of preparedness and anxiety that often occurs after someone has been personally attacked.

perpetrators: Individuals who purposefully victimize and intimidate others, usually for purposes of gaining power and relieving feelings of frustration and anger.

phases of community disaster: Conceptualization that communities experience certain stages during and after a serious disaster: heroic phase, honeymoon phase, disillusionment phase, and reconstruction phase.

PTSD (posttraumatic stress disorder): Condition that occurs when people have been severely traumatized and are not functioning effectively. They demonstrate a variety of anxiety and depressive symptoms.

Red Cross: An international organization established to assist people worldwide when disaster strikes.

shell shock: A term used for the veterans of World War II who showed symptoms of PTSD.

12 | CHAPTER CHILD ABUSE, SPOUSAL ABUSE, AND SEXUAL ASSAULT

As was discussed in Chapter 11, personal threat can be a cause of **posttraumatic stress disorder (PTSD)**. This chapter deals with three very prevalent forms of personal threat that continue to occur in the United States and worldwide. The survivors of these forms of victimization frequently suffer from the delayed type of PTSD because they are prevented from or inhibited in seeking professional help. Unlike the victims of a natural disaster or a bombing, these victims are sometimes not believed and are blamed for the assaults against them. This leads to feelings of shame, guilt, and suppression of the victimization. Additionally, because these forms of victimization are often committed by family members and acquaintances, victims and their families have real reasons not to report the assault; namely, that they may be dependent on the perpetrator for survival. Lastly, and unfortunately, even when these forms of victimization are reported, the judicial system does not always provide justice for the victim, though judicial decisions in favor of victims have become much more common over the past 20 years.

CHILD ABUSE

Child abuse may come to a crisis worker's attention in several ways. In each case, the person's feelings of shame, fear, guilt, and anger exist and need to be identified, so he or she can begin to understand the family or individual dynamics that led to the abuse. Once the person understands why and how the abuse occurred, there is hope that he or she can overcome the emotional trauma created by the abuse.

Prevalence

The National Center on Child Abuse Prevention Research (2005), a program of the National Committee to Prevent Child Abuse, estimates that in 2002 there were 1,800,000 referrals alleging child abuse or neglect accepted by state and local child protective services agencies for investigation or assessment. These referrals included more than 3 million children, and of those, approximately 896,000 children were determined to be victims of child abuse or neglect by the child protective services agencies. The U.S. Department of Justice reported a total of 861,602 substantiated child abuse reports in 1998. Of these substantiated cases during that year, 461,274 were neglect cases; 195,891 were physical abuse cases; 99,278 were sexual abuse cases; and 51,618 were emotional abuse cases (U.S. Department of Justice, retrieved 11/04/01).

The discrepancy between reported cases and cases considered actual cases of child abuse by the judicial system could be the result of a variety of factors, such as false reporting, inaccurate reporting, or lack of evidence; also, children sometimes change their minds about reporting the abuse. Counselors must be aware of the emotional ramifications of child abuse reports, whether substantiated or not. Even a false report could be a signal that a family is in crisis. The crisis worker can use the feelings and perceptions associated with both false and substantiated reports as a way to identify unmet needs and other problems in a family unit.

Sometimes the crisis interventionist will be called on to work with a child, the child's parents, or the entire family when a child is being abused by the parents. The abuse may or may not be the presenting problem. At times, a social worker will refer the family for counseling after a teacher or doctor reports the case to the district's child protective agency. On the other hand, the crisis counselor may discover abuse to exist in a family that came in for other reasons. In these cases, the crisis worker will have to report the case to the state's child protective agency.

Types of Child Abuse

Child abuse can be categorized into four types. **Physical abuse** occurs when damage to tissues or bones is inflicted on a minor by other than accidental means. Whenever parental discipline causes marks on a child, it is typically considered abuse. **Sexual abuse** occurs when an adult or individual several years older than the minor engages in any sexual contact. This can include intercourse, oral sex, anal sex, exhibition, fondling, or kissing. When a family member sexually abuses the minor, the contact is considered incest and is reported to child protective services. When the sexual abuse is perpetrated by someone other than a family member, the offender is usually dealt with by law enforcement. **General neglect** occurs when parents fail to provide for the minor's basic needs, such as food, shelter, clothing, and proper medical care.

Society and the law expect a child to be properly supervised, fed, and protected from bad weather by clothing and housing. **Emotional abuse** is the hardest to prove, but probably the most prevalent type of abuse. In this type, a minor is repeatedly criticized and demeaned, receives no love or nurturance, and is not allowed to develop a sense of self. Parents who treat their children this way are usually the most psychologically disturbed of all types of child abusers, except perhaps for some sexual abusers.

How to Detect Child Abuse and Neglect

There are many clues for identifying child abuse and neglect. One sign alone may not necessarily indicate abuse, but if a number of signs are present, it is prudent to consider the possibility of abuse. A counselor should suspect abuse or neglect if a child exhibits any of the following behaviors or signs:

- Is habitually away from school and constantly late; arrives at school very early and leaves very late because the child does not want to go home
- Is compliant, shy, withdrawn, passive, and uncommunicative
- Is nervous, hyperactive, aggressive, disruptive, or destructive
- Has an unexplained injury, a patch of hair missing, a burn, a limp, or bruises
- Has an inordinate number of "explained" injuries, such as bruises on arms and legs over a period of time
- Has an injury that is not adequately explained
- Complains about numerous beatings
- Complains about the mother's boyfriend doing things when the mother is not at home
- Goes to the bathroom with difficulty
- Is inadequately dressed for inclement weather; for example, is wearing only a sweater in winter for outerwear
- Wears a long-sleeved top or shirt during the summer months to cover bruises on the arms
- Has clothing that is soiled, tattered, or too small
- Is dirty and smells, has bad teeth, hair is falling out, or has lice
- Is thin, emaciated, and constantly tired, showing evidence of malnutrition and dehydration
- Is unusually fearful of other children and adults
- Has been given inappropriate food, drink, or drugs

Other signs may relate to the parents rather than the child. Some possible indicators that parents are being abusive are these:

- Parents show little concern for their child's problems.
- Parents take an unusual amount of time to seek health care for the child.
- Parents do not adequately explain an injury the child has suffered.
- Parents give different explanations for the same injury.
- Parents continue to complain about irrelevant problems unrelated to the injury.

- Parents suggest that the cause of the injury can be attributed to a third party.
- Parents are reluctant to share information about the child.
- Parents respond inappropriately to the seriousness of a problem.
- Parents are using alcohol or drugs.
- Parents have no friends, neighbors, or relatives to turn to in crises.
- Parents are very strict disciplinarians.
- Parents were themselves abused, neglected, or deprived as children.
- Parents have taken the child to different doctors, clinics, or hospitals for past injuries (doctor shopping).
- Parents are unusually antagonistic and hostile when talking about the child's health problems. (Orange County Social Services Agency, 1982)

The San Francisco Child Abuse Council (1979) has identified specific indicators of physical abuse to watch for: bruises on an infant; bruises on the posterior side of a child's body; bruises in unusual patterns (belt buckle, loop from wire); human bite marks; clustered bruises; bruises in various stages of healing; burns from cigarettes or ropes; dry burns; lacerations of the lip, eyes, gum tissues, or genitals; possible fractures; absence of hair; bleeding beneath the scalp.

How to Detect Sexual Abuse of Children

Sexual abuse has several specific indicators. When one or more of these are present, abuse should be considered.

Presumptive Indicators of Sexual Abuse

1. Direct reports from children. False reports from young children are relatively rare; concealment is much more the rule. Adolescents may occasionally express authority conflicts through distorted or exaggerated complaints, but each such complaint should be sensitively and confidentially evaluated.
2. Pregnancy. Rule out premature but peer-appropriate sexual activity.
3. Preadolescent venereal disease
4. Genital bruises or other injuries. Remember that most sexual abuse is seductive rather than coercive and that the approach to small children may be nongenital. The presence or absence of a hymen is nonspecific to sexual abuse.

Possible Indicators of Sexual Abuse

1. Precocious sexual interest or preoccupation
2. Indiscreet masturbatory activity
3. Vaginal discharge; more often masturbatory or foreign body than abusive
4. Apparent pain in sitting or walking. Be alert for evasive or illogical explanations. Encourage physical examinations.

Behavioral Associations of a Nonspecific Nature

1. Social withdrawal and isolation
2. Fear and distrust of authorities

3. Identification with authorities. Too-willing acquiescence to adult demands may represent a conditioned response to parental intrusion
4. Distorted body image; shame, sense of ugliness, disfigurement
5. Depression
6. Underachievement, distraction, daydreaming
7. Low self-esteem, self-deprecation, self-punishment, passiveness
8. Normal, peer-appropriate behavior. Children may show no signs and carefully avoid risk of detection. (Orange County Social Services Agency, 1982)

Infant Whiplash Syndrome   In the past couple of decades, a potentially life-threatening injury to children has been identified and described: **infant whiplash syndrome,** or **shaken baby syndrome.** It is a serious injury, and the results can be devastating.

Most of the time, infant whiplash syndrome occurs when adults become frustrated and angry with a child and shake the child. Most people are not aware how seriously this can hurt a child. Children have received whiplash injuries at other times also, such as at play and in car accidents. Such an injury can be sustained when anxious adults try to wake a child who is unconscious after a fall or a convulsion.

Young infants have very weak neck muscles and only gradually develop the strength to control their heavy heads. If they are shaken, their heads wobble rapidly back and forth. The result can be somewhat like the whiplash injury an adult suffers in a car accident. Usually, however, the injury to the infant is much more severe. The back-and-forth vigorous movement of the head may cause damage to the spinal cord in the neck and bleeding in and on the surface of the brain. It is very important that parents and other adults know about this kind of injury and never shake an infant or child for any reason.

Association of Child Abuse with Posttraumatic Stress Disorder

If child abuse is not detected and brought to the attention of mental health workers, the abused individual often develops symptoms of PTSD following the abuse, symptoms that often continue into adulthood. The trauma of being abused often affects a person's functioning in work and personal relationships. Often, adults who were sexually abused as children (**AMACS,** or adults molested as children) may unwittingly repeat the abuse with their own children or perpetuate abuse on themselves. Suicide and substance abuse are commonly associated with these individuals as well. As children, denying the abuse helped in their daily survival, but as adults, denial often works against their surviving daily stress.

Children who are repeatedly abused develop a condition referred to as **child abuse accommodation syndrome.** In order not to feel the emotional torment of being abused, neglected, and sexually abused, the child protects himself or herself by accepting the abuse and not fighting it. Abuse can continue for many years before it gets reported. Sometimes it is never reported, and victims die with the secret of having been a victim of abuse. When it does get

TABLE 12.1 | CHILD ABUSE ACCOMMODATION SYNDROME

Abuse

Secrecy

Accommodation

Disclosure

Suppression

All family members use defenses: dissociation, repressions, denial, minimization, externalization

reported, it is often by accident. The family is not ready psychologically to handle the disclosure and everyone goes into a crisis state. Table 12.1 describes the child abuse accommodation syndrome and the defenses used to maintain an abusive relationship.

The key for all child abuse is providing crisis intervention for abused children and their families. If intervention comes early, many children will not have to suffer from delayed PTSD as adults, and the abused children and their parents, siblings, and other relatives have the chance of salvaging some form of satisfying relationship.

Reporting Child Abuse

Mandated reporting of child abuse nationwide began after passage of the Child Abuse Prevention and Treatment Act in 1974. This federal legislation required every state to adopt specific procedures for identifying, treating, and preventing child abuse and to report the efficiency of these procedures to the federal Department of Health, Education, and Welfare.

Currently, all 50 states have mandated reporting laws, although the person required to report differs from state to state. Professionals who are involved with children, such as teachers, nurses, doctors, counselors, and day care workers, have become increasingly important in the detection and treatment of child abuse (Tower, 1996, pp. 13–14). Any professional who works with children must be knowledgeable about the mandated reporting laws in his or her state.

In most states, when a crisis worker suspects that abuse is occurring or has occurred, the worker must call the local child abuse registry or other welfare or law enforcement agency and report the information to a peace officer or social worker. Next, the worker usually submits a written report. Once the abuse is reported to the **child protective services agency,** a social worker becomes responsible for investigating the case. Most reports are unsubstantiated; others result in referral for crisis intervention. The goal is to remove the risk from the child rather than remove the child from the risk. When child abuse is reported, the parent enters a major crisis state and often needs intervention to get through the ensuing social services investigations, the judicial system process, and the reality of having a child taken out of the home. Most people are not prepared to deal with these things and need support and education to cope with them and continue functioning. When a report is false, the crisis state is even worse, and these parents are often in extreme distress. Many have tremendous fear that their child will automatically be taken away when a report of suspected abuse is made, so the crisis worker needs to educate the parents on the probabilities of this not happening.

When the child has been abused by someone other than a family member, the police are to be notified. In most states, this type of abuse becomes a criminal case, and children are usually not taken from the home unless it is determined that the parents cannot protect the child.

Interventions with an Abused Child

When a crisis worker suspects that a child may be a victim of abuse, the worker must first, as gently as possible, confirm the abuse, and second, treat the problem. An abused child is not likely to come right out and confess being abused, because the child has been taught not to tell. Colao and Hosansky (1983) propose eight reasons why children do not tell people they are being abused or sexually molested:

1. The child is physically, financially, or emotionally dependent on the abuser.
2. The abuser has threatened the child's safety or that of another family member.
3. The child blames herself or himself for what happened.
4. The child has been taught that the good are rewarded and the bad are punished and therefore assumes responsibility for the assault.
5. The child fears that no one will believe her or him, either because the abuser is a known and trusted adult or because the child has no proof.
6. The child has been given the message that sexual issues are never discussed.
7. The child does not have words to explain what happened, and adults in the child's environment are not sensitive to what the child means.
8. The child totally blocks the incident from his or her memory because of the trauma of the assault.

The crisis worker must provide a very safe atmosphere and assure the child that he or she will be protected by the counselor and other helpers who will be contacted. A helpful reframe is to point out that the child's parents just need guidance or help so they can learn better ways to discipline. If the child is being sexually abused, the counselor can point out that "Mommy (or Daddy) is sick and needs professional help from a doctor to stop what she (or he) is doing." Another effective comment is to tell the child that "many other children go through this, and when the helpers get involved, usually things start getting better."

If the crisis worker believes that the parents, when they have the child alone, will coax him or her to deny the abuse, the worker should call the child protective agency and detain the child if possible. However, if the worker is going to continue working with the family, it is often helpful to reframe the reporting so it appears to be for rather than against the parents. To prevent outrage from parents, it is a good idea to have every client sign a form before treatment outlining the limits of confidentiality and mandatory reporting requirements. This can be used when informing them of a report.

Reframing for the abusing parents or for the spouse of a perpetrator can help reduce defensiveness also. A counselor can point out to the parents that they should be glad someone cares enough about their child to take the time and energy to protect her or him, even if the abuse doesn't really exist.

Educate the parent about the system; explain that the social services agency does not want to take their child if there is any other way to resolve the crisis. If, however, the parents are guilty of severe abuse, they may remain hostile. In these cases, it is better to lose a client and get protection for the child.

Reporting child abuse to the state protective agency can be reframed as opening a way the family can gain access to resources and services they might not otherwise get. Saying "I need all the help I can get in serving you" will help reduce their defensiveness.

In cases of neglect, it is fairly easy to convince parents that the social services agency is there to teach or provide resources. In incest and severe physical abuse cases, parents are often more resistant, and they need classes, groups, and marital and individual counseling. Sometimes, these perpetrators may go to jail, which leads to different issues for the children, nonperpetrating parent, and incarcerated parent. Children may feel guilt; the nonperpetrating parent may suffer financially; and the incarcerated parent will experience loneliness. Counselors may need to deal with any or all of these various problems.

Play Therapy   Abused children respond well to play therapy, especially very young, preverbal children who don't often respond to verbal therapy. Their concrete mental abilities prevent them from benefiting from insight-oriented verbal therapy. In play, they can work out their feelings symbolically and unconsciously. Coloring, painting, molding clay, telling stories, and playing with dolls can help clear up nightmares, acting-out behaviors, and withdrawal behaviors. If the abuse was reported early enough, 3–7 sessions of play therapy for a young child (age 4–10 years) may be all that is needed, providing that parents are supportive and the risk of further abuse is eliminated. Crisis workers should refer children to therapists with expertise in play therapy when it seems appropriate. Although crisis workers may not be trained to provide play therapy, they may be able to explain the purpose and process of play therapy to a child or parents and encourage participation in it.

Family Therapy   Sometimes, children need to confront their parents so the children can hear an apology and acknowledgment of responsibility. These sessions can also be used to set up contracts between parents and children. An abused child may feel less afraid to be around a perpetrating parent if he or she is assured that the parent has a nonabusive plan of action that the parent will follow during times of stress or just daily life, which has been and will be monitored by a third party (the therapist).

The Battering Parent

Counselors can work more easily with abusive parents if they have some idea of why the parents behave as they do. The Orange County Social Services Agency (1982) has developed an outline, adapted below, that attempts to explain the **battering parent.** Remembering this information may be helpful for crisis workers trying to empathize with batterers, who often repulse them.

Battering parents often share these characteristics: They were violently or abusively treated physically or emotionally, or both, as children. They had insufficient food. They often lived with dirt and disease. As children, they suffered repeated fractures, burns, abrasions, and bruises. They commonly experienced overwhelming verbal onslaughts. They knew sexual abuse by molestation, incest, or aberrant sexual acting out. They engaged in little two-way communication. They tend to repeat the same behavior with their children.

As children, these parents developed a deep loss of worth and experienced intense, pervasive demands and criticism from their parents. They were convinced that regardless of what they did, it was not enough, not right, at the wrong time, or a source of irritation or disgrace to the parents. They never had the opportunity to work out their anger toward, and forgiveness of, the parents. These people tend to perpetuate those feelings into adulthood; they are often lonely and friendless, whether living an active or a lonely life.

When confronted with suspicions of battery, some parents display these behaviors:

- They show little concern, guilt, or remorse for the child's battered condition.
- They are fearful or angry about being asked for an explanation of the child's injuries.
- They make evasive or contradictory statements about the circumstances of the mistreatment, whether emotional or physical battery.
- They place blame on the child for any injuries.
- They criticize the child and say little that is positive about him or her.
- They see the worker's interest in the child's injuries or problems as an assault on themselves and their abilities.
- They refuse to participate in treatment.
- They cooperate out of fear for themselves rather than concern for the child, while they try to conceal as much as possible.
- They don't touch or look at the child.
- They have unrealistic expectations of the child's capabilities and behavior, disregard for and minimization of the child's needs, and no perception of how a child can feel.
- They show overwhelming feelings of the child's worthlessness as well as their own worthlessness.
- They express guilt over or expectation of another failure, or both.

The family unit of which the battering parent is a part often has these characteristics:

- There is little communication and understanding among family members.
- The family unit is vulnerable to any and all stresses or ill winds.
- The family generally fails in problem solving.
- The family uses the child as a scapegoat for pent-up frustrations resulting from personal and marital conflicts.
- Parents demonstrate their frustrations by child abuse that is only rarely premeditated. (Orange County Social Services, 1982)

The crisis worker can reframe therapy to these people as an opportunity to correct their own behavior and do better for their children than their parents or others did for them. Providing parenting information and skills will be a part of crisis interventions. Many parents will for the first time be educated on how to talk rather than yell; restrict rather than hit; and understand rather than discipline. Learning new skills will empower them to be more effective parents and be more successful in getting their children to do what they want them to do.

They will learn how to have a social relationship rather than a functional parent-object relationship. Giving them specific alternative behaviors to use when stressed with a child is helpful. Here are some suggestions:

1. Call a friend or neighbor.
2. Put the child in a safe place and leave the room for a few minutes.
3. Take 10 deep breaths and 10 more.
4. Do something for yourself, such as play your favorite music, make a cup of tea or coffee, exercise, take a shower, read a magazine or book.
5. Change your activity into productive energy, such as shaking a rug, doing dishes or laundry, scrubbing a floor, beating a pan or pillow, or throwing away unwanted trash.
6. Sit down, close your eyes, think of a pleasant place in your memory. Do not move for several minutes.

Interventions for Adults Who Were Sexually Abused as Children

As mentioned earlier, many adults molested as children seek crisis intervention. Sexual abuse is often repressed so well by children that it may not be detected even by skilled clinicians. When sexual abuse started in early childhood and continued for years and was accompanied by physical abuse, ritual abuse, or emotional abuse, the surviving child or adult may need long-term therapy. Crisis workers may be needed to provide short-term counseling for these people to help them through the crisis of remembering and having to deal with their parents, knowing what they now know. This moment often has an emergency quality to it, and the counselor must watch for suicide closely. Once the initial crisis state has begun to subside, the client may choose to continue in long-term therapy.

Other molestation survivors can respond well to participating in support groups and reading books designed for them. Crisis workers are encouraged to become familiar with books about the topic and refer them to clients.

Perpetrators of sexual abuse need a different intervention plan than battering parents. Typically, sexual abuse perpetrators abdicate their responsibility for themselves, feel victimized by the family, and lash out all at once. Perpetrators must take full responsibility for their actions and work to reclaim the parts of themselves that they have disowned (Caffaro, 1992). A male perpetrator often views his child as a substitute wife, caretaker, and sexual partner; these demands require far more emotional energy than a child has.

Although controlling the sexually abusive behavior may be the initial goal of crisis intervention, at some point the offender will have to focus on the origins of his problem. According to Caffaro (1992), sexually abusive behavior by a father stems from his relationship with his own father. This relationship can be characterized as one of physical abuse, neglect, rejection, and abandonment. Because his largely absent father frequently did not display tender emotions toward him, the perpetrating father must learn to develop empathy in himself. Belonging to a men's group can be helpful. The members can serve as substitute fathers and can mirror the man's growing sense of self as well as demonstrate how to bond appropriately with others.

The crisis worker would do well to help this father express feelings of shame, fear, anger, and guilt in an accepting climate. Then, groups need to be created that focus on early childhood relationships with the man's father and his need to express his feelings and develop his sense of self. Although women sometimes sexually abuse children, it is more common for men to do so.

ELDER ABUSE

According to the National Center on Elder Abuse (1994), this abuse can be categorized as domestic elder abuse, institutional elder abuse, and self-neglect or self-abuse. Domestic elder abuse refers to mistreatment by someone who has a special relationship with the elder; it includes physical abuse, sexual abuse, emotional abuse, neglect, and financial or material exploitation. Most states collect data on these types of abuse and have mandatory reporting laws. Institutional abuse refers to the same types of abuse when they occur in residential facilities for elders, such as nursing homes and board and care homes. Self-neglect refers to elders' abuse or neglect of themselves, often because of mental impairment, that threatens their health or safety.

One of every 20 older Americans may be victims of abuse each year; nearly 1.57 million older people became victims of domestic elder abuse during 1991 (National Center on Elder Abuse, 1994). A survey of 30 states in 1991 reported the following types of elder abuse, with percentages of occurrence: physical abuse, 19.1%; sexual abuse, 0.6%; emotional abuse, 13.8%; neglect, 45.2%; financial exploitation, 17.1%; other types, 4% (National Center on Elder Abuse, 1994). The crisis worker needs to understand why some caretakers abuse the elderly. Crisis intervention may focus not only on helping the victim but also on helping the abuser, who is probably a caregiver.

Stress in the caregiver is often a cause of abuse. Dealing with elderly people who are mentally impaired is frustrating, especially for caregivers without proper equipment or skills. If this is the case, the crisis counselor may refer the caregiver to a support group, offer education about mental impairments, or help the caregiver find low-cost medical equipment. Respite care may be very useful for some caregivers. It gives them a break, allowing them to have a vacation from caregiving while a paid caregiver comes to the residence and cares for the elderly person.

In some facilities, the elderly can be kept for the entire day. The crisis counselor often helps the caregiver work through guilt feelings caused by the sense of abandoning the elderly relative. A useful reframe is to suggest that without getting a break, the caretaker is abandoning the elder in other ways, such as emotionally. A really loving husband, wife, or child would take a break in order to be refreshed and offer appropriate caregiving.

Remember that caregivers have other life stressors to deal with, and they may be taking out their frustrations on the elder because the elder is an easy target. If this is the case, the crisis worker can help caregivers cope better with life problems; these issues should be addressed as part of crisis counseling.

In cases of physical abuse, some suggest that the cycle-of-violence theory holds, in that the children of the elderly parents were abused by them when they were children. They then act out their anger on the dependent elder parent because the use of violence has become a normal way to resolve conflict in their family. The crisis worker must help adult child caregivers address their own past history of child abuse to stop the cycle.

In some cases, the abuser has personal problems, such as substance abuse, financial problems, emotional disorders, or other addictions. Adult children with such problems are dependent on their elderly parents to support them and provide a home for them. This situation increases the likelihood of conflict and abuse. Many states provide training for caregivers; some hospitals have support groups for caregivers; and the state's adult protective agency may offer support services for caregivers. The crisis worker needs to be aware of what is available in the community.

Interventions with Abused Elderly People

Dealing with elder abuse is a multifaceted process. It includes interventions by physicians, social workers, nurses, psychiatrists, psychologists, and other professionals and paraprofessionals, all working together to protect and heal the damage done to the elderly person. The crisis worker must be knowledgeable about community support groups for abused elders and the array of supportive and protective services that are available.

Public guardianship programs, financial planning, and transportation are just a few of the services available to help the elderly be more autonomous and be taken care of by people who are closely monitored. Mental health providers can also use an empowerment model with the elderly, teaching them assertiveness skills and self-advocacy. The crisis worker can encourage the elder abuse victim to join with others in educating the public and elders about the prevalence of the problem so the elderly won't feel shame and guilt in coming forward with reports of abuse.

As with all forms of abuse, crisis counseling must be supportive as the person speaks, always validating the shame and pain of abuse but always later focusing on the survival aspect that allows the person to move forward.

Family counseling may be an option, especially if the abuser and the abused will continue living together after the abuse has been reported. This counseling may focus on airing and resolving resentments, improving communication, and defining roles and expectations.

INTIMATE PARTNER ABUSE AND DOMESTIC VIOLENCE

Although it is against the law to batter one's spouse, it is sometimes difficult to press charges and secure justice even in severe cases of spousal abuse. In 1989, police officers were given the right to press charges if they observed spousal abuse, even if the battered spouse did not press charges. This change of attitude is partially because of recent acknowledgment of the **battered woman syndrome** (a type of PTSD), which often inhibits the battered partner from pressing charges. In 1994, a new bill was passed in California requiring health practitioners who are employed in a health care facility, clinic, or doctor's office and who have knowledge of a woman being battered by a partner to report this behavior to a law enforcement officer. The reason for external control is the relatively new idea that a battered woman cannot adequately make the decision to get out of the dangerous situation if she suffers from battered woman syndrome. An additional bill was also passed in California that requires applicants for several professional licenses to show that they have completed course work in spousal abuse. Since the terrorist bombing on September 11, 2001, what formerly had been referred to as a "terrorist threat" (a batterer threatening to kill his partner) was instead referred to as a "criminal threat" (Arambarri, 2005). Although a criminal threat does not physically harm a victim, it is a form of emotional abuse and often prevents a victim from leaving a batterer.

Since the murder of Nicole Brown-Simpson in June 1994, the entire nation has been alerted to the reality of spousal abuse. The famous O. J. Simpson trial has probably been the primary reason for the abundance of spousal abuse movies, talk show topics, and legislative proposals that came in the mid-1990s. A major change prompted by the Simpson case has been a focus on providing counseling services for the batterer. The obvious flaws in the judicial system have been looked at, and instead of simply ignoring a batterer's behavior, as in years past, funding is now available to help prevent repeat battering by requiring that the batterer go to diversion groups.

Prevalence

Physical assault against both women and men is astonishingly common in our country. In a 1995–1996 survey (Tjaden & Thoennes, 1998), 8,000 women and men were asked about their experiences of being assaulted in their lifetime. The results indicate a very high prevalence of physical violence in our society. Fifty-two percent of the women and 66% of the men stated they had been physically assaulted in their lifetime. The type of assaults ranged from being pushed, grabbed, or shoved; having hair pulled; being slapped, hit, kicked, bitten, choked, hit with an object, or threatened with a gun or knife; or having a gun or knife used on them. Although it may be true that men are assaulted more than women throughout their life, violence against women by a spouse or partner is more prevalent than it is for men. In fact, 25% of surveyed women, compared with 8% of men, stated that they had been raped or assaulted by a current or former spouse or partner.

It is widely accepted that violence against women is primarily partner violence, with 76% of the women reporting that a rape or physical assault was perpetrated by a current or former husband or partner, compared with 18% of the men. Additionally, women are significantly more likely than men to be injured during an assault.

Stalking is another form of violence against men and women. The victim feels high levels of fear at the thought of the former spouse or lover following and perhaps inflicting injury on her or him. About 8% of the surveyed women and 2% of the men said they had been stalked during their lifetime. It is estimated that 1 million women and 371,000 men are stalked annually in the United States.

Violence against women by a significant other is so prevalent in our country that many websites have been created to disseminate information about this topic. The National Women's Health Information Center through the Office on Women's Health in the U.S. Department of Health and Human Services (2000) offers a variety of services for Internet users. Its purpose is to increase awareness of the problem, sponsor research, and provide information about facts and statistics regarding violence against women. It defines domestic violence (intimate partner violence) as acts of violence against women within the context of family or intimate relationships that include physical abuse, psychological abuse, sexual assault, emotional abuse, isolation, and economic abuse.

Some interesting facts about domestic violence provided by this organization follow:

- Domestic violence is the leading cause of injury for American women age 15–44 years.
- An estimated 1.1–4 million are victims of partner abuse per year.
- 1 in 4 women will be assaulted by a domestic partner in her lifetime.
- Nearly one-third of women report being physically abused by a husband or boyfriend.
- Thirty percent of female murder victims have been killed by their intimate partners.

Although battering of a male partner by a woman occurs, this is not discussed in this chapter. Typically, the dynamics of PTSD don't exist in male victims as they do when a woman is being battered. (Examine the current literature on abuse of males by their female partners to learn more about this phenomenon.) About 97% of partner abuse cases are male to female battering, so it makes more sense to focus on these. Additionally, partner violence occurs in gay and lesbian couples. The reader is encouraged to refer to literature about this specific type of intimate partner violence.

How Are Children Affected?

Each year an estimated 3.3 million children are exposed to violence by seeing a family member abuse their mother or female caretaker (American Psychological Association, 1996, p. 11). Children are more likely to be abused themselves in homes where partner abuse occurs (U.S. Department of Justice, 1993). Although not all men who abuse women abuse children, about 40–60% of men who abuse women also abuse the children (American Psychological Association, 1996, p. 80). Sadly, when children are killed during a domestic dispute, 90% are under age 10 years and 56% are under age 2 years (Florida Governor's Task Force on Domestic and Sexual Violence, 1997, p. 51).

Common Myths

A surprising number of misconceptions exist about domestic violence. Here are five of the most common myths:

1. Battering happens only to minorities and in lower socioeconomic families.
   (Domestic violence occurs among all races and in all socioeconomic backgrounds.)
2. Women are masochistic and achieve unconscious satisfaction in being beaten.
   (This antiquated concept has not been accepted for many years. If women liked being beaten, they wouldn't suffer from battered woman's syndrome, depression, and PTSD.)
3. The battered woman has a dependent personality disorder.
   (Not all battered woman demonstrate dependency traits. Many are self-sufficient and highly capable of self-care and autonomy. The batterer is often dependent on the partner.)
4. Battering is caused by alcohol and drug abuse.
   (Although substance abuse is correlated to violence, it is not always involved in domestic violence. There are many causes for battering.)
5. Batterers are mentally ill.
   (Although batterers certainly have anger and control issues, they do not necessarily meet the criteria for mental illness.) (Woods, 1992)

A Historical Perspective

Many feminists have examined the beginnings of wife abuse in an attempt to understand this social problem. As part of a grassroots movement in the 1970s, women began to propose an alternative causality model for wife battering to that offered by traditional psychiatric theories. Battering became viewed as a social illness rather than the result of a man's or woman's individual psychopathology. Women, according to these pioneer feminists, have always been portrayed as subservient in the media and have been trained to be so by parents and men alike since ancient times.

As far back as 750 BC, laws were written that sanctioned wife abuse, making a woman property and the husband responsible for her. A "rule-of-thumb law" existed until 1864 stating that a man was allowed to beat his wife so long as the stick he used was no wider than a thumb (Fenoglio, 1989).

In 1974, the first battered women's shelter was created in Minnesota. Since that time, about 700 such shelters have been established throughout the United States. This is not enough, but at least it is a start. Feminists are now proposing that more emphasis be placed on making the man leave the home, as he's the one with the problem, rather than sending the wife and children out to a shelter for safety (Woods, 1992).

Women in Western industrialized nations are more fortunate than those in certain South American countries, where wife battering is legally sanctioned. One example is the case of a Brazilian man who was acquitted of murdering his wife by using the defense of machismo. The blow to his honor from having to live with the fact that she had committed adultery was more than a man should have to bear, according to the rules of this male-dominated society.

Why Do Women Stay?

You can probably make a few guesses why a woman would stay with a man who verbally, emotionally, physically, or sexually abuses her. How many of the following had you thought of?

- She is afraid that he'll kill her, the pets, her children, her family. He often threatens to do this.
- Her religious beliefs forbid her leaving (til death do us part).
- She is influenced by the profamily society (stay together at all costs).
- She is economically dependent on the man. He often has forced her to quit school or her job, or never allowed her to work or know about their finances.
- She has no resources (no place to go, no transportation, no money).
- The children need a father.
- She gets no support from her family; many of these women are told to stick it out.
- She hopes he'll change because she loves him when he's not abusive.
- She believes him when he says it is her fault he beats her.
- She sees no other options.
- She feels insecure and unable to take care of herself (psychological dependence).

Denial can be so strong in these relationships that the battering may not be mentioned unless you inquire about it. This is not to say a counselor should question the partners in a harsh, judgmental manner, but if signs of battering start to become evident, the counselor should consider abuse a possibility.

The Battering Cycle

Spousal abuse can be understood as a recurrent three-phase pattern. According to Woods (1992), the battering cycle usually starts out in the honeymoon phase.

Honeymoon Phase   The man may show jealousy, which makes the woman feel special and important at first. They feel love and, often, dependency on one another. Mutuality, which is often a part of healthy intimacy, is not present, however.

Tension-Building Phase   At this point, there may be minor incidents such as criticizing, yelling, and blaming. The woman often walks on eggshells because she believes it may be her fault that he's upset. He says it's her fault, and she spends her time trying to figure out how she can prevent any violence from happening. The batterer may still feel in control of himself at this point. He may see that he has a problem, and if intervention could be given at this point, there might be a window of opportunity for preventing the next stage. Unfortunately, the tension usually escalates into a violent episode.

Explosive Phase   The tension will be released in a variety of ways, depending on the history of violence in the relationship. Typically, it gets worse over time. At this point, the batterer is out of control. He may terrorize his wife for hours, break things, hit, spit, push, choke, burn, tie up, rape, or kick her. She will often survive this stage with bruises and broken bones and may end up in a hospital. Sometimes the police will be called at this stage.

It is after this violent episode that the window of opportunity exists for the woman before denial sets in. However, in most situations, denial does set in for both, and there is a return to an adapted honeymoon stage.

Honeymoon Stage Again   Now the batterer apologizes and begs her to believe the violence won't happen again. She can't believe it actually happened and is in shock. This leaves her vulnerable to accepting his apologies and flowers. After all, she loves him and has hope that it won't happen again. There is a false resolution based on denial and minimization, and life goes on. He may encourage her to go shopping or throw a party; he treats her well for a while. Then, as is normal in any relationship, tension develops, and without appropriate stress management and communication skills, the cycle continues. Sadly, the honeymoon stage is the first to be eliminated, and battering relationships end up being a tension-violence cycle.

Battered Woman Syndrome

After this pattern has been experienced for more than a couple of cycles, the woman often develops battered woman syndrome. This is a type of PTSD that needs to be addressed and treated by the crisis counselor.

Three components of battered woman syndrome can be identified:

1. **PTSD Symptoms:** Because of the traumatic effects of victimization by violence, various symptoms develop, as this violence is outside the range of normal human experience. The woman may re-experience the trauma in dreams, avoid stimuli associated with the trauma, avoid feelings, and experience a numbing of general responsiveness. She may be detached, experience loss of interest, show increased arousal and anxiety, and have difficulty sleeping.
2. **Learned Helplessness:** A state of learned helplessness develops after she attempts to leave or get help and meets with no success because of system failure or other factors. She defends against this frustration by learning to survive rather than by escaping the battering.
3. **Self-Destructive Coping Responses to Violence:** Because she may perceive that her only choice is to stay (she may fear getting killed or has no place to go), she often uses drugs and alcohol to escape or may attempt suicide; at least, electing to die would be her choice (Fenoglio, 1989).

After determining that a client is a battered woman, a counselor must attempt to understand the phenomenological view of the woman without judging her. It may be helpful for you to have an idea of some of the beliefs these women have based on previous cases of counselors working at battered women's centers and shelters. Woods (1992) says that many of these women were brought up to take care of men and believe it is their role to nurture their partner when he's hurt.

Also, the woman may have been convinced by books, the media, or other mental health professionals that she is a co-dependent and is the sick one for deciding to stay. Rather than acknowledging that women in our society are socialized to be dependent, she may be judging herself and calling herself weak for staying.

Other women may not even be aware they are in an abusive relationship, and you may have to ease the client into accepting this idea and giving up denial. The Southern California Coalition on Battered Women (SCCBW) (1989) offers some useful questions to ask a woman who may be unsure if her relationship is truly abusive (Table 12.2):

Other questions that may help the woman decide if she is in an abusive relationship:

*   Do you often doubt your judgment or wonder if you are crazy?
*   Are you often afraid of your partner and do you express your opinion less and less freely?
*   Have you developed fears of other people and tend to see others less often?
*   Do you spend a lot of time watching for your partner's bad, and not-so-bad, moods before bringing up a subject?
*   Do you ask your partner's permission to spend money, take classes, or socialize with friends?

If she answers "yes" to many of these questions, the woman has probably been abused and has changed as a result of being abused (Southern California Coalition on Battered Women, 1989).

TABLE 12.2 | QUESTIONS THAT MAY HELP CLARIFY
WHETHER A RELATIONSHIP IS ABUSIVE

How many of these things has your partner done to you?

- Ignored your feelings
- Ridiculed or insulted women as a group
- Ridiculed or insulted your most valued beliefs, religion, race, heritage, or class
- Withheld approval, appreciation, or affection as punishment
- Continually criticized you, called you names, shouted at you
- Humiliated you in private or public
- Refused to socialize with you
- Kept you from working, controlled your money, made all decisions
- Refused to work or share money
- Took car keys or money away from you
- Regularly threatened to leave or told you to leave
- Threatened to hurt you or your family
- Punished or deprived the children when angry at you
- Threatened to kidnap the children if you left
- Abused, tortured, or killed pets to hurt you
- Harassed you about affairs he imagined you were having
- Manipulated you with lies and contradictions
- Destroyed furniture, punched holes in walls, broke appliances
- Wielded a gun in a threatening way

You may also need to educate her on common behaviors that indicate a battering relationship. Inform her that she may be a battered woman if these statements fit her:

- Is frightened of her partner's temper
- Is often compliant because she is afraid to hurt her partner's feelings or is afraid of her partner's anger
- Has the urge to rescue her partner when or because her partner is troubled
- Finds herself apologizing to herself or to others for her partner's behavior when she is treated badly
- Has been hit, kicked, shoved, or had things thrown at her by her partner when he was jealous or angry
- Makes decisions about activities and friends according to what her partner wants or how her partner will react
- Drinks or uses drugs (Southern California Coalition on Battered Women, 1989)

Intervening with Battered Women

The purpose of intervention with a battered woman is to encourage her to act for her own well-being and safety. The five goals of intervention with a battered woman are these:

1. Let her know help is available.
2. Give her specific information about resources.
3. Document the battering with accurate medical records.
4. Acknowledge her experiences in a supportive manner.
5. Respect her right to make her own decisions.

While you are helping her identify the battering and her perspective, you will also be offering her your knowledge of battering and reframing some of her ideas. In addition, the crisis worker will offer empowering and supportive comments as well as suggest resources such as books, shelters, or groups.

Education   Woods (1992) believes it is also important to give the woman various facts about battering presented at the beginning of this section. This will help her see she is not alone. She needs to be told as well that the violence usually increases in intensity and frequency and that her batterer needs professional help if he is ever to change.

Reframes   Woods (1992), like most feminists working in the battered women's movement, believes that someone needs to tell the woman that the batterer has the problem and nothing she can do will prevent the next battering episode. This goes against the woman's belief that if she only had dinner ready, had the kids quiet, made the bed, and so on, he wouldn't get upset. Pointing out to her that he is sick and needs help from a professional may be accepted by her.

Another **reframe** has to do with her belief that she is weak for staying and for using drugs and alcohol. The crisis worker might reframe these behaviors as evidence of strength. Her behavior can be equated to that of a prisoner of war who learns how to get what he or she needs to survive. Her weakness is now strength. This new perspective can often turn her perspective around, so she starts to believe that she has strength to take new action with the crisis worker's support.

Cusick (1992) also agrees that the "therapist must show the client that she has orchestrated her own survival and has the skills to continue to do so" (p. 48).

Empowerment and Support   The last thing the battered woman needs is for someone else to make decisions for her about what she should do. The crisis worker may find it very stressful *not* to make decisions, because often the battered woman client will choose to stay with her batterer and be abused again. Crisis workers must pay attention to their own frustrations and feelings of helplessness with this population. It is easy for a counselor to fall prey to secondary PTSD while working with clients who have been assaulted repeatedly. Remember to consult with other counselors when you become aware of these feelings.

Typically, a battered woman has had every decision made for her by the batterer, so the best thing the counselor can do is provide her with choices and support them. The counselor can give her names, phone numbers, and suggestions. The woman's main concern will often be "How am I going to be safe?" The counselor may let her know she is most at risk when she leaves her batterer but that if she wishes, a plan can be made that will ensure her safety.

Helping her explore her own resources, such as family, friends, or church associates, is a good idea before you offer your own ideas. Battered women's shelters are usually free and should be used as a last resort. They are not like resort hotels, and a considerable amount of freedom is lost in a shelter. However, if there is nowhere else to go or no funds, the shelter is a great resource.

Following is an outline presented by Judy Bambas, volunteer coordinator at the Women's Transitional Living Center, on how to provide effective support for a battered woman:

1. Let her know you believe her.
   "Many women have been beaten by their partners."
   "I'm glad you've told me about the abuse."
2. Let her express her feelings. She has a right to be angry, scared, and so on. This may be the first time she is feeling safe enough to express anger over the abuse.
   "You seem very afraid of your partner."
   "You seem nervous talking about being abused."
   "You seem very angry about being abused."
3. Express your concern for her safety and the safety of her children. She may deny that abuse occurs or deny the level of danger to herself or her children.
   "This injury shows you are in great danger. You have a right to be safe."
   "Your safety is important. I'm very concerned about you and your children."
4. Let her know that help is available. Keep information at hand to share with her about help lines, shelters, counseling, and other resources. Ask her if she wants to report the abuse to the police. Explain slowly and carefully the choices available to her. She may need time and a safe place before she makes any decisions.
   "I have information that can help you."
   "There are many people in the community who can help you."
5. Reinforce the idea that nobody deserves to be beaten. She tends to believe some of the myths about domestic violence even though they may contradict her own reality. Remind her that she is not the cause of the beatings.
   "No one deserves to be hit."
   "You aren't the reason he hits you."
6. Realize that she may be embarrassed and humiliated about the abuse. She may worry that those who have offered to help in the past (e.g., family and friends) will be too burned out to help this time. Support her desire for help now.
   "You may feel embarrassed, but there are many women who have told me they are abused."

7. Be aware of the effects of isolation and control through fear. The woman may be physically or socially isolated, or both, due to location, language, intimidation, economic dependence, and other factors. Remind her that she is not alone. Connecting with others, through services such as support groups, can help break the isolation that battered women experience. Support her efforts to reach out to others.

   "You are not alone. Others can help and understand. I have information that may help you."

8. Assure her that you will not betray her trust.

   "What you share with me is confidential. My concern is for your safety."

9. Document the battering with specific information in her medical record. Her medical records may be used as evidence if she decides to press charges against the batterer. Be specific in description and sites of injuries. If the patient says that abuse is the source of the injuries, note, "Patient stated . . . ," then continue the statement with who injured whom with what. If the patient refers to an instrument or weapon used by the abuser, note that in her record. If the injuries are inconsistent with the patient's explanation, make a note of it. If you suspect battering but the patient denies it, note "suspected abuse" in her record. Your notes may help identify her as battered on a future visit.

10. Remember that she may have other problems that demand immediate intervention. She may lack food or housing or be unable to care for her children or herself. Make appropriate referrals. If she is staying in a hospital, she may fear that the batterer will visit her. She may want her location to be kept confidential.

    "It seems you have a concern about housing. I have information about other resources."

The Batterer

Is there ever hope for a batterer? Can he be cured? Can marriage counseling help? The answers to these questions are tricky because they depend on the man and his motivation. According to Woods (1992), there is only a 1% success rate for batterer treatment programs. Despite this very low estimate, some studies do show that court-ordered counseling may help.

A 1990 outcome study compared 120 court-referred abusers with a group of 101 nonreferred abusers. Results indicated that 75% of court-referred men who attended court-sponsored counseling reduced their recidivism rate. Another 1990 study found that after counseling, abusive men had not committed violent acts for 1 year. Based on these studies, the Family Service Center of the Marine Corps in San Diego established a model program to combat domestic violence (Barnett & LaViolette, 1993, pp. 126–127).

Other studies have suggested that short-term (6–12 weeks) psychoeducational batterer-intervention programs have helped some batterers to stop physical violence in the short term but were inadequate in stopping abuse over time. Some of the batterers even became more sophisticated in their psychological abuse and intimidation after attending such programs (American Psychological Association, 1996, p. 85).

More and more battered women's shelters are including batterers' programs in their facilities. Many more therapists are offering groups for this population, who really need the help. Judges are mandating counseling instead of jail time when a man is charged and convicted of battering his partner, a trend that demonstrates a greater focus on the man's part in the problem.

Arambarri (2005) suggests that these groups should focus more on power and control rather than anger management. Many times these batterers are referred to anger management groups led by therapists who are not specifically trained in domestic violence. She believes that unless the power and control issues are dealt with, the batterer may not be dealing with the real problem.

The alternative to counseling and jail may be a restraining order, by which the man is prohibited from physical proximity to the woman. However, recent statistics indicate that more than two-thirds of the restraining orders obtained by women against intimates who raped or stalked them were violated, and approximately one-half of the orders obtained by women against intimates who physically assaulted them were violated (U.S. Department of Justice, 2000). Although protection orders are a good idea, they aren't sufficient in preventing further violence. It would seem then that counseling is still an essential aspect of domestic violence prevention.

A Phenomenological View of the Batterer   It is possible that crisis workers will on occasion interview a batterer. This man may or may not see himself as a batterer, may or may not have chosen to seek help, and may or may not be amenable to intervention, depending on his personal and social resources.

Recently, a batterer was brought to counseling by his wife of 2 years after he had hit her with a broomstick. He didn't perceive himself as a wife beater but was willing to accept whatever the counselor told him. The therapist proceeded to suggest to him that he might be a batterer if the following behaviors fit him:

- You are very jealous.
- You sulk silently when upset.
- You have an explosive temper.
- You criticize and put down your partner a lot.
- You have difficulty expressing your feelings.
- You drink or use drugs.
- You believe that it is the male role to be in charge and have contempt for women.
- You are protective of your partner to the point of being controlling.
- You are controlling of your partner's behavior, money, decisions.
- You have broken things; thrown things at your partner; hit, shoved, or kicked your partner when angry.
- You were physically or emotionally abused by a parent.

After realizing how many of these behaviors described him, the man began to define himself as a wife beater and realized he needed help to change. As with many batterers, he had a history of poor role modeling by his own father and was in fact abused as a child.

Interventions with the Batterer

With his wife present, the therapist began to educate the man about the dynamics of power and control typically found in abusive relationships. The client agreed that most of these were present in their relationship. Woods (1992) offers an outline of the patterns the husband used to maintain power and control. They have general applications for many batterers.

Intimidation: Putting her in fear by using looks, actions, gestures, a loud voice, smashing things, destroying her property.

Isolation: Controlling what she does, who she sees and talks to, where she goes.

Emotional abuse: Putting her down or making her feel bad about herself; calling her names; making her think she's crazy; using mind games.

Economic abuse: Trying to keep her from getting or keeping a job. Making her ask for money; giving her an allowance; taking her money.

Sexual abuse: Making her do sexual things against her will; physically attacking the sexual parts of her body; treating her like a sex object.

Using children: Making her feel guilty about the children; using the children to give messages; using visitation as a way to harass her.

Threats: Making or carrying out threats to do something to hurt her emotionally; threatening to take the children away; threatening to commit suicide; threatening to report her to welfare.

Using male privilege: Treating her like a servant; making all the big decisions; acting like the master of the castle.

Physical abuse: Twisting, biting, tripping, pushing, shoving, hitting, slapping, choking, pushing down, punching, kicking, using a weapon, beating, grabbing.

After educating this man on the destructive patterns he was using, the therapist attempted marital counseling and contracted for 12 crisis intervention sessions. They worked on communication skills and compromise, as is done with other couples. An odd thing was occurring, though. Nothing ever satisfied the man, and he was still angry. His wife, he said, wouldn't give him sex, didn't spend enough time with him, spent money wrong, and was sick too much. It soon became apparent that his needs were not being met by anyone. After 2 months, he reoffended. He told his wife this was how he was and would always be! She then decided she would have to divorce him. (Later she changed her mind, and they continued to try to work things out with periodic marriage counseling sessions.)

Despite education and many attempts by others to empathize with his needs, he still was not cured. Why? Most feminists and clinicians who work in the field of domestic violence believe that traditional family therapy is not an appropriate intervention in domestic violence cases (Segel-Evans, 1991). They believe that the batterer is completely responsible for the violence, and that he should be the one in therapy to work on his violence problem. Marriage counseling gives him the message that his wife has a part in creating the violence, thereby exonerating him from full responsibility for his sickness. With this perception, the recommended treatment for domestic violence cases is twofold. First, the woman should be assessed for safety and given choices and support. It should be emphasized to her that her symptoms evolved only after the trauma of being abused. Second, the man should be the one to leave and attend groups for battering men or enter individual therapy, or both, to work on his violence. He must accept responsibility and learn more appropriate ways to communicate, deal with stress, conquer his insecurities, and learn to meet his own needs.

Not all clinicians would agree with this perspective. Kugler (1992) agrees with many of the ideas but believes the battered woman is not the passive, helpless victim she is often portrayed to be. He holds the victim accountable for her own violence toward the husband, which may provoke his violence. Also, he believes therapists need to point out to the woman that the abuse won't stop unless she makes the man accountable—legally and morally. He suggests that mental health workers help empower the woman by assisting her to "realistically evaluate the situation and understand the interactional dynamics of the relationship" (p. 45). Then she can learn to alter her behavior, which may help alter his behaviors.

Kugler feels that too many women get weakened by well-meaning counselors who set the boundaries for them. This, he says, doesn't help the woman in the long run, for she is likely to enter another abusive relationship without having learned effective limit-setting behaviors.

Kugler does not believe that the woman gets blamed for the battering simply by understanding the abusive behavior in the context of the violence. He says that those who dogmatically say that couples' counseling is never an appropriate crisis intervention modality greatly limit help, especially for the woman who truly believes she has a part in the abuse and wants to work on changing her behavior.

As with all crisis work, counselors must keep all this information in mind as they interact with each client, using what will be helpful and putting aside parts that are not relevant.

RAPE

Rape is the common term used when discussing sexual assault. It is a frequent form of assault in our society. In the past decade, there have been several rape trials publicized in the media, and talk shows are exploring date and acquaintance rape.

Some of the clients who seek crisis intervention will have just recently been raped. Others will have been raped many years ago but have been motivated to come for help by a recent triggering event. For example, watching the Tyson trial brought out the anger of a 69-year-old woman who had been raped by her fiancee 40 years earlier (Heller, 1992). Victims of rape often go through similar stages called **rape trauma syndrome** (another type of PTSD). This syndrome is recognized in California courts as a condition that occurs following a rape. The crisis worker must help the rape victim proceed through these stages, which will be discussed later.

Common Myths and Facts about Rape

Like so many other common topics, rape has generated its own set of myths. Wesley (1989), a rape crisis counselor with the Orange County Sexual Assault Network, listed the following typical myths and facts during a presentation to a crisis intervention class at California State University, Fullerton.

1. *Myth:* Rape is rare and will never happen to me.
   Fact: Every 6 minutes a rape takes place. The FBI estimates that 1 in 4 women and 1 in 10 men will be sexually assaulted in their lifetime. Most rapes are not even reported.
2. *Myth:* Rape is about sexual desire.
   Fact: Sex has little to do with it. Sex becomes the weapon, the vehicle to accomplish the desired end result, which is to overwhelm, overpower, embarrass, and humiliate another person. Also, looking at typical rape victims shows clearly that this crime is not about sex: Ninety percent of disabled women will be raped. Children and the elderly are also at high risk of being raped because of their vulnerability. An attacker can easily overpower these victims.
3. *Myth:* Only strangers commit rape. Forced sex among acquaintances is not rape.
   Fact: In 60–80% of rapes, the victim and the assailant know each other. In addition, for women 15–25 years of age, 70% of the assaults are date rape. The woman is vulnerable at these ages because she is starting to have sexual feelings, set limits, and pursue intimate relationships.
4. *Myth:* Rapists are psychotic or sick men.
   Fact: Less than 5% of convicted rapists are clinically diagnosed as psychotic. The media present these cases to the public because of the bizarre nature of the rapes, but the rapist can be anyone.
5. *Myth:* Women who get raped are asking for it.
   Fact: Women who try to look attractive and sexy are asking for attention, approval, and acceptance—not victimization. Babies in diapers and fully clothed grandmothers being raped are evidence that rape is not caused by sexy clothes.
6. *Myth:* He can't help it; once he's turned on, he can't stop.
   Fact: Could he stop if his mother walked in? Humans can control their sexual behaviors. (Adapted from Wesley, 1989)

What Is Rape?

Rape is a sexual act against one's will; it is sexual violence. It might be intercourse, oral sex, anal sex, or penetration with any foreign object. Rape is a felony that carries a sentence of 1–16 years for each count. Most rapists don't go to prison because most rapes aren't reported. About 95% of rapists are men. Almost none of the men who are raped report it because of the homosexual aspect of male-to-male rape. This is unfortunate because male rape victims underuse crisis services, leaving a population of men who will be struggling emotionally with feelings of humiliation and loss of masculinity. In a 1995 survey (U.S. Bureau of the Census), 1 of 6 women and 1 of 33 men has experienced an attempted or completed rape as a child or adult. Specifically, 14,903,156 women and 1,947,708 men reported having been raped at some time in their life (Tjaden & Thoennes, 1998). An estimated 683,000 women are forcibly raped each year in the United States, that is, 1.3 women are raped every minute (Kilpatrick, Edmunds, & Seymour, 1992). Rape remains the most dramatically underreported crime; 70–84% of rapes are not reported to law enforcement.

Rape Trauma Syndrome

Rape victims often experience three identifiable stages after the assault; together, these stages comprise the rape trauma syndrome. A crisis worker is well advised to understand these stages so as to better join with the client at any given point in the crisis.

Stage 1: *Immediate Crisis Reaction*   During this acute phase, which lasts 2–6 weeks, the victim experiences emotional pain, specific physical pain, and general soreness. As with PTSD, sleep disturbances are common. The person often feels vulnerable when asleep or is fearful of nightmares. Eating disturbances will also be seen, evidenced by nausea and loss of appetite. Emotional reactions encompass hysteria, fear, anxiety, humiliation, shame, embarrassment, guilt, anger, and an acute sense of vulnerability. How the victim copes has a lot to do with her previous coping style.

Stage 2: *Reorganization*   As the initial feelings start to subside, victims realize they may get through it. They may tell themselves they need to get back to normal and can't keep dwelling on the attack. This type of thinking leads to a state of denial whereby the experience is minimized or blocked altogether.

If victims don't get professional help, they may stay stuck in this phase. They may be able to function somewhat, but it will be at a lower level than before the rape. Mood swings, depression, psychosomatic illnesses, substance abuse, phobias, failed relationships, sexual dysfunctions, suicide attempts, and revictimization may be part of this phase. The crisis worker is likely to encounter victims who have been stuck in this phase for several years because they just can no longer function.

As discussed in Chapter 1, it is easier to work with victims who are in Stage 1 because they haven't invested energy in denial yet. The longer they wait, the longer the intervention will have to be.

Stage 3: *Reintegration*   In reintegration, clients move from being victims to being survivors. With proper crisis intervention, they can emerge as stronger, more assertive persons, more aware of themselves and with increased self-esteem. After all, they have survived an extremely traumatic experience—evidence of their strength (Wesley, 1989).

Interventions with a Rape Victim

Much of the material about how to work with rape victims originally came from literature produced by the Orange County Sexual Assault Network (OCSAN). What follows is an integration of that agency's treatment approach to sexual assault with the ABC model presented in this book.

If rape victims contact a crisis worker immediately after the rape, they are likely to be confused about what steps to take. They may feel guilty and not consider themselves a victim who has the right to medical attention and police assistance (Heller, 1992). A counselor can help survivors decide what to do by providing information and resources. Overall, an empowerment model is suggested with this population. It encompasses the steps described next.

A: Achieving Contact   During the first 5 minutes or so, survivors are probably sizing up the crisis worker and thinking, "Can this counselor handle what I've got to say?" It is important for the helper to be calm, clear, and trustworthy and somehow convey the message, "I'm not going to be shocked."

During this early contact, reassure and validate clients for seeking help. Ask questions to get a clear picture of what happened; doing this helps to get the interview moving and calms clients. At this point, it isn't important to attain a full graphic picture of every detail. Reflecting, paraphrasing, and asking open-ended questions are excellent strategies for this stage.

Assessing for symptoms is also important in case a client needs help from a physician. Sometimes a client will be severely depressed and needs medication to function at even a minimum level.

B: Boiling Down the Problem to Basics   At this point, it is appropriate to identify how clients are feeling now, keeping them in the present. To understand what makes the rape a crisis for them, a good question is this: "What is the hardest part for you?" The answer gives the counselor a place to begin, a focus for reframing, educating, empowering, and supporting the client. The statements following are models of the types you might find helpful at this time.

Supportive Statements   Every rape victim needs to be believed and the experience legitimized. People rarely make up stories about being raped. Statements like the following will help to restore the victim's dignity and reduce his or her sense of embarrassment:

"It must have been frightening."

"It wasn't your fault; you didn't ask for this to happen and you deserve to be taken care of and treated with dignity and respect."

"It's difficult to scream when you're frightened."

"Sure, you were hitchhiking, but not in order to get raped."

Educational Statements   Clients can benefit from learning about rape trauma syndrome. This information helps to normalize their experience so they don't think they're reacting unnaturally. Clients also benefit from knowing that rape is not about sex but about power. The rapist just happened to use sexual behavior as the weapon of assault.

Empowering Statements   Constantly help clients focus on being in control of their decisions:

"You weren't in control during the assault, but now you are in control. You've already chosen to seek help from me. Let's look at some other options so you have more choices."

Reframing   The crisis worker can offer a different way of interpreting victims' behavior while being raped. She can help clients see that in no way should they consider themselves stupid for not resisting the rapist.

"It sounds as though you were very wise to keep still and quiet rather than risk further injury by fighting."

C: Coping   By exploring the ways clients have coped with other crisis situations, you can activate their strengths and further empower them. Encourage them to think of other ways to cope. Perhaps they can use their current support systems and reach out to such new systems as support groups.

After clients have presented all the ways of coping they can think of, the crisis worker can suggest other resources and brainstorm additional ways. The worker might recommend literature, taking a self-defense course, or calling a hot line; she might also offer to accompany the client to the police station or doctor's office. As long as the client makes the decision, many options are possible for the crisis worker.

One of the newer approaches to working with rape victims is EMDR (eye movement desensitization and reprocessing). Most communities have certified EMDR therapists who have had considerable success in helping sexual assault victims. EMDR therapy targets all of the information related to the trauma, allowing the cognitive elements and emotional elements to be reprocessed. Often, the end result is increased feelings of control and power. "Part of the treatment includes facilitating the emotional adoption of positive self-beliefs, such as 'I'm now in control,' 'I now have choices'" (Shapiro & Forrest, 1997, p. 135). This approach would appear to fit with the empowerment model previously discussed.

Date and Acquaintance Rape

Recently, there has been a lot of attention directed toward **date rape**—a situation in which a woman voluntarily goes out with a man and may even engage in some form of sexual conduct but at some point is overpowered by the man. It brings up some especially difficult issues because the woman is confused. At a certain point, she wanted to be with this person. However, when the situation gets out of control, she often doesn't know what to do. Women are most often raped between 16 and 24 years of age. The peak rate of victimization occurs in the 16- to 19-year-old age group, with the next highest rate in the 20- to 24-year-old age group (Koss, 1992). About 90% of college women surveyed report that their attacker was a boyfriend, ex-boyfriend, friend, acquaintance, or co-worker. Nearly 13% of the women surveyed reported being the victim of date rape, and 35% the victim of attempted rape while on a date (Fisher, Cullen, & Turner, 2000).

Steiner (1994), the clinical supervisor at Mariposa Women's Center in Orange, California, offers some valuable thoughts on how to educate and support women who are survivors of date rape or any woman at risk of date rape:

- First, no one can predict how [she] will react in a threatening situation. Nor can she blame herself for not reacting differently. Too much of a survivor's recovery is spent trying to redo what has already happened. We all can change only our future, not our past.

- Don't be afraid to be seen as rude or paranoid. If he gives you a hard time or humiliates you because you don't want to go into his room, or to his apartment, or for a drive, he is exhibiting a behavior common to date rapists—no respect for your feelings.

- Go ahead, wreck his stereo or anything else you can reach if he doesn't stop when you say no. When it's all over, he'll have a hard time saying "You know you wanted it and no one would believe you anyway" if his room is in a shambles. If somehow you were wrong about him, a new stereo is a lot cheaper than a year of recovery from rape.

- When you don't report it and you don't tell your close friends, you increase the damage inflicted by the rape by isolating and blaming yourself. If your friends don't react the way you had hoped, don't blame yourself. Remember that what happened to you is bad, and they are afraid to believe it could happen to them. They need help in facing it.

- Everybody needs help in recovering from traumatic events. Ask for what you need from friends, family, rape support centers, and others trained to help.

- People do recover from rape, and they are never the same. They can be stronger, more compassionate to others, and more respectful of themselves.

CASE VIGNETTES

Practice using the ABC model with the following cases. Use the reframes, educational statements, empowerment statements, and support statements provided throughout the chapter. Pay attention to your feelings of frustration, anger, helplessness, and fear. Try to approach each case without judgments or a preset agenda. *Remember, mandatory reporting might be an issue (child abuse). Make sure to assess for suicide when appropriate. Lastly, keep in mind any legal or medical issues.*

Child Abuse and Spousal Abuse

Case 1   A very upset 25-year-old woman comes to you. Her husband has threatened to kill her 4-year-old son. Her son is not the child of her husband. Last night her husband was drinking and her son was bothering him. He hit the boy and gave him a black eye. It is the first time he has hit her son. Usually, he takes his frustrations out on her. She tells you not to tell anyone because she is afraid of what her husband would do if he found out that he had been reported.

Child Sexual Abuse

Case 2   A 14-year-old girl comes to this clinic because her mother believes something is wrong; her daughter's grades have been going downhill and she does not like the people her daughter hangs around with at school. The girl's father has been having a sexual relationship with her since she was 7 years old. She does not want to tell anyone because he threatened to throw her out of the house if she told. Her mother appears to be happy with him.

Child Physical Abuse

Case 3   A 47-year-old man, who is an elder at his church, comes to counseling. He runs his own business, which is very successful. He lives in a high-class neighborhood and everyone believes he is an ideal citizen and parent. He is raising three children on his own because his wife died 2 years ago. He has come in because for the last year he's been taking out his frustrations on his oldest child, who is 9 years old. He has broken the boy's arms twice and has hit him with a board on several occasions. He realizes he needs help.

Child Neglect

Case 4   A woman brings her family in because she and her spouse were reported for child neglect. She tells the interviewer that she is very upset by the false statement. She is a very religious person, and her children are very well taken care of. They eat at specific times and are not allowed to snack. During the interview, the children are going through the wastepaper baskets looking for food. The mother tells you that they missed breakfast this morning and will have to miss another meal because good children do not miss meals.

    Hint: Maintain a nonjudgmental attitude.

Spousal Abuse

Case 5   A 27-year-old nurse comes to you. She is working to put her husband through medical school. She is complaining about being unassertive. She sits uneasily in the chair. When she moves, she sometimes grimaces in pain. She loves her husband and wants to please him but does not think she can. Due to her lack of sexual responsiveness, he sometimes gets extremely angry and does things.

Spousal Abuse and Elder Abuse

Case 6   A 65-year-old woman comes to you. She lives in a retirement trailer village with her husband, who is a retired salesman. She comes to the session crying. Her mouth is cut and her right eye is swollen and bruised. She expresses anger and hatred toward all men. Her husband beat her last night because there was too much grease on his plate. She wants to leave but is afraid. He has threatened to kill her if she tries to leave.

Acquaintance Rape

Case 7   A young woman who has recently been raped by an old friend comes to counseling. She went to a party and had a few drinks. The friend walked her to her car and then forced her into the car and raped her. She has told no one. Her biggest problem is that this friend works for the same company she does.

Rape

Case 8   A 32-year-old male was raped by two men. He is feeling a great deal of shame because he thinks he's the only male this has ever happened to. He is also very angry because he was unable to do anything to stop the rape. One of the men had a gun. He is afraid no one will believe his story. He feels that he might just end it all now because his life won't be worth living after this.

Rape

Case 9   A 19-year-old co-ed was walking across campus when four men forced her into their van and raped her. There were other people around when it happened, but no one did anything to stop the event. When she told her parents, they became upset with her and believed she was to blame. Her father told her that if she would just stop wearing such sexy clothes, these things wouldn't happen. She is confused and feels unable to study, and she has thoughts about suicide.

KEY TERMS FOR STUDY

AMACS (adults molested as children): Adults who often manifest PTSD because of the unresolved emotional residue of childhood sexual abuse. Support groups for this population are increasing.

battered woman syndrome: A form of PTSD frequently manifested by women who are continually beaten by their domestic partners. Often, the woman develops a sense of helplessness and hopelessness. She does not consider leaving her abuser; rather, she focuses on surviving the abuse. She is often in a daze.

battering cycle: The events leading to, through, and away from domestic violence. The cycle begins in the honeymoon period, when both partners are in love and feel happy. The tension builds and eventually an explosion happens, either verbally or physically. After the explosion, the batterer feels relieved and seeks forgiveness, and the honeymoon begins again. Eventually, the honeymoon period goes away, and the couple oscillates between tension and violence.

battering parent: Parent who beats a child as a disciplinary action, out of frustration, or for other reasons. This parent was probably abused as a child and lacks the skills to properly communicate with and discipline a child. The parent's anger is out of control, and the parent is using the child to relieve stress.

child abuse: One type of trauma that can cause PTSD (too prevalent in our society). The four most common kinds of child abuse are these:

> **Physical abuse:** Indicated by tissue damage, broken bones, or organ damage from nonaccidental means. Burns, welts, bruises, and other marks are also indications.

> **Sexual abuse:** Occurs when an adult gratifies himself or herself sexually with a minor. Abuse ranges from fondling to voyeurism to intercourse.

> **General neglect:** Indicated when a parent or guardian fails to provide for a child's basic needs, such as food, shelter, clothing, and medical care.

> **Emotional abuse:** Occurs when a child is continually humiliated, criticized, and deprived of love. Usually leads to severe psychiatric symptoms and is difficult to prove.

child abuse accommodation syndrome: A protective condition in which an abused child maintains secrecy about the abuse, permits it to reoccur, and, even if the abuse is accidentally disclosed, tries to suppress it.

child protective services agency: A county or state agency established to protect children from abuse by investigating reports of child abuse and intervening when necessary.

date rape: The most common form of rape for women between the ages of 15 and 24 years. While out with a friend or date, or while at a gathering with acquaintances, a woman is sexually assaulted. Often, the man does not realize he is raping her.

empowerment model: An intervention model for clients in crisis that helps to restore a person's sense of control. In working with survivors of rape, crisis interventionists use this type of approach when issues of power and feelings of helplessness are discussed. The survivor is presented with alternative ideas that help him or her feel more in control and powerful. The worker may want to point out choices and decisions that are still under the person's control, even though the sexual assault may not have been.

infant whiplash syndrome: A very serious form of child abuse that results when a baby is shaken. The shaking causes the brain to roll around in the skull cavity. This abuse can lead to brain damage or death.

mandated reporting laws: Laws requiring professionals such as counselors, teachers, and medical personnel who work with children to report any suspicions of child abuse to either a child protective agency or a law enforcement agency. Exactly who is required by law to report and the procedures for reporting vary from state to state.

posttraumatic stress disorder (PTSD): A state in which a person re-experiences a traumatic event as flashbacks or in nightmares, feels anxious and hypervigilant, and has impaired functioning.

rape trauma syndrome: A form of PTSD commonly found in women and men after a sexual assault. First, there is the immediate crisis reaction, with all the symptoms of anxiety one would expect. Then, the rape survivor attempts to reorganize. Without help, the survivor reorganizes by using ego defense mechanisms. With help, the survivor learns to cope with her or his feelings and works through the trauma to move to the third phase: reintegration. Finally, the survivor comes to terms with the assault and integrates it into his or her life.

REFERENCES

Administration on Aging. (2000). *Profile of older Americans*. Web site: www.aoa.dhhs.gov/aoa/stats/profile/default.htm

Aguilera, D. C. (1990). *Crisis intervention: Theory and methodology,* 6th ed. St. Louis: Mosby.

Altman, B. M., Cooper, P. F., & Cunningham, P. J. (1999). The case of disability in the family: Impact on health care utilization and expenditures for nondisabled members. *Milbank Quarterly* 77(1):39–75.

Alzheimer's Association of Orange County. (1998). *Alzheimer's disease fact sheet*. Author.

Alzheimer's Disease and Related Disorders Association, Inc. (1995). *Caregiver stress: Signs to watch for . . . Steps to take.* Author.

American Association of Suicidology. (1999). *U.S.A. suicide: 1997 official final data*. Washington, DC: Author.

American Psychiatric Association. (1994). *Diagnostic and Statistical Manual of Mental Disorders, Fourth Edition* (DSM-IV). Washington, DC: Author.

American Psychiatric Association. (2000). *Diagnostic and Statistical Manual of Mental Disorders, Fourth Edition, Text Revision* (DSM-IV-TR). Washington, DC: Author.

American Psychological Association. (1996). *Violence and the family: Report of the American Psychological Association Presidential Task Force on Violence and the Family,* p. 85.

American Red Cross. (2001). *Emotional health issues for victims*. Web site: www.trauma-pages.com/notalone.htm

Ansello, E. F. (1988). The intersecting of aging and disabilities. *Educational Gerontology 14*(5):351–363.

Ansello, E. F., & Eustis, N. N. (1992). A common stake? Investigating the emerging "intersection" of aging and disabilities. *Generations 16*(Winter):5–8.

Arambarri, P. (2005). Domestic violence 101. Presentation given at the 7th Annual Conference on Domestic Violence and Victim Advocacy: Through the Lens of Culture. Fullerton, CA: Western State University College of Law.

Arredondo, P., Toporek, R., Brown, S. P., Jones, J., Locke, D. C., Sanchez, J., & Stadler, H. (1996). Operationalization of the multicultural counseling competencies. *Journal of Multicultural Counseling and Development 24*:42–78.

Association for Advanced Training in the Behavioral Sciences. (2005). *Eating disorders: A brief guide.* Author. Web site: www.aatbs.com

Association for Continuing Education. (1997). Phone: 1–800–777–6839.

Baker, C. (1991). An AIDS diagnosis: Psychological devastation! *California Therapist 3*(5):66–67.

Bambas, J. (1994). Interventions with battered women. Presentation at California State University, Fullerton.

Barnett, O. W., & La Violette, A. D. (1993). *It could happen to anyone: Why battered women stay.* Newbury Park, CA: Sage.

Beck, A. T. (1976). *Cognitive therapy and emotional disorders.* New York: International Universities Press.

Behrman, R. E., & Quinn, L. S. (1994). Children and divorce: Overview and analysis. *The Future of Children 4*(1):4–14.

Bell, T. (1999). Divorce. Presentation given at California State University, Fullerton.

Bien, T. H., Miller, W. R., & Tonigan, J. S. (1993). Brief interventions for alcohol problems: A review. *Addiction 88*(3):315–336.

Boehnlein, J. K. (1987). Culture and society in posttraumatic stress disorder: Implications for psychotherapy. *American Journal of Psychotherapy 41*(4):519–528.

Bowen, M. (1985). *Family therapy in clinical practice.* Northvale, NJ: Jason Aronson.

Bowlby, J. (1980). *Attachment and loss.* Vol. 3: *Loss, sadness, and depression.* New York: Basic Books.

Boyd, V. D., & Klingbell, K. S. (1979). Behavioral characteristics of domestic violence. Unpublished paper.

Brenner, C. (1974). *An elementary textbook of psychoanalysis.* Garden City, NY: Anchor Books.

Briere, J., & Gil, E. (1998). Self-mutilation in clinical and general population samples: Prevalence, correlates, and functions. *American Journal of Orthopsychiatry 68*:609–620.

Brown, M. (1990). *AIDS awareness survey.* Fullerton, CA: California State University Press.

Bugental, J. F. T. (1978). *Psychotherapy and process: The fundamentals of an existential-humanistic approach.* New York: Random House.

Bulnes, A. (1989). AIDS crisis intervention. Presentation at California State University, Fullerton.

Caffaro, J. V. (1992). A room full of fathers. *California Therapist* 4(2):37–44.

California Treatment Advocacy Coalition. (Retrieved 10/27/2005). Key reforms of assembly Bill 1800. Available at http//www.org/State Activity California About CTAC.htm

Caplan, G. (1961). *An approach to community mental health.* New York: Grune & Stratton.

Caplan, G. (1964). *Principles of preventive psychiatry.* New York: Basic Books.

Centers for Disease Control and Prevention. (2002). Guidelines for preventing opportunistic infections among HIV-infected persons: Recommendations of the U.S. Public Health Service and the Infectious Diseases Society of America. *MMWR 51:*(RR-8).

Centers for Disease Control and Prevention. (2003). *STD surveillance 2003.* Author.

Clarke, R. D. (2000). Burned down to the wick? *Black Enterprise 31.*

Cohen, E. (1992). What is independence? *Generations (Winter):*49–52.

Colao, F., & Hosansky, T. (1983). Your child should know. Handout from M. Wash of the California Department of Social Services at California State University, Fullerton.

Cole, C. (1993). Psychiatric emergencies. Presentation at California State University, Fullerton.

Comer, R. J. (1995). *Abnormal psychology,* 2nd ed. New York: Freeman.

Coogle, C., Ansello, E. F., Wood, J. B., & Cotter, J. J. (1995). Partners II: Serving older persons with developmental disabilities: Obstacles and inducements to collaboration among agencies. *Journal of Applied Gerontology 14*(September 3): 275–288.

Corey, G. (1991). *Theory and practice of counseling and psychotherapy.* Pacific Grove, CA: Brooks/Cole.

Corey, G. (1996). *Theory and technique of counseling and psychotherapy.* Pacific Grove, CA: Brooks/Cole.

Corey, G., Corey, M. S., & Callanan, P. (1993). *Issues and ethics in the helping professions,* 3rd ed. Pacific Grove, CA: Brooks/Cole.

Corey, G., Corey, M. S., & Callanan, P. (1998). *Issues and ethics in the helping professions,* 4th ed. Pacific Grove, CA: Brooks/Cole.

Cormier, L. S., Cormier, W. H., & Weisser, R. J., Jr. (1986). *Interviewing and helping skills for health professionals.* Portola Valley, CA: Jones and Bartlett.

Corsini, R. J., & Wedding, D. (1989). *Current psychotherapies.* Itasca, IL: F. E. Peacock.

Cusick, M. (1992). When your client has been battered. *California Therapist* 4(4): 47–49.

Darche, M. A. (1990). Psychological factors differentiating self-mutilating and non–self-mutilating adolescent inpatient females. *The Psychiatric Hospital* 21:31–35.

Darwin, C. (1965). *The expression of emotions in man and animals.* Chicago: University of Chicago Press. (Originally published in 1872).

Davidson, P., Cain, N. N., Sloane-Reeves, J., Giesow, V., Quijano, L., Van Heyningen, J., & Shoham, I. (1995). Crisis intervention for community-based persons with developmental disabilities and behavioral and psychiatric disorders. *Mental Retardation* 33:21–30.

Davidson, P. W. (1999). Characteristics of older adults with intellectual disabilities referred for crisis intervention. *Journal of Intellectual Disability Research* 43(1):38–47.

Davis, H. (1982). Enabling behaviors. Unpublished paper from Recovery Services/Family Recovery Services. Orange, CA: St. Joseph Hospital.

DiClemente, R. J., Ponton, L. E., & Hartley, D. (1991). Prevalence and correlates of cutting behavior: Risk for HIV transmission. *Journal of the American Academy of Child and Adolescent Psychiatry* 30:735–739.

Drass, D. (1993). *Dreams under fire: The gang crisis.* New York: KNABC-TV, Franciscan Communications.

Ellis, A. (1994). *Reason and emotion in psychotherapy revised.* New York: Kensington.

Fact sheet on the criminalization of people with mental illness. 2001. Web site: www.bazelon.org/crimjustfactsheets.html

Fair Oaks Hospital. (1984). *The coke book.* Summit, NJ: Author.

Federal Interagency Forum on Aging. (2005). *Related statistics.* Available at: http://www.agingstats.gov/

Fenoglio, P. (1989). Battered women and their treatment at the Woman's Transitional Living Center. Presentation at California State University, Fullerton.

Fischer, M. A. (2000). Hell's speedway. *GQ(July)*:141–145.

Fisher, G. S., Cullen, F. T., & Turner, M. G. (2000). *The sexual victimization of college women.* U.S. Department of Justice, National Institute of Justice.

Fleming, M. G., Barry, K. L., Manwell, L. B., Johnson, K., & London, R. (1997). Brief physician advice for problem alcohol drinkers: A randomized trial in community-based primary care practices. *Journal of the American Medical Association* 277(13):1039–1045.

Florida Governor's Task Force on Domestic and Sexual Violence. (1997). *Florida Mortality Review Project*, p. 45.

Francis, K. (1998). Substance abuse treatment at Gerry House West. Presentation at California State University, Fullerton.

Freudenberger, H. J. (1975). The staff burnout syndrome in alternative institutions. *Psychotherapy: Theory, Research and Practice* 12:73–82.

Garfield, S. L. (1980). *Psychotherapy: An eclectic approach.* New York: John Wiley.

Gilliland, B. E., & James, R. K. (1988). *Crisis intervention strategies.* Pacific Grove, CA: Brooks/Cole.

Gomez, J. S., & Michaelis, R. C. (1995). An assessment of burnout in human service providers. *Journal of Rehabilitation* 61:23.

Graham, R. (1989). Adult day care: How families of the dementia patient respond. *Journal of Gerontological Nursing* 15(3):27.

Grant, B. F., Harford, T. C., Dawson, D. A., Chou, P., Dufour, M., & Pickering, R. (1994). Prevalence of DSM–IV alcohol abuse and dependence: United States, 1992. *Alcohol Health and Research World* 18(3):243–249.

Hackney, H., & Cormier, L. S. (1988). *Counseling strategies and interventions.* Englewood Cliffs, NJ: Prentice Hall.

Haley, J. (1976). *Problem-solving therapy.* San Francisco: Jossey-Bass.

Harvard Mental Health Letter. (December 1996). Suicide. Part II. pp. 1–4.

Harvard Mental Health Letter. (1998). Alzheimer's disease: The search for causes and treatments. Part I. *MDMA 15*(2):1–4.

Harvard Mental Health Letter. (2001). *MDMA 18*(1):5.

Health Communications. (n.d.). *Facts about cocaine.* Hollywood, FL: Author.

Heller, M. (1992). Sexual assault. Presentation at California State University, Fullerton.

Hesley, J. W. (February 2000). Reel therapy. *Psychology Today 33*:55–57.

Hogan, D., Ebly, E. M., & Fung, T. S. 1999. Disease, disability, and age in cognitively intact seniors: Results from the Canadian study of health and aging. *Journal of Gerontology: Medical Sciences 54A*(2):77–82.

Hong, G. K. (1988). A general family practitioner approach for Asian-American mental health services. *Professional Psychology: Research and Practice 19*(6):600–605.

Hovey, J. D. (2000). Psychosocial predictors of acculturative stress in Mexican immigrants. *Journal of Psychology 134*:490–502.

Ivey, A. E., Gluckstern, N. B., & Ivey, M. B. (1997). *Basic attending skills,* 3d ed. North Amherst, MA: Microtraining Associates.

Jacobs, J. (1994). Gender, race, class, and the trend toward early motherhood. *Journal of Contemporary Ethnography 22*(4):442–462.

Janicki, M. P. (1991). *Building the future: Planning and community development in aging and developmental disabilities.* Albany, NY: New York State Office of Mental Retardation and Developmental Disabilities.

Janosik, E. H. (1986). *Crisis counseling: A contemporary approach.* Monterey, CA: Jones and Bartlett.

Johnson, A. B. (1990). *Out of bedlam: The truth about deinstitutionalization.* New York: Basic Books.

Johnston, J. R. (1994). High-conflict divorce. *The Future of Children 4*(1):165–182.

Jones, W. (1968). The A-B-C method of crisis management. *Mental Hygiene 52*:87–89.

Kanel, K. (2000). Mental Health Needs of Spanish-Speaking Latinos in Southern California. *Hispanic Journal of Behavioral Sciences 24*(1):74–91.

Kashiwagi, S. (April 1993). Addiction and the Asian family. *Treatment Today,* pp. 43–76.

Kenner, K. L. (1996). *Gangs.* Santa Barbara, CA: ABC-Clio.

Kinzie, J. D., Fredricksone, R. H., Ben, R., & Fleck, J. (1984). Posttraumatic stress disorder among survivors of Cambodian concentration camps. *American Journal of Psychiatry 141*:645–650.

Koss, M. (1992). Rape on campus: Facts and measure. *Planning for Higher Education 20*(3):21–28.

Koss-Chioino, J. D. (1999). Depression among Puerto Rican women: Culture, etiology and diagnosis. *Hispanic Journal of Behavioral Sciences 24*(1):74–91.

Krames Communications. (1995). Marijuana: Are the highs worth the isolation? San Bruno, CA: Author.

Kruger, L. J., Bernstein, G., & Botman, H. (1995). The relationship between team friendships and burnout among residential counselors. *Journal of Social Psychology 135*:191.

Kübler-Ross, E. (1969). *On death and dying.* New York: Macmillan.

Kugler, Daniel. (1992). An opposing view on partner abuse. *California Therapist 41*:43–45.

Ladrech, J. (2004). Serving on CAMFT's Trauma Response Network. *The Therapist 16*(6):20–21.

Lancer, D. (2004). Recovery in the twelve steps. *The Therapist 16*(6):68–71.

Leick, N., & Davidson-Nielson, M. (1991). *Healing pain, attachment, loss, and grief therapy.* London: Rutledge.

Leiter, M. (1991). The dream denied: Professional burnout and the constraints of human service organizations. *Canadian Psychology 32*:547–558.

Liebowitz, M. R., Salman, E., Jusion, C. M., Garfinkel, R., Street, L., Cardenas, D. L., Silvestre, J., Fyer, A. J., Carrasco, J. L., Davies, S., Guarnaccia, P., & Klein, D. (1994). Ataque de nervios and panic disorder. *American Journal of Psychiatry 151*(6):871–875.

Lindemann, E. (1944). Symptomatology and management of acute grief. *American Journal of Psychiatry 101*:141–148.

Lloyd, E. E. (1998). Self-mutilation in a community sample of adolescents. (Doctoral dissertation, Louisiana State University, 1998). *Dissertation Abstracts International 58*:5127.

Lopez, S. R., Grover, K. P., Holland, D., Johnson, M. J., Kain, C. D., Kanel, K., Mellins, C. A., & Rhyne, C. (1989). Development of culturally sensitive psychotherapists. *Professional Psychology: Research and Practice 20*(6): 369–376.

Los Angeles County Department of Mental Health. (2001). *Critical incident stress information sheet.* Available at: www.trauma-pages.com/cisinfo.htm

Ludt, N. (1993). Bereaving parent support groups. Presentation at California State University, Fullerton.

Maslach, C., & Jackson, S. E. (1986). *Maslach burnout inventory: Manual,* 2d ed. Palo Alto, CA: Consulting Psychologists Press.

Maslow, H. A. (1970). *Motivation and personality* (revised edition). New York: Harper & Row.

McGoldrick, M., Pearce, J. K., & Gordana, J. (1982). *Ethnicity and family therapy.* New York: Guilford Press.

McQueen, A., Getz, J. G., & Bray, J. H. (2003). Acculturation, substance use, and deviant behavior: Examining separation and family conflict as mediators. *Child Development 74*(6):1737–1759.

Meichenbaum, D. (1985). *Stress inoculation training.* New York: Pergamon Press.

Mental Health Center of North Iowa, Inc. *Background phases of disaster.* Author. Retrieved 6/8/2005 from: http://www.mhconi.org/Topic-disasterBkgrd.htm

Miller, W. R., & Sanchez, V. C. (1993). Motivating young adults for treatment and lifestyle change. In: G. Howard, editor: *Issues in alcohol use and misuse in young adults.* South Bend, IN: University of Notre Dame Press.

Minuchin, S. (1974). *Families and family therapy*. Cambridge, MA: Harvard University Press.

Moline, M. (1986). Lecture notes. California State University, Fullerton.

National Center on Child Abuse. (2005). *Statistics on child abuse during 2002*. U.S. Department of Health and Human Services. Available at: http://nccanch.acf.hhs.gov/pubs/statsinfo/nis3.cfm

National Center on Elder Abuse. (1994). *Elder abuse: Questions and answers*. Washington, DC: Author.

National Center for Health Statistics. (1998). National and state patterns. *National Vital Statistics Reports 47*(12).

National Center for Posttraumatic Stress Disorder. *Phases of traumatic stress reactions in a disaster*. Author. Retrieved 6/8/2005 from: http://www.ncptsd.va.gov/facts/disaster/fs-phases-disaster.html?rintable=yes

National Center for Posttraumatic Stress Disorder. (2005). *Treatment for PTSD*. White River Junction, VT: National Center for Posttraumatic Stress Disorder, VA Medical Center. Available from: http://www.ncptsd.org/facts/treatment/fs_treatment.html

National Center for State Courts Research Report. (1997). *CPOs: the benefits and limitations for victims of domestic violence*.

National Council on Alcoholism. (1986). *Facts on alcoholism and alcohol-related problems*. New York: Author.

National Council on Alcoholism and Drug Dependence. *Alcoholism and alcohol-related problems*. Retrieved 11/6/01 from: www.ncadd.org/facts/problems.html

National Council on Alcoholism of Orange County. (1986). *Facts on crack*. Santa Ana, CA: Author.

National Incidence Studies of Missing, Abducted, Runaway or Thrown-Away Children Bulletin. (October 2002). *Runaway/thrown-away children: National estimates and characteristics*. Retrieved 5/11/05 at: www.ncjrs.org/html/ojjdp/nismart/04/nsl.html

National Survey on Drug Use and Health: National Findings (2003). Substance dependence and abuse. Retrieved 5/12/2005 at: http://www.drugabusestatistics.samhsa.gov/NHSDA/2k3NSDUH/2k3results.htm

National Women's Health Information Center. (2000). Violence against women. Office on Women's Health: U.S. Department of Health and Human Services. Retrieved 11/5/01 at: www.4woman.gov/violence/index.htm

Nelson-Jones, R. (1990). *Thinking skills: Managing and preventing personal problems*. Pacific Grove, CA: Brooks/Cole.

Nephew, T. M., Williams, G. D., Stinson, F. S., Nguyen, K., & Dufour, M. C. (2000). *Surveillance Report #55: Apparent per capita alcohol consumption: National, state and regional trends, 1970–98*. Rockville, MD: National Institute on Alcohol Abuse and Alcoholism, Division of Biometry and Epidemiology.

Nock, M. K., & Prinstein, M. J. (2004). A functional approach to the assessment of self-mutilative behavior. *Journal of Counseling and Clinical Psychology 72*(5):885–890.

Nowinski, J. (2000). *Twelve-step facilitation*. Bethesda, MD: National Institute on Drug Abuse, National Institutes of Health, U.S. Department of Health and Human Services. Available from: http://www.drugabuse.gov/ADAC/ADAC!).html

Obusnsha's Handy English-Japanese Dictionary (1983).

Oquendo, M. A., (1995). Differential diagnosis of ataque de nervios. *American Journal of Orthopsychiatry* 65(1):60–64.

Orange County Register. (September 20, 1990). *What are the treatments?* P. M3.

Orange County Social Services Agency. (1982). *Battering parent syndrome: Handout #7*. Santa Ana, CA: Author.

Peake, T. H., Borduin, C. M., & Archer, R. P. (1988). *Brief psychotherapies: Changing frames of mind*. Newbury Park, CA: Sage.

Pines, A., & Maslach, C. (1978). Characteristics of staff burnout in mental health settings. *Hospital and Community Psychiatry* 29:223–233.

Price, R. E., Omizo, M. M., & Hammitt, V. L. (October 1986). Counseling clients with AIDS. *Journal of Counseling and Development* 65:96–97.

Roberts, A. R. (1990). *Crisis intervention handbook: Assessment, treatment, and research*. Belmont, CA: Wadsworth.

Rogers, J. R., Gueulette, C. M., Abbey-Hines, J., Carney, J. V., & Werth, J. L., Jr. (2001). Rational suicide: An empirical investigation of counselor attitudes. *Journal of Counseling and Development* 79:365–372.

Rosen, A., Zlotnik, L. Z. (2001). Social work's response to the growing older population. *Generations (Spring)*:69–71.

Ross, S., & Heath, N. (2002). A study of the frequency of self-mutilation in a community sample of adolescents. *Journal of Youth and Adolescence* 31:67–77.

Rouse, B. A. (ed.). (1995). *Substance abuse and mental health statistics sourcebook*. Washington, DC: U.S. Department of Health and Human Services, Public Health Services.

Saadatmand, F., Stinson, F. S., Grant, B. F., & Dufour, M. C. (2000). *Surveillance Report #54: Liver cirrhosis mortality in the United States, 1970–97*. Rockville, MD: National Institute on Alcohol Abuse and Alcoholism, Division of Biometry and Epidemiology.

San Francisco Child Abuse Council. (1979). *Identifying children at risk*. San Francisco: Author.

Schechter, D. S., Marshall, R., Slaman, E., Goetz, D., Davies, S., & Liebowitz, M. R. (2000). Ataque de nervios and history of childhood trauma. *Journal of Traumatic Stress* 13(3):529–534.

Schneider, B. (1988). Care planning: The core of case management. *Generations* 12(5):16–18.

Segel-Evans, K. (July–August 1991). The dangers of traditional family therapy when intervening in domestic violence. *California Therapist*, pp. 45–48.

Sequoia YMCA Youth Development Department. (1987). *AIDS education project for sheltered and incarcerated youth*. Redwood City, CA: Author.

Shapiro, F. (2002). EMDR twelve years after its introduction: Past and future research. *Journal of Clinical Psychology* 58:1–22.

Shapiro, F., & Forrest, M. S. (1997). *EMDR*. New York: Basic Books.

Shoham-Vardi, I., Davidson, P., Cain, N. N., Sloane-Reeves, J. E., Giesow, V. E., Quijano, L. E., & House, K. D. (1996). Factors predicting re-referral following crisis intervention for community-based individuals with developmental disabilities and behavioral and psychiatric disorders. *American Journal of Mental Retardation 101*(2):109–117.

Simpson, C., Pruitt, R., Blackwell, D., & Sweringen, G. S. (April 1997). Preventing teen pregnancy: Early adolescence. *ADVANCE for Nurse Practitioners*, pp. 24–29.

Singer, E. (1970). *Key concepts in psychotherapy.* New York: Basic Books.

Slader, S. (1992). HIV/IV drug users. Presentation at California State University, Fullerton.

Slaikeu, K. A. (1990). *Crisis intervention: A handbook for practice and research,* 2nd ed. Boston: Allyn & Bacon.

Southern California Coalition on Battered Women. (1989). *Am I in a battering relationship?* Santa Monica, CA: Author.

Sparks, P. J., Simon, G. E., Katon, W. J., Altman, L. C., Ayars, G. H., & Johnson, R. L. (1990). An outbreak of illness among aerospace workers. *Western Journal of Medicine 153*:28.

StayWell Company. (1998). *Cocaine in the family: Is everyone's strings being pulled?* San Bruno, CA. Author.

Steiner, L. (1990). Suicide assessment and intervention. Presentation at California State University, Fullerton.

Steiner, L. (1994). Date rape. Presentation at California State University, Fullerton.

Stern, S. M., (2001). Poverty and Health Statistics Branch of the U. S. Census Bureau, HHES Division. Washington, DC.

Stuck, A., Minder, C. E., Peter-Weist, I., Gillmann, G., Eglit, C., Lesselring, A., Leu, R. E., & Beck, J. C. (2000). A randomized trial of in-home visits for disability prevention in community-dwelling older people at low and high risk for nursing home admission. *Archives of Internal Medicine 160*:986–987.

Sullivan, H. S. (1954). *The psychiatric interview.* New York: Norton.

Sutton, E. (1992). "Retirement" for older persons with developmental disabilities (aging and disabilities). *Generations (Winter)*:63–64.

Szasz, T. (1986). The case against suicide prevention. *American Psychologist 41*(7):806–812.

Talecxih, L. (2001). The impact of sociodemographic change on the future of long-term care. *Generations (Spring)*:7–11.

Tjaden, P., & Thoennes, N. (1998). *Prevalence, incidence, and consequences of violence against women: Findings from the National Violence Against Women Survey.* National Institute of Justice, Centers for Disease Control and Prevention: Research in Brief.

Tower, C. C. (1996). *Child abuse and neglect,* 3rd ed. Boston: Allyn & Bacon.

Turning Point. (1994). Channel 7 news program. Los Angeles.

Tustin Community Hospital. (1987). *Progression and recovery of alcoholism: Handout.* Tustin, CA: Author.

U.S. Bureau of the Census. (1998). *Statistical abstract of the United States.* Washington, DC.

U. S. Bureau of the Census. (2001). *Number of women 15–50 years who had a birth in the past 12 months by marital status by age.* Census 2000 Supplementary Survey Summary Tables. Available at:

http://factfinder.census.gov/servlet/DTTable?ds_name=D&geo_id=D&mt_name=ACS_C2S

U.S. Bureau of the Census. (2001). *Statistical abstract of the United States.* Washington, DC. Available at: www.census.gov

U.S. Bureau of Justice Statistics. *Intimate partner violence.* Retrieved 11/5/01 at: www.ojp.usdoj.gov/bjs/abstract/ipv.htm

U.S. Census Bureau. *Statistical abstract of the United States: 2004–2005. Vital Statistics of the United States, annual: National Vital Statistics Report*, and unpublished data. See also: http://www.cdc.gov/inchs.htm

U.S. Centers for Disease Control Division. (2005). *Divisions of HIV/AIDS prevention basic statistics.* Author. Available at: http//www.cdc.gov/hiv/stats.htm

U.S. Department of Health and Human Services: Office of Applied Studies. (2000). *Substance abuse statistics.* Retrieved 11/5/01 at: www.samsha.gov/oas/oasftp.cfm

U. S. Department of Justice. (2000). *National violence against women survey.* Author.

U. S. Department of Justice. (2000). *Rates of substantiated child abuse reports.* Office of Victims of Crime. Retrieved 11/5/01 at: www.childstats.gov

U.S. Department of Justice, Bureau of Justice Assistance. (1993). *Family violence: Interventions for the justice system.*

U.S. Department of Justice, Office for Victims of Crime Bulletin. (2001). *Working with victims of crimes with disabilities.* Author.

U. S. Public Health Service. (1985). *Cocaine users: A profile.* Chicago: Dupont.

Vettor, S. M., & Kosinski, F. A., Jr. (2000). Work-stress burnout in emergency medical technicians and the use of early recollections. *Journal of Employment Counseling* 37:216.

Vocational Education Act Amendments. (Pub. L. 94–492). October 12, 1976.

Walker, S. (1994). Health promotion and prevention of disease and disability among older adults: Who is responsible? *Preventive Healthcare and Health Promotion for Older Adults (Spring):*45–50.

Wesley, J. (1989). Rape. Presentation at California State University, Fullerton.

Westefeld, J. S., Range, L. M., Rogers, J. R., Maples, M. R., Bromley, J. L., & Alcorn, J. (2000). Suicide: An overview. *The Counseling Psychologist* 28:445–510.

Williams, G. D., Grant, B. F., Harford, T. C., & Noble, J. (1989). Epidemiologic Bulletin #23: Population projections using DSM–II criteria: Alchohol abuse and dependence, 1990–2000. *Alcohol Health and Research World* 13(4):366–370.

Woods, K. (1992). Domestic violence fact sheet. Presentation at California State University, Fullerton.

Worden, W. (1982). *Grief counseling and grief therapy.* London: Tavistock.

Wright, J. W. (1993). African-American male sexual behavior and the risk for HIV infection. *Human Organization* 52(4):421.

Wyman, S. (1982). Suicide evaluation and treatment. Presentation at seminar sponsored by Orange County Chapter, California Association of Marriage and Family Therapists.

Yang, A. (1999). *Wrongs to rights: Public opinion on gay and lesbian Americans moves toward equality.* Washington, DC: Policy Institute of the National Gay and Lesbian Task Force.

Yi, H., Stinson, F. S., Williams, G. D., & Dufour, M. C. (2000). *Surveillance Report #53: Trends in alcohol-related fatal traffic crashes, United States, 1977–98.* Rockville, MD: National Institute on Alcohol Abuse and Alcoholism, Division of Biometry and Epidemiology.

Young, M. E., Nosek, M. S., Howland, C. A., Chanpong, G., & Rintala, D. H. (1997). Prevalence of abuse of women with physical disabilities. *Archives of Physical Medicine and Rehabilitation* 78:534–538.

Zager, G. (1998). Teenage runaways: Life at a youth shelter. Presentation given at California State University, Fullerton.

Zimbardo, P. G. (1992). *Psychology and life,* 3rd ed. New York: HarperCollins.

Zola, I. K. (1988). Aging and disability: Toward unifying an agenda. *Educational Gerontology* 14(5):365–367.

NAME INDEX

SUBJECT INDEX

TO THE OWNER OF THIS BOOK:

I hope that you have found *A Guide to Crisis Intervention,* Third Edition useful. So that this book can be improved in a future edition, would you take the time to complete this sheet and return it? Thank you.

School and address: _____

Department: _____

Instructor's name: _____

1. What I like most about this book is: _____

   _____

   _____

2. What I like least about this book is:

   _____

   _____

3. My general reaction to this book is:

   _____

   _____

4. The name of the course in which I used this book is:

   _____

5. Were all of the chapters of the book assigned for you to read? _____

   If not, which ones weren't? _____

6. In the space below, or on a separate sheet of paper, please write specific suggestions for improving this book and anything else you'd care to share about your experience in using this book.

   _____

   _____

   _____

DO NOT STAPLE. PLEASE SEAL WITH TAPE.

FOLD HERE

BROOKS/COLE
CENGAGE Learning

BUSINESS REPLY MAIL
FIRST-CLASS MAIL   PERMIT NO. 34   BELMONT CA

POSTAGE WILL BE PAID BY ADDRESSEE

Attn: *Counseling Editor*

Brooks/Cole
10 Davis Drive
Belmont, CA   94002-3098

FOLD HERE

OPTIONAL:

Your name:_____ Date: _____

May we quote you, either in promotion for *A Guide to Crisis Intervention*, Third Edition, or in future publishing ventures?

Yes: _____ No: _____

Sincerely yours,

Kristi Kanel